Samuel Harvey Taylor

Classical Study

Its Value Illustrated by Extracts from the Writings of Eminent Scholars

Samuel Harvey Taylor

Classical Study

Its Value Illustrated by Extracts from the Writings of Eminent Scholars

ISBN/EAN: 9783337178451

Printed in Europe, USA, Canada, Australia, Japan

Cover: Foto ©Thomas Meinert / pixelio.de

More available books at **www.hansebooks.com**

CLASSICAL STUDY:

ITS

VALUE ILLUSTRATED

BY EXTRACTS FROM THE

WRITINGS OF EMINENT SCHOLARS.

EDITED, WITH AN INTRODUCTION,

BY

SAMUEL H. TAYLOR, LL.D.

PRINCIPAL OF PHILLIPS ACADEMY.

ANDOVER:
WARREN F. DRAPER,
MAIN STREET.
1870.

INTRODUCTION.

OPPOSITION to the Study of the Classics is not new. It has existed in every country where they have formed a part of the educational course. In Germany and Prussia the conflict was at one period long and spirited between the supporters and opposers of classical learning. Temporarily the latter triumphed; but at length the influence of the government, and of the people generally, advocated the study. Since that time, however, the subject has been agitated anew there; and the dispute is not yet settled, nor may we expect it soon to be, though the study is very generally and successfully prosecuted. Of late in England the war has been bitter; and more recently the strife has revived in Scotland. In our own country the discussion began early. More than eighty years ago, Dr. Benjamin Rush published "Observations on the Study of the Latin and Greek Languages," in which he says: "The expulsion of Latin and Greek from our schools would produce a revolution in society and in human affairs. That nation which shall first shake off the fetters of those ancient languages will advance further in knowledge and happiness in twenty years than any nation in Europe has done in a hundred."

Forty years later, a series of spirited papers, bearing the signature "Rumford," appeared in the Boston Centinel, which were collected and published in 1824, making a pamphlet of one hundred and forty pages. The author of these Essays maintains 'that the dead languages are no guide to the signification of English words'; 'no guide to English grammar'; 'no benefit to style'; 'that classical literature is of little value as a source of knowledge'; 'that classical studies are not the best means of strengthening the understanding'; 'and of not much value as a facility to foreign living languages.'

Hon. Thomas S. Grimke, of Charleston, South Carolina, an accomplished scholar, long a faithful and successful student of the Classics, says, in a note to an address on the Character and Objects of Science, delivered in 1827 : "The reflections and experience of twenty years have led me gradually and irresistibly to the conclusion that the best interests of education require a total revolution on this subject" — the study of the Classics. "I would rather have a young man deeply imbued with the spirit, thoroughly instructed in the principles, and enriched with the knowledge to be gathered from the eminent authors of the British school, than that he should be the most accomplished classical scholar in the Union, nay in the world." " I desire to record here emphatically my opinion, founded on the history of my own mind, and the experience of twenty years, that I have derived no substantial improvement from the Classics." And in an address delivered seven years later, he says : " The whole system of education is destined to undergo an American Revolution, in a higher and holier sense of the term than that of '76, by the substitution of a complete Christian American education for the strange and anomalous compound of the spirit of ancient, foreign, heathen states of society, with the genius of modern, American Christian institutions."

In view of the high position and scholarship of the author, sentiments like these, earnestly uttered in different parts of the country, had considerable influence, and shook the faith of some in the old curriculum. These views mainly were the occasion of the able Article, in defence of the Classics, in the Southern Review, by Hon. Hugh S. Legaré, a part of which forms the third chapter of this volume. Other chapters owe their origin to similar causes.

In 1827, a resolution was passed at a meeting of the President and Fellows of Yale College, appointing a committee to consider the expediency of dispensing with the study of the *dead languages*. Though this committee reported against any change in the course, the appointment itself is evidence of a difference in the public mind in relation to classical learning. At nearly the same time Amherst College proposed two parallel courses for graduation — one to include, the other to omit, the Classics, but substituting other studies for them. The parallel course, however, was soon abandoned and the Classics required as a part of the curriculum.

The general agitation of the subject of classical study at this time, forced upon the conductors of the American Educational Society the consideration of the question of requiring candidates for the ministry under its patronage to study the Classics. Professor Stuart, of the Theological Seminary, Andover, was requested by the officers of the Society to publish his views on the subject. This he did in an able Essay on the value of Classical Study, which was published in the Quarterly Journal of the American Education Society for July, 1828.

The discussions elicited by the objections raised against the study of the Classics settled the question in their favor for many years. A considerable number of addresses in their defence were published ; and able articles of the same tenor appeared in the journals of the day.

Within a few years past the discussion has been

revived. The English Schools Commission in prosecuting their investigations found great defects and abuses in the study ; and the inference was too readily and too illogically drawn here that there was a similar perversion and waste of time in the acquisition of classical learning among us. The developments in England called forth " Classical and Scientific Studies," by Professor W. P. Atkinson. Soon after, " Remarks on Classical and Utilitarian Studies," by Dr. Jacob Bigelow, appeared ; and at nearly the same time the collection of Essays on " The Culture demanded by Modern Life," edited by Dr. Youmans ; and still later, from the other side of the Atlantic, " Essays on Liberal Education," edited by Rev. F. W. Farrar. The tone and tendency of all these is to depreciate the value of Classical Study, and to dissuade rather than to incline the young to enter upon it, though the writers referred to concede, to some extent, the advantages to be derived from the study. Besides, the popular journals often question and disparage the usefulness of such studies, and create in the public mind a distrust in courses of study which, in the judgment of the most competent teachers, are deemed necessary for the best discipline of the mind. Within the last year three journals, within the space of three weeks said : " Scientific education will steadily supplant classical education during the next half century. Step by step the champions of classical training are retreating from their oldest, if not their strongest, positions." "Our educational institutions, as far as classical education is concerned, have no apologists, but are assailed equally by men of science and by scholars." "The sciences are of infinitely more consequence to young men of the country than Greek roots." A teacher at the annual meeting of the Massachusetts Teachers, one year ago, said that the study of the Classics was conducting us back to barbarism; and a member of the School Committee in one of the towns in the State, and occupying one of the highest positions as a teacher, has affirmed that six months was sufficient for the study of Latin, and three months was better. And from abroad we hear the bold position taken by a gentleman[1] of distinguished ability and culture : "Our education does not communicate to us knowledge, does not communicate to us the means of obtaining knowledge, does not communicate to us the means of communicating knowledge."

The views thus strongly and confidently expressed against the utility of classical studies, need to be met by counter statements and opinions, or many of the young will be misled and prejudiced against a course of study which is adapted to give the best training and the broadest culture. It is fitting, therefore, to

[1] Hon. Robert Lowe, on Primary and Classical Education.

present here in brief the expressed opinions of eminent scholars who look at the subject from a point of view wholly different from that given above. In the fair balancing of the evidence, it will not be difficult to determine on which side the weight of authority rests :

"Classical studies are, in truth, beyond comparison, the most essential of all; conducting, as they do, to the knowledge of human nature, which they bring us to consider under all its variety of aspects and relations; at one time in the language and literature of nations who have left behind them traces of their existence and glory; at another, in the frequent vicissitudes of history which continually renovate and improve society; and finally, in the philosophy which reveals to us the simple elements and the uniform organization of that wondrous being whom history, literature, and language successfully clothe in forms the most diversified, and yet always bearing on some more or less important part of his internal constitution. Classical studies maintain the sacred tradition of the intellectual and moral life of our species. To cripple, far more to destroy them, would in my eyes be an act of barbarism, an audacious attempt to arrest true civilization, a sort of high treason against humanity." [1]

"The study of ancient literature, if properly directed, is absolutely the best means towards a har-

[1] Victor Cousin, as quoted by Professor Pillans, Lectures, p. 38.

monious development of the faculties — the one end
of all liberal education; yet this means is not always
relatively the best, when circumstances do not allow
of its full and adequate application." [1]

" There are other advantages besides the intrinsic
merit of the ancient Classics, amply sufficient to repay
us for devoting a few years to the study of Greek and
Latin." " We know no kind of labor so well adapted
to the general improvement of the faculties in early
youth." [2]

" Familiarity with the Greek and Roman writers is
especially adapted to form the taste, and to discipline
the mind, both in thought and diction, to the relish of
what is elevated, chaste, and simple. The compositions
which these writers have left us, both in prose and
verse, whether considered in reference to structure,
style, modes of illustration, or general execution,
approach nearer than any others to what the human
mind, when thoroughly informed and disciplined, of
course approves; and constitute what it is most desirable to possess, a standard of determining literary
merit." " Classical discipline forms the best preparation for professional study." " The study forms the
most effectual discipline of the mental faculties." [3]

" Is the pursuit of classical literature worth the time

[1] Sir William Hamilton, Discussions on Philosophy, p. 329, Eng. ed.
[2] Edward Everett, North American Review, Vol. xi. pp. 415, 416.
[3] Professor Kingsley, Silliman's Journal, Vol. xv. pp. 329, 330.

expended on it? From the deepest and fullest convictions of my heart, I answer, Yes. I would I could
answer so loud as to be heard in every part of my
country." "I have never yet engaged in any exercise
which afforded more salutary discipline of this sort"—
the ability to command words to express exactly the
shades of ideas — "than that of translating difficult
passages from a foreign language. I have sometimes
spent whole hours on even a preposition or an adverb;
but I am very certain that few of my hours have been
spent to better purpose, in their influence over the
habits of the mind." [1]

"It is our glorious privilege to follow the track of
those who have adorned the history of mankind, to
feel as they have felt, to think as they have thought,
and to draw from the living fountain of their genius.
Wonderful and mysterious is the intellectual communion we hold with them." [2]

"Destroy the ancient Greek and Latin authors, if
you aim at absolute dominion; because, if those are
read, principles of liberty and just sentiments of the
dignity and rights of mankind must be imbibed." [3]

"With one voice we should respond to every ruth-
less attempt to tear from our college course the study

[1] Professor Stuart, Journal of American Education Society, July, 1828,
pp. 89, 91.

[2] Professor Adam Sedgwick. A Discourse on the Studies of the University. [3] Hobbs.

of the Greek and Latin languages: Procul, O procul
este profani." [1]

"I [have] labored to remove unfounded prejudices
that exist against such [classical] studies, and to place
them in their true light, as a fruitful source of pleasure
and instruction; as laying the most solid foundation
of every other part of learning; as calculated to refine
our taste, strengthen our mental faculties, humanize
our manners and conversation, grace and adorn all our
other acquirements." [2]

"I hope the day is far distant when the study of
classical literature will cease to be essential to the
education of the English gentleman; and that whatever
changes, in this reforming age, may be made in our
universities and public schools, classical literature will
stand as the foundation on which everything else is
based. For, whether we regard the language as a
means of sharpening the intellectual faculties, or the
literature as a means of elevating and purifying the
taste, it would be easy to show that no subject could take
their place, or accomplish the objects which they effect." [3]

"Let not the University, however, be understood as
placing a slight value on the ancient Classics, and as
implying that the study of them may be dispensed with

---

[1] Professor R. B. Patton, Biblical Repository, January, 1837.
[2] Professor N. F. Moore, Columbia College, Lectures, p. 35.
[3] Dr. William Smith, in Davidson's Classical Scholarship, p. 241.

as generally unprofitable. By no means. We have a
veneration for them, deep and abiding. We esteem
classical learning as one of the most pure and elevating
pursuits in which the mind of man can be engaged.
He who would imbibe a lofty spirit of generous and
heroic virtue, a true and ardent love of civil and religious liberty, a refined taste, a well-ordered intellect,
and a free exercise of the combined graces and strength
of oratorical language, let him drink deep and long
at the full fountain of Greek and Roman literature." [1]

"I know of no mental operation more widely and
generally wholesome than the rendering of a compact
Latin paragraph into nervous, idiomatic English;
unless it be that of rendering a passage from a good
native author into terse, pointed, accurate Latin." [2]

"For my part, believing that the greatest achievements of philology are yet to be won, and her most
powerful instruments yet to be forged, I hold, with
Max Müller, that educationally and socially the study of
antiquity is more important than ever it was, and with
Rothe, that no substitute can ever be found for it." [3]

"I am fully conscious of the great value of classical
education, if it can be carried far enough. If a man
can continue his general education to the age of two

---

[1] Hon. James Talmadge, at the Dedication of the Chapel of the University of New York.

[2] Professor D'Arcy W. Thompson, Wayside Thoughts, p. 249.

[3] John E. B. Mayor, in Preface to Greek Reader, pp. l, li.

or three and twenty, it is well worth his while to be a classical scholar. Those who wish a superior education cannot neglect the Classics."[1]

" The study of science cultivates only one faculty, or set of faculties, but cultivates it more effectually than the study of language, — gives it, so to speak, a finer edge. The study of language, if properly conducted, besides its peculiar uses, cultivates all the faculties; though it cannot cultivate any one of them so effectually as the science appropriate to that faculty would do. Hence the study of languages, properly conducted, will do more for intellectual culture than any other single study; nevertheless, the culture attainable by the study of languages alone is very defective."[2]

Question. " Why do you attach importance to Latin ? "

Answer. " A boy can scarcely learn any science without the aid of Latin; in fact, in every turn he takes there is a difficulty. He cannot even pick up a botanical book but he is at sea, if he does not know Latin; and it is the same with chemistry. In fact, a third of our own language is more or less connected with it. If he wants to learn French, and has learned Latin, he has half learned his French. Unless a boy

[1] D. R. Fearon's Report, English Schools Commission, Vol. vii. p. 292.
[2] Rev. R. I. Bryce, LL.D., Principal of Belfast Academy — Schools Commission Reports, Vol. v. p. 869.

learns a dead language, I have come to the conclusion that if you give him ever so much mathematics, he never gets the faculty of expressing himself as if he had learned one of the dead languages; and, of the two, I should prefer Latin. ..... If you take a book like Caesar, and take one of those long sentences, and make a boy carry on his mind the connection from the beginning to the end of it, you have done a great deal; you have brought the boy to think more than you could in any other way." [1]

"You would, then, like to teach Greek and Latin to those who are destined to become small tradesmen, and so on?" "I would teach those languages to peasants, if I had the means and the staff." [2]

"I could not put any subject that I am accustomed to teach before Latin in point of utility to the mind." [3]

"The Classics give by far the best mental training." [4]

"I should not be at all inclined to impair the teaching of Latin in any way; because I consider that Latin is a most valuable thing to teach. It is the most precise language. Therefore I should not give

[1] Mr. Edmond Edmunds, a resident of Rugby — Schools Commission Reports, Vol. v. p. 487.

[2] Fred. W. Walker, M.A., Head Master of Grammar School at Manchester — Ibid. Vol. v. p. 216.

[3] Rev. Wm. Charles Williams, B.D., North London Collegiate School — Schools Commission Reports, Vol. iv. p. 500.

[4] Rev. Joshua Jones — Ibid. Vol. iv. p. 591.

English as much time as Latin, for the simple reason that I think it might be taught more easily." [1]

" Schoolmasters were almost unanimous in regarding Latin as their chief educational instrument." [2] So, too, " lawyers, medical men, farmers, engineers, agreed in wishing that a certain amount of Latin should form a part of the preliminary education for their several occupations." [3] Indeed, the great bulk of the witnesses before the Committee of the Schools Commission gave a preference to the study of language as a means of mental discipline.

The value of classical study is illustrated still further by statements which go to show more directly its adaptation to discipline the mind, and prepare it for the practical duties of life.

Dr. Jäger, director of the Frederic William Gymnasium, at Cologne, a mixed school, with both the classical course and classes in *real* or practical studies, and, from being at the head of the two different departments, well qualified to judge, " assured me it was the universal opinion that the *Realschulen* were not at present successful institutions. He declared that the boys in the corresponding forms of the classical school beat the *Realschule* boys in matters which both do alike, such as history, geography, the mother tongue,

<hr>

[1] G. W. Dasent, D.C.L., Ibid. Vol. v. p. 528.
[2] Ibid. Vol. i. p. 24. [3] Ibid. Vol. i. p. 25.

and even French, though to French the *Realschule* boys devote so far more time than their comrades of the classical school. The reason for this, Dr. Jäger affirms, is that the classical training strengthens a boy's mind so much more. This is what, as I have already said, the chief school authorities everywhere in France and Germany testify. I quote Dr. Jäger's testimony in particular, because of his ability, and because of his double experience." [1]

" Even mathematicians find that students from a good gymnasium make better progress than those who come from practical high schools where the Classics are excluded." [2]

" I have known cases where the leading prizes in French and German have been monopolized by leading prize-holders in Latin and Greek, although among their competitors have been lads whose linguistic studies have been confined almost entirely to the modern tongues." [3]

" Not a few [schoolmasters] declared that boys who had learned Latin beat boys who did not know Latin, even in other subjects in which Latin had no direct connection." [4]

" I have heard tradesmen express their gratitude

[1] Matthew Arnold's Schools and Universities on the Continent, p. 221.
[2] Professor Frederic Thiersch.
[3] Professor D'Arcy W. Thompson, Wayside Thoughts, p. 346.
[4] Schools Commission Reports, Vol. i. p. 24.

for the training of a classical school; they had found it of practical benefit in after life." [1]

" Do you think that, looking to the position of those who go behind the counter at the age of fourteen or fifteen, you would still make Latin generally one element in their education ? Yes, I would." [2]

It has also been said by a writer of high authority, that business men in Germany prefer those who have been educated in the regular gymnasia to those educated in the *Realschulen*.

The following statements, made at the Philological Association at Poughkeepsie, in July last, by Professor Boise of Chicago University, but for many years of the University of Michigan, are valuable here; the more valuable from the fact that the two parallel courses of study have not had so fair a trial elsewhere in our country. Two such courses were organized at Ann ·Arbor about seventeen years since. " The so-called scientific course embraces the modern languages, sciences, history, etc. — all those studies which are claimed to be specially practical, but excluding the ancient languages. All the Professors have given a fair share of their time and strength to that course, except the two Professors of the ancient languages.

[1] John E. B. Mayor, Preface to Greek Reader, p. xliv.
[2] Rev. J. Collingwood Bruce, LL.D.— Schools Commission Reports, Vol. v. p. 761.

The results, after a long and fair trial, have been somewhat as follows:

" 1. The number of the students in the scientific course has generally, I think always, remained considerably less than in the classical.

" 2. Nearly every year several students have left the scientific course, have gone back and begun the study of Latin and Greek, and prepared themselves for the classical course.

" 3. The classical graduates have been much more fortunate in obtaining responsible and lucrative positions than the scientific.

" A member of the last class with which I was connected at Ann Arbor, that of '68, has given me the names of ten men — nearly a third of the classical section — who obtained at once on their graduation salaries ranging from one thousand to seventeen hundred dollars a year. Not one of the scientific men, so far as he has been able to ascertain, obtained so large a salary. Thus in financial value a classical education is superior, not to speak of its superiority in other and far more important respects."

The recent opposition to classical study, both in England and this country, is due in part to the practical character of the age, which attaches special value to studies that meet its immediate demand;

partly to the rapid progress of physical science, which has given unwonted interest to that always attractive department of study; but chiefly to the fact that, generally, the study has not been conducted in such a manner as to give the best results of classical training. Rich as the mine is, it does not yield its treasures without the right kind of working. The highest benefits of classical study fail to be attained on several grounds:

1. The end to be aimed at is often overlooked. The study is in many cases undertaken and prosecuted with a view of gaining admission to college, and of completing the course there required. This end may be gained with very little critical scholarship, and very little mental discipline. Our system of education looks too much to the more immediate results, and too little to the more permanent and more valuable. Education is not so much knowledge as the preparation for knowledge. The course of study referred to, therefore, should have no such narrow end in view. It should be so conducted as to lay the broadest foundation for subsequent studies, and for the best results of life: to secure the most critical scholarship, the best discipline, and the finest culture at every step in the course.

2. There is often a misapprehension and neglect of the kind of work to be done. The feeling is widely

prevalent that the mere reading is the chief thing to be attained, while all that gives the most critical training, and cultivates the taste — peculiarities in construction, or modes of expression — are looked upon as of minor importance. This sacrifices some of the most valuable elements of the study; it overlooks the roots of the language, which photograph indelibly the habits, views, and conceptions of the people of the past. It overlooks the nicer distinctions in the meaning of words, the difference of thought as indicated by different cases, moods, tenses, as well as by all the other more delicate machinery of language, which are designed to mark with precision the picture or view just as it lay in the mind of the author.

Most of those who study in this defective way are disappointed in the results of their labors, and are pretty likely to increase the number who think that the time devoted to classical study might more wisely have been given to other subjects.

3. Another obstacle to the successful study of the Classics is the habit, in the early part of the course, of going over too much ground in a given time. As the preparatory course is the first effort of the pupil in the critical study of language, and is to lay the foundation on which the succeeding superstructure is to be erected, anything which prevents the formation of right habits of study, gives a wrong bias, or interferes

c

with the thoroughness of the work, may prove fatal to the whole. A Professor in one of our colleges says: "If there must be defect in any part, let it be in the superstructure. I do not hesitate to utter my deliberate and matured conviction that more importance should be attached to the preparatory than to the collegiate course of study. I mean that the destiny of the student, and of the world through him, is more affected by the preparatory course. A failure in this is wont to be so fatal, so irretrievable, that no pains should be spared to avoid it."[1] Now, when it is borne in mind how much is implied in the proper preparation for the college course, how many subjects for study are embraced, it will at once be evident that more work is involved than can properly be done in the time usually allotted to it. Hence the temptation to do it superficially. But it is not the mere going over the ground that secures the end sought. Haste here emphatically makes waste. It is the last place to try a system of cramming. There must be time to investigate and make the way luminous at every step; to reason and compare, to adjust delicate questions, to discriminate between apparently similar words, modes of expression and construction, and to get clear and well-defined ideas, or there is little progress or profit. Many a student, driven over ground hurriedly

[1] Professor Stanton, Union College.

because so much must be done in a given period, with no time to take in the spirit and beauties of what he is studying, without strengthening his memory, quickening his perceptions, refining his taste, or invigorating his reasoning powers, loses all interest in the study, charges his failure to the Classics, while it belongs only to the hurried, confused, and ill-directed manner of studying them. There can be little doubt that, if the pupil attempted only what he could thoroughly master in this part of his course, the benefit to him in his future studies, and its influence on his future success, would be much greater than it is as the study is usually pursued. It is clear, also, that this slow and thorough method at the outset, mastering all forms, the laws which determine them, as well as what they express, reviewing, re-reviewing, and reviewing again, making the portions studied as familiar as if in our own language, that such a method will keep up an unabated interest, and in the end enable the student to go over vastly more ground, and with greater pleasure and profit, than according to the usual methods of study.

4. Another reason why classical education does not yield its best fruits is the want of properly qualified teachers. Many of these are just from college without experience and without a critical knowledge of what they are to teach. Much of the elementary instruction therefore is necessarily defective, and fails to awaken

interest in the student, or to lay the foundation for subsequent success. The highest benefits of classical study are generally not attained without a right start; and such a start is not to be expected unless there are persons competent to give the proper direction. There are honorable exceptions to such defective teaching; but it must be admitted that to a great extent the early part of the classical course is by no means what it might be under more favorable circumstances.

Then, too, in the higher institutions there is not always the experience and thoroughness necessary to give the highest value to the instruction. If greater experience and thoroughness should take the place of any such defects, and the style of teaching be made broader and more critical, and the demand upon the student's efforts so increased as to require new earnestness and to awaken new interest in the study, the estimate placed upon the worth of classical study would be greatly enhanced. This would soon correct the excuse sometimes given for not investigating thoroughly all the topics involved in the lessons, that the critical points and the broader relations of the subjects are not called up at the recitations ; it would also silence the plea not unfrequently made against a thorough preparation for College, that it leaves the scholar too little to do there.

If the pupil is to reap the choicest fruits of classical

study, he must first learn the symbols of the language—
the words and their roots, their forms and modifications;
the force of cases, moods, and tenses; the arrangement
of words and sentences — the reason for one position
rather than another, and the 'general laws of agreement
and construction. Then he should be carried forward
to higher topics — to the finished rendering of his
author, the study of synonyms, antiquities, the manners
and customs of the times; the prominent subjects of
thought at the period studied, and the circumstances
which gave them their peculiar coloring; the influences
under which his author wrote; the logic, rhetoric, oratory, and poetry of the writers; the history and civilization, the science, philosophy, and religion of the
time; the connection between the past and the present;
in a word, everything which will serve to photograph
to his mind the busy and strange scenes of the past, the
thinkers and actors with their surroundings, and to
make him a conscious sharer in the movements of a
world so different from his own. The student who is
carried forward, from term to term, in the investigation
of subjects like these, treading with a firmer and surer
step as he advances, will be constantly introduced into
new fields of thought and investigation, will find new
beauties and attractions in the compositions of the great
masters of antiquity; will never be listless in the study
so conducted, nor complain that he learns little that

c*

is new year after year, or that the same questions are propounded in the later as in the earlier years of his course, or that he hears nothing beyond the common rules of syntax.

It has already been stated that one of the chief difficulties in realizing the best results of classical training in our country is the want of well-qualified teachers. The course of collegiate education embraces such a variety of studies, that the best preparation for so difficult a department of instruction as that of the Classics, could not reasonably be expected from it. The Germans owe their high distinction in classical learning, in a great degree, to their philological seminaries, where the masters of the higher. schools acquire a ·thorough knowledge of classical antiquity. Wolf long conducted such a seminary at Halle, in which he was assisted by Immanuel Bekker. The philological seminary at Berlin has been under the direction of such men as Boeckh, Buttmann, Bernhardy, Lachmann, Haupt ; that at Bonn under Professors Näke, Welcker, Ritschl, and Otto Jahn. Every Prussian university has a philological seminary.[1] The advantage of this provision to those who are to enter upon the work of classical instruction is very great. They have a more critical and comprehensive acquaintance with the subjects they are to

[1] See Arnold's Schools and Universities on the Continent, p. 192.

teach; the ancient world is opened to them in its genius and spirit, in all the elements that made it what it was, more fully than the usual university course would have secured to them. Of course the fruits of a classical training under such instruction are vastly greater than they could have been without these advantages.

The want of similar facilities for the preparation of classical teachers, particularly for our preparatory schools, is a serious hinderance to the highest success in classical culture. The mere grammatical knowledge of the ancient languages, or a verbal acquaintance with their literature, or the ability to render them into idiomatic English are not sufficient qualifications for a teacher of Latin and Greek; he needs all the varied knowledge which goes to make these living languages and himself a conscious actor in the scenes which he interprets to his pupils. If some provision could be made, either for the establishment of independent training schools for classical teachers, or in connection with institutions already existing, by which those who are to give direction and tone to the earlier classical studies, can be properly educated for their work, the benefits of the training would be more manifest, and the popular clamor against the ancient languages, or the demand that they should no longer form a part of the curriculum of a liberal education, would cease. Our

country can boast of many rich fruits of classical culture, but we need to show still more and better. And
with the proper facilities, it can be done. It is not
reasonable, therefore, to reject from our course of instruction a study, which, wisely conducted, has great
and varied educational power.

The present collection of Essays has been made with
a view of correcting the popular misapprehension in
regard to the value of classical study; to check, if may
be, the prejudices against it; to show to the student
who enters upon it, what it can do for him, and to
stimulate him to prosecute it with such thoroughness
and earnestness as to gather from it the rich treasures
it contains. The Essays, as will be seen, are the productions of distinguished scholars of England, Scotland,
Germany, and different parts of our own country.
They were written at times considerably remote from
each other, by men in different pursuits of life, yet they
all have one general tone, setting forth with emphasis,
and sometimes with rhetorical beauty, the value of the
study which they recommend. We need to be re-
called by their arguments from our doubts, and to take
counsel of them rather than of the popular sentiment.
We need to give a broader interpretation to what are
called useful studies. It is not the practical sciences
only that are to be regarded as useful, such as aid us

in guiding the ship across the ocean, or in running the steam-car, or flashing information along the wires, or in disarming the lightning of its power; nor such only as minister to our daily wants, to the conveniences· and comforts of life; we must learn to regard every study as useful which imparts increased vigor to the mind, forms the character more perfectly, gives a more cultivated taste, or makes us know ourselves better. "It will be a bad day for moral and political amelioration when the faculties of the soul are balanced against a certain value in counters, and when the stores of moral knowledge are rated only at their auction prices. We can conceive of no train of habitual thought and conversation more hostile to individual elevation of mind, and more paralyzing to everything generous and noble in national character, than the perpetual reference of everything to its equivalent in common or ordinary estimation. The principle carried out would reduce the earth to a hive, and every fragrant and beautiful flower upon its surface to the mere aliment of its inhabitants. It is a coarse and selfish doctrine, worthy of man only in an early stage of his progress, and always indicative, when found in more advanced communities, of a sordid and grasping spirit. Reducing every pursuit and enterprise to a single aim, and trying it by a single test, it strikes all that is disinterested from motive, all that is lofty from society, all that is courteous from manners. It asks a certificate of character from every undertaking, pausing upon it, with its chilling and sneering philosophy, till it can lay its hand upon the evidence of its practicability and profit. All high studies, all purely literary culture, all that warms the imagination and clusters round the heart, it neglects or despises. Nay, it would almost teach its disciples to tear away those gentle affections which unite them to their kind, and those sublime emotions which lead them to their Creator — a new Iconoclast, trampling upon the shattered symbols of ancient hope." [1]

In selecting these extracts, only such parts of the original Essays have been taken as related more especially to the subject. Sentences, paragraphs, or whole pages have been omitted, as the object in view seemed to require. But in no case, so far as is known, have the sentiments and arguments of the authors been changed or modified by the form in which they are here presented. The usual marks, indicating the omission of sentences or paragraphs, etc., have been purposely dispensed with.

In the Essays selected there will be found some repetition of thought and illustration. But the diversity in the treatment of the common subject, the richness and variety of the illustrations, will more

---

[1] American Quarterly Review, Vol. xvii. p. 4.

than compensate for the occasional instances of repetition. There is no one of the papers which does not present the subject with new force and freshness.

It is in no way intended, either by the remarks made in this Introduction, or in presenting the Essays themselves to the public, to cry up classical study to the detriment of any other; but only to give it its true place and importance, which it is in danger of losing in an age that looks so largely at immediate practical results. A full and symmetrical education is what is needed. Any diminished interest in scientific or kindred subjects, or in the study and literature of our own rich language, is greatly to be deprecated; we need more, rather than less, devotion to these. But, while we assiduously cultivate such departments of study, and devise the best means of teaching them with still greater success, let us not fail to drink more largely than ever at the refreshing and inexhaustible fountains which the great minds of antiquity have opened for us.

ANDOVER, December 1, 1869.

CLASSICAL STUDY.

I.

No educational question has been more keenly debated than that of the position which the Classics ought to occupy in our scholastic curriculum. By some it has been held that they should be the exclusive, or almost the exclusive, instruments of intellectual education; while others have entertained the opinion that they should have no place among the ordinary subjects of study. Between these two extreme opinions lie others, modified in various degrees according to the points of view, intellectual tastes, and varying circumstances of the condition of life, or state of mind and feeling, of those who have held them. From the time of Locke until the present day this question has formed a battle-ground upon which rival educational factions have fought, both eager for the strife, and, as is generally the case in all controversies, too often heedless of the cause of truth, and caring for little else except victory over their opponents.

This Essay, entitled "Classical Studies: their true position and value in Education," was originally read before the Literary and Philosophical Society of Liverpool by Rev. Joshua Jones, M.A., Principal of King William's College, Isle of Man. It was first published in the Transactions of the Society, and afterwards in a pamphlet by itself.

It may seem to some a superfluous task to attempt
to say anything further upon a subject about which so
much has already been said, and consequently to advance anything new is so difficult.   It appears to us,
however, that it has been too generally treated in the
one-sided spirit of the advocate or the partisan, and
that writers have hitherto for the most part written
upon it exclusively from the one point of view which
they may have happened to adopt.   It is the purpose
of this paper rather to take a review of the whole
question in all its aspects, to consider the arguments,
and compare what has been said on both sides, to
modify objections and qualify assertions; and, though
we cannot hope to bring forward, in a matter which
has been so often and keenly discussed, much that is
altogether novel, yet we do hope to be able to present
the whole subject in a new form, and to shed a somewhat clearer light upon it.   We may add that the subject is particularly pressed upon our attention at the
present time by the circumstance that Her Majesty's
Public School Commissioners have, in their report
recently published, recommended that the Classics
should still be retained as the leading subject of instruction and the educational basis in the Public
Schools of England ; and it is therefore just now an
interesting and useful matter for inquiry whether this
recommendation, after a due consideration of the facts
of the case, and of the arguments *pro* and *con.*, be a
wise and judicious one or not.

It is not difficult to account for the high position
which the Classics have so long occupied in our system

of education. At the revival of learning in the sixteenth century there was no literature worthy of the name, except that of Greece and Rome. The middle ages had produced a few great intellects ; but they had expended their energies for the most part on theological or philosophical subtleties, calculated indeed to exercise and develop the logical powers of the mind, but of little value, either in themselves or for the purpose of general intellectual discipline. There had been a conflict between human reason and ecclesiastical authority; the latter had fixed certain limits beyond which intellectual inquiry might not go ; and the former, active and struggling, but yet constrained by outward force to obey, had expended its energies on every minute point within the narrow sphere assigned to it. The mind of man has perhaps but rarely manifested such intense power and acuteness as it exhibited in the works of some of the great schoolmen, c.g. Anselm and Thomas Aquinas ; and but rarely, perhaps, has it ever produced results of so little value to the intellectual progress of mankind. Scholasticism, then, having supplied no general literature, the classical writers of Greece and Rome were the only authors suitable for general study, when the human mind began to emancipate itself from the fetters in which it had been so long bound. Again, Latin was at the time, and had been for centuries, the language of the Church, and of the schools of law and physic ; so far from being a dead language, it was the vernacular of the churchman and of the learned ; and it had thus established a sway from which it could not easily be displaced. It must also be remembered that at the period spoken of, and for some time after, classical subjects would have formed natural and interesting materials of thought and conversation to the educated, from the entire absence of those numerous and absorbing topics which the vast increase of knowledge, and the wide-spread diffusion of information, scientific, literary, political, and general, and the brilliant and extensive literature of modern times, supply to us in our age. Then further, it must be borne in mind that contemporaneous with the revival of learning was the foundation in our own country of many of the great seminaries of learning, which naturally adopted the classical languages and literatures as the then only general subjects of study worthy of pursuit. Thus it happened that the Classics got exclusive possession of the educational field ; they formed the only unprofessional studies of the great seats of learning ; they became the sole media through which professional instruction was conveyed ; they were fostered by scholastic endowments devoted to, and often founded for, their exclusive pursuit, in virtue of the principle inherent in all endowments of perpetuating that for the support of which they were originally bestowed or have been subsequently applied ; they were the only studies with which the majority of the learned were acquainted, and consequently they were the only ones which they were disposed, or indeed able, to teach. And so they were propagated from generation to generation of students ; they had the advantage of possession, and in time, too, the prestige which the tradition of long-continued pursuit, and all the associations and

prejudices connected therewith, never fail to give — a
prestige which inclines people to acquiesce even in that
of which they do not quite approve; they had enlisted
on their side the best minds of each age, and the ardent
feelings of able and zealous votaries; and it is not a
matter of wonder that what had thus been the great
study of the men of any one generation, and of their
fathers and forefathers for many previous ones, should
not at any time be dethroned from its position but after
a hard and desperate struggle.

But while it is easy to account for the commanding
position which classical studies have so long held in
our educational system, the real question for us to
decide is, how far that position is at the present time
tenable. For it must be remembered that the circumstances of our age are very different from those of the
sixteenth century. Then the Classics contained the
only philosophy, history, poetry, and oratory worthy of
the name; but now that philosophy is in many respects
superseded by the deeper and truer philosophy which
the enlarged speculations and wider experience of
modern times have produced; that history is, if not
altogether supplanted, yet rendered less valuable by
reason of the far wider range of facts differing often in
kind from those of the classical records which modern
history unfolds; and that poetry and oratory if unsurpassed, can still be equalled, or nearly so, by the
productions of modern authors. The point for our
decision then is, whether in the present condition of
society, and the existing state of knowledge, classical
studies ought to fill the exclusive and exalted position

in education which they have hitherto done; and if not, what place, if any, they ought to be permitted to occupy. This is the question which has been so long and keenly debated, and to the solution of which we hope in the present paper to contribute something.

Before proceeding to discuss the proposed subject, we shall find it convenient for our purpose to fix our ideas upon two preliminary points.

First, then, it will be useful for us to determine the proper object of education, because this is a point which lies at the foundation of our present inquiry, and will subsequently help us in the investigation of one of the most common objections to classical studies. This matter has formed the subject of an earnest controversy between those, on the one hand, who advocate the training and development of the faculties as the aim and end of education, and those, on the other hand, who maintain that education should rather have as its object professional training, or the imparting of knowledge which can be directly turned to account in the business of after life. Now we may take it as a fundamental principle, that the object of general education is not so much to impart information, as to call into exercise, and develop and discipline faculties; not so much to store with knowledge, as to awaken the desire, and supply the power, of acquiring knowledge; not to afford special training for particular pursuits in life, but to furnish general culture; not to train a man for his future calling, but to make him fit for any calling, by giving him the power of taking up any subject that presents itself, comprehending its principles, and mastering its details, — by making his intellect broad, clear, vigorous, and active, — by imparting to him a sound and accurate judgment, able to decide aright the various questions which occur in business or ordinary life ; — in short, by educing and training those powers and habits of mind which enable a man in his social and business capacity to deal successfully with his fellow-men, and to exert a wholesome and useful influence on all within his sphere of action. To confine education, then, within the limits afforded by the imparting of the preparatory knowledge, or training, necessary for a profession or business, is grievously to narrow its limits and to impair the prospect of its ultimately bringing forth the desired fruit. For, we must remember, a man has other duties to perform besides those of his profession, trade, or calling ; he has to be the ruler and counsellor of a home circle, to whom wife and children and domestics will look for advice and direction ; he has to meet his fellow-creatures in social intercourse ; he has perhaps to take some part in political or civic affairs ; and for all these duties, domestic, social, and political, his education ought to fit him, as well as for his profession or trade. Now it is obvious that so wide a culture as that of which we have been speaking, which has to influence the whole man in all his capacities, faculties, and feelings, cannot be effected by the mere acquisition of knowledge as knowledge ; no attainable amount of knowledge can enable him to grasp all the subjects, and grapple successfully with all the difficulties, which meet him in his ordinary life ; nothing short of the vigorous and healthy action of all his faculties, as far as may be, will stand him in good stead in the great world-battle in which every true man has to engage. General culture, then, is the best preparation for a man's special work in life, whatever that work may be, and should therefore be the primary object aimed at in his education.

We must be careful, however, to guard against any misapprehension in this matter; though it be true that the imparting of knowledge for its own sake is not the primary object of education, yet it must be remembered that education must be based on knowledge, and cannot be carried on without it; intellectual grasp and acuteness can only be attained by exercising the faculties in the acquisition, the contemplation, and the comparison of the various branches of human learning. Education is not instruction indeed, but without instruction education is impossible.

The second preliminary point upon which it seems desirable to say something is the distinction between the different kinds of education. Now there are three kinds of education — Primary, Secondary, and Higher:

Primary Education consists in the imparting of the mere elements of learning, or rather of those branches of knowledge which are indispensable for every one in civilized life, or which are necessary for the subsequent acquisition of all knowledge — I mean reading, writing, and arithmetic. Under proper methods of teaching these elements, some amount of intellectual discipline may be imparted; but that discipline is not very considerable in amount, nor is it of a very high quality.

This, however, is all the mental culture attainable by the great mass of our population, who are forced at an early age to forego all systematic education, and engage in hard manual toil for the sustenance of life. Secondary Education is that of the vast majority of our middle classes, who are enabled to stay longer at school than our working population, say until their fourteenth, fifteenth, or sixteenth year, and have therefore the opportunity of receiving a more thorough mental discipline, and acquiring a higher intellectual culture. They have time and opportunity for the pursuit of many of the higher branches of study, and of those which are the most efficacious for the training and cultivation of the mind ; and the great object in educating them, after first of all securing their acquisition of those elements of knowledge which are necessary, or eminently useful, for the successful carrying on of the ordinary business of men in their position of life, should be to educe and discipline the various powers of their minds. The Higher Education is that of those who have the means, opportunity, and desire of prolonging their studies up to the period of early manhood. Its object is the complete and harmonious development, and the calling forth into healthful, vigorous action, of all the mental faculties ; in short, the general cultivation of the whole intelligence ; and this is to be effected by the study of the higher, more refining, and more recondite branches of knowledge.

Leaving out of sight Primary Education, as not connected with our present subject of discussion, we have to consider only the Secondary and the Higher.

We assume, then, as essential conditions, first, that in both, the branches of study which appertain specially to Primary Education have been secured; next, that in both so much extra information has been imparted as is necessary or useful for a man who has to occupy a position above that of the mechanic or day-laborer, and earn his living in any other way than by the work of his hands; and we assert that afterwards, in both alike, the object in view should be mental discipline and culture, — the only difference between the two being, that in Secondary Education this discipline and culture can only be carried on to a certain point, and must stop at a much lower level than the one attainable in the Higher Education. The difference then between the Secondary and Higher Education is one rather of degree than of kind; the instruments used in the one must be, with certain modifications and with some exceptions, pretty much the same as those used in the other; the main distinction being that in the one they may be somewhat inferior in quality, as they have to do less accurate work, and cannot be used long enough to bring their work to that degree of perfection which they are able to attain in the other. The conclusion at which we have arrived, and which concerns immediately our present purpose, is, that in the education of both the middle and upper classes of society the same subjects of study and the same course of instruction should, with certain modifications and under certain limitations, be adopted; the leading exception being, that in the case of those who have the opportunity of pursuing their studies to a more advanced age, some subjects which are unsuitable for immature minds, or less developed faculties, may be added, while those which are being pursued in common by all, can by them be studied more deeply, widely, and thoroughly.

So then, taking into account intellectual education only — for it is with this alone we are at present concerned — we shall have to consider what subject, or subjects, of study are best calculated to educe and supply healthful exercise to the various mental faculties, and to secure the harmonious development and perfect culture of the mind of man. No doubt that, if the human intellect were sufficiently vigorous and capacious to comprehend and retain it, this would be best effected by the study of the whole cycle of human knowledge; but as the acquisition of all that can be known by man is plainly impossible, even to the highest and most vigorous intellect, and we have to form an educational system which will suit minds of average grasp and power, it is quite plain that we must make a selection from among the various branches of human learning; and while we take into our course as many of these as can be fairly acquired by the student, not as a mere possession of the memory, but as part of his mental furniture, and in such a way as to expand and invigorate his mental powers, we must lay chief stress upon those which are most likely to promote the object which in education we have in view.

Now, the subject which first presses its claims for selection upon our attention is that of Language. Language is the expression of thought, and if not

actually co-extensive with it, yet it is the only medium
by which thought can be embodied in a definite form
in our own minds, and by which it can be conveyed to
others. In studying language, then, we are to a considerable extent contemplating those mental processes
of which it is the expression; in investigating its laws,
we are investigating at the same time in no small
degree the laws of thought; and therefore it is that
Grammar may be regarded as, to use the words of Her
Majesty's Public School Commissioners,[1] " the logic of
common speech." There must be a mutual action
and reaction always going on between the inward
process and its outward exponent; what calls forth
and disciplines our faculty of language must also
develop and train in no small degree our faculties of
thought; vigor and clearness of verbal expression must
be the counterpart of a certain force and lucidity of
mind, corresponding in kind, if not co-extensive in
degree. Thus it is clear, from a *priori* considerations,
that the study of language, in some form or other, is
of essential importance as an intellectual discipline;
and it follows, as a natural corollary, that the more
perfect the language studied, the more perfect will be
the discipline resulting therefrom.

When we speak of Language as a subject of study,
we cannot exclude from our idea the subject-matter
which it conveys; the thought conveyed, as well as
the mode of conveying it, the " matter," as well as
the " form," must come under consideration. With
language, then, literature must ever be closely allied;

------

[1] Report, p. 28.

for, though we may in idea dwell more sometimes on the one, and sometimes on the other, yet in fact they are indissolubly connected. And the study of literature commends itself to our notice independently, on its own merits, as "the study of the intellectual and moral world we live in,"[1] and therefore suitable for the culture of the intellectual and moral beings who inhabit that world.

We have arrived, then, at this point in our inquiry — language and literature seem to have a primary claim for a leading position among our subjects of study. We shall have hereafter to examine more fully how far this claim is tenable, by a comparison between the classical languages and literatures and other leading branches of learning, in respect of their educational value. We say the classical languages and literatures, because we shall show that — whereas we cannot possibly study all, or even any considerable number of languages, and their accompanying literatures, but must make a selection from among them of those most suitable for the discipline and culture of the mind — these are plainly entitled to this pre-eminence.

Now in whatever we may say in favor of the Classics occupying a prominent place in our educational course, we must carefully guard against being supposed to suggest that they ought to hold that exclusive position therein which they for so many generations have maintained. We shall not attempt for one moment to defend the untenable opinion, which has been fostered by the system so long, and even still to a considerable

---

[1] Report of Public School Commissioners, p. 28.

2

extent pursued in our public schools, that they are the only subjects suitable for mental discipline. On the contrary, it will be at once acknowledged that the languages and literatures of Greece and Rome form collectively but one among many subjects suitable for the development and training of the mind of man. The only point proposed for discussion is, — whether they are the best adapted instruments for this purpose; whether they ought to occupy in our educational system the central position around which all other subjects should be arranged; whether, in other words, the place which these other subjects ought to take be one of equality with, or one (as Her Majesty's Public School Commissioners recommend) of subordination to, the Classics, as the foundation of the educational super-structure. Mr. Gladstone puts the matter at once on a right issue, when, in his letter to one of the Commissioners, he requires that the question whether " the classical training is the proper basis of a liberal education " should receive " a distinct affirmative, or a substantial negative," and expresses a wish that " the relation of pure science, natural science, modern languages, modern history, and the rest to the old classical training ought to be founded on a principle"; denying, at the same time, on his part, " their right to a parallel or equal position," and maintaining that " their true position is ancillary, and, as ancillary, it ought to be limited and restrained without scruple, as much as a regard to the paramount matter of education may dictate."[1]

[1] Report of Public School Commissioners, Vol. ii. pp. 42, 43.

Whether it may be desirable, indeed, to have a principal subject of study at all is a matter which may at first sight admit of considerable doubt. It cannot be denied that true mental culture is the result of the blending together of many studies, each filling its own proper position, and each harmonizing with every other. But it must be remembered that, for the purpose of effecting this harmonious blending, there should be some central study around which all should be gathered, and with reference to which each one should be placed, instead of all being left to pursue, as it were, their own ways, and follow erratic orbits — a course likely to lead to intellectual chaos and confusion, rather than to a harmonious composition and action of the intellectual elements. And further, it would appear that, in order to bring out the mental powers in their full vigor and development, they ought, in consequence of their limited nature and capacity, to be exercised in a limited sphere — a sphere not so narrow indeed as to impede their full expansion and free action, and yet not so wide as to render their energies aimless and discursive. And this seems to indicate the desirableness of selecting some one leading branch of study to which all others should be subordinated.

This point, then, having been ascertained, the question immediately arises: Ought the Classics to be this principal subject, which is to form the centre of our educational course? It must be at once admitted that classical studies cannot discipline and expand all our mental faculties, and therefore that they can only effect a part of our mental culture; yet, if it can be shown

that they train a larger number of faculties in a more
effective way, and that they are, in short, more potent
instruments of culture than any other class of studies;
if it can be ascertained that they form a real centre,
about which a large number of branches of learning
can naturally be arranged, their right to fill the leading,
central position spoken of will have been satisfactorily
established.

The course of our inquiry, then, has brought us now
to the consideration of the influence of the study of
the Classics in the exercise, expansion, and cultivation
of the faculties of the intellect.

1. The study of the Classics exercises and strengthens
the *memory.* The learning of grammatical paradigms
and rules; the act of remembering words and phrases;
the learning by rote passages of authors; the constant
necessity of bearing in mind a large mass of historical,
antiquarian, mythological, and philological information,
with a view to the right understanding and appreciation
of the meaning of the classical writers (all of which
are essential elements of good classical training), afford
constant practice to this important faculty, and thereby
invigorate and develop it.

2. It cultivates the *judgment*, by constantly exercising that faculty in the investigation of the appropriate
meaning of words; in the selection of the most exact
methods of rendering sentences, by giving each word
and phrase and particle its full force and interpretation,
in the examination of difficulties; in the comparison
of rules with their exemplifications, and of passages
with their parallel passages from the same or other

authors; for all this requires discrimination and decision, which are essentially acts of the judgment.

3. It educates the *analytical* faculty, by necessitating on the part of the student the tracing up of words to their roots, — the division of compound words into their component elements, — and the analysis of sentences, and those, too, sentences unusualy complicated and involved, with many clauses, whose connection with, and dependence on, one another are not at once obvious, and in which the words, which in sense are consecutive, are often widely distant from one another in position.

4. It develops the *reason*. "Correct syntax is," as it has been well said, "nothing but a correct process of reasoning." Syntax consists in the arrangement of words and their inflections in such a way as to be correspondent with the operation of the reasoning faculty within, and therefore the study of syntax must be a discipline of that faculty. Then, again, the student of a language has constantly to be tracing out the connecting links of sentences and paragraphs, all of which are counterparts of a ratiocinative process in the mind of the author whose work he is studying; and he has to resolve philological principles into the conclusions, which from time to time he needs, deducible therefrom. Add to this, that the classical authors supply us in history, oratory, and philosophy, with some of the most perfect specimens of reasoning which any literature can produce; and it will be seen in how great a degree classical studies tend to call out and expand the reason.

5. It educates the *taste*, through the instrumentality

of translation and composition, which involve the constant necessity of carefully considering how the idiom of the classical languages may be best expressed by that of our own, and, conversely, how idiomatic English may be best turned into idiomatic Greek or Latin ; the task of determining how to represent all the nice distinctions which exist in the words and inflections of one language, without loss of force or meaning in the words and inflections of another — a task of especial difficulty, and therefore calling for the exercise of nicer discrimination and more refined taste, where the classical languages have to be turned into our own, or *vice versa*, because of their great difference from our own language in point of structure and mode of expression ; and lastly, in the case of verse composition, the necessity of deciding how to clothe the ideas and language of modern poetry in the most appropriate forms which the poetry of Greece or Rome can suggest or supply.

6. It exercises and cultivates the *imagination*, because classical literature contains some of the most perfect works of imagination which the world can produce ; and the length of the time which, in consequence of the difficulty of the languages, must necessarily be spent over each passage of these works for the understanding of its construction and meaning, affords the student a better opportunity of entering into and appreciating its imagery or sentiment, than if it were hurried over in a mere cursory reading.

7. It gives precision to, and cultivates the faculty of, *language*. The careful study of the complex and yet perfectly constructed sentences of the best Greek

and Latin authors, and the habit of turning those sentences into good idiomatic English, which shall fully express as far as possible the most minute shade of difference in the meaning of the original, are perhaps the best possible exercises which the student can anywhere find, in the art of discerning the exact force of words and phrases, and of clothing ideas in appropriate symbols, wherein consists the perfection of the operation of the faculty of language.

Such is the efficacy of classical studies regarded as a discipline of the mental faculties.

Let us now view the Classics as a central subject, and examine whether they can fairly be regarded as a natural centre, around which a considerable number of other branches of learning can be easily and without undue force aggregated. What are the subjects, then, which an efficient classical teacher can connect, and to some extent teach, together with his own special subject?

1. First, in teaching the grammar of the classical languages to beginners, if he endeavor to impart, not a mere rote-acquaintance with declensions and conjugations, but a sound and accurate knowledge of the accidence — a knowledge based indeed upon the paradigms contained in the text-book, and acquired by the memory, but illustrated by his own oral teaching; if he be careful to mark all the leading inflections, contrasting them with the corresponding grammatical forms of their own or any other language, or languages, known to his pupils, and illustrating by appropriate examples the points to which he is calling their attention; he will

be teaching principles and facts common to the etymology of all languages, imparting much valuable instruction about the grammar of those particular languages to the analogies of which he is directing notice, and thus be clearing away many difficulties which impede the student in the direct study of them, and help him in the acquisition of them, or indeed of any others which at any time he may have occasion to learn. Similarly, in explaining and illustrating the rules of syntax to more advanced pupils, by pursuing the same method of comparison between the syntactical rules of Greek and Latin, and the corresponding ones in English, or in any other modern language they may be learning, while he is imparting an accurate knowledge of the construction of Latin and Greek sentences, he is also supplying a considerable amount of information upon the principles of construction of language in general, and upon their practical exemplifications in his own, or some other language with which his pupils are concerned. And when, in the reading of a Greek or Latin author, he calls attention to those inflections and syntactical rules as they are practically exhibited, and by parsing and analysis impresses them upon the minds of the students, he has a further and an ever-recurring opportunity of doing much in the same direction. Thus with the teaching of Latin and Greek grammar (whether from the textbook, or practically in the reading of an author), the teaching of English, or any other grammar, acquaintance with which is desirable for the learner, and the imparting of the leading principles of universal grammar, may be readily associated.

2. Again, in the translation of Greek and Latin authors into English, by avoiding the absurd and injurious practice, so common in schools, of what is technically called " construing " (a practice which by accustoming the student to a distorted caricature of his own tongue, with an utter neglect of its own proper idioms, impairs his power of using it aright), and by requiring his pupils to render each sentence in good readable English, while at the same time he insists upon an exact interpretation of every inflection, word, and clause, he is supplying the best possible exercise in English composition. Add to this that the Classics afford abundant suitable topics, upon which the student may be required to reproduce in his own words, what he has learned from his teacher, together with such additional ideas as his own reflection or reading may furnish; and it will be seen that classical instruction naturally fosters that most important branch of education, composition in our own mother tongue. Classical studies tend also in another way to help the student in the acquisition of a thorough mastery of his own language; because, in the practice of Latin and Greek composition, he learns many of its characteristic peculiarities, has his attention especially directed to its idioms, and is constantly occupied in the discovery, and the accurate reproduction in different language, of the exact force and meaning of its words and modes of expression. Thus, necessarily, is the art of composition in the vernacular imparted with the teaching of the classical languages.

3. But, besides the influence which classical studies thus have in promoting the more exact knowledge of

our own and other tongues, they can also be used as the occasion for arousing an interest in many other branches of learning, and be made, as it were, the basis upon which the superstructure of knowledge in those branches may be easily and surely built. Thus, any geographical allusion in the text of an author may be used by the teacher as the starting-point from which he may convey, and by the student as a centre around which he may gather, much information about the past and present political or local divisions, physical or general features, trade and productions, of the country or locality referred to ; and in this way the student may acquire a considerable knowledge of commercial, political, and physical geography, both ancient and modern. By seizing in a similar manner upon the occasion afforded by any biographical or historical allusion, explaining its meaning and reference, adding information where it may be necessary, and comparing, where comparison may be possible and appropriate, events of national or personal history recorded or referred to, in the text, the classical teacher may not only awaken a taste for, and inculcate the principles of, historical and biograpical research, but also teach a great deal about the history of other countries, and the biography of other men. Then, again, any reference to manners and laws, customs and usages, civil, military, or religious, would afford a natural ground for drawing a comparison between them and those of other countries and times in general, and of our own country and age in particular; and thus give an occasion for supplying much interesting antiquarian knowledge, and much valuable information about the condition of society, laws, customs, and modes of government which prevail among ourselves or other nations, in our own times.

4. Further, by referring, wherever opportunity offers itself to parallel passages in other authors — comparing them with those in the classical writers which he wishes to illustrate, and occasionally criticising, pointing out their respective merits and defects — the classical teacher is calling attention to, awakening an interest in, and conveying some knowledge about general literature, both ancient and modern, and inculcating the first principles of literary criticism.

Thus, independently of the knowledge of the facts, arguments, and ideas conveyed in the classical writings themselves, in the course of classical instruction much knowledge about languages generally, our own language in particular, history, geography, antiquities, and indeed almost every subject which comes within the scope of a literary education, may incidentally be introduced as naturally suggested by the main subject. And therefore it follows that, in any educational system in which the Classics occupy a place, these subjects would, in virtue of a natural connection, be associated with them as direct branches of instruction. Add to this, that in Logic, Moral and Metaphysical Philosophy, the Classics furnish models perhaps unsurpassed by modern writers, certainly better suited than any other to form the basis of a philosophical culture. The conclusion, then, to which we are forced by these considerations is, that classical studies form a natural centre around which a considerable number of the branches of instruction, necessary or desirable in a liberal education, are readily congregated.

So, then, it would appear that classical studies are extensively efficacious in the discipline of the mental faculties, and are fitted to occupy a central position in our educational system.

But it may be urged, as it has been frequently, that the same advantages appertain in an equal or in a greater degree to the study of our own, or at all events some other modern language, e.g. French or German; and that other branches of study, e.g. Mathematics, Natural Science, or even, as it has been gravely suggested, History, are to be regarded as equally or more efficacious, and as having a similar or greater claim to the position of pre-eminence. We shall now, therefore, proceed to compare the Classics with the above-mentioned subjects in respect to their relative educational value.

I. First, we shall institute a comparison between the study of our own and the classical languages.

Now, in doing so, we grant, at the very outset, that it is an indispensable part of a youth's education that he be thoroughly instructed in the theory, and made expert in the practical use, of his own mother tongue. That a boy, who has gone through a sufficiently prolonged educational course, should be ignorant of the grammar of his own language, deficient in its orthography, and destitute of the power of writing pure grammatical English, is altogether inexcusable. Instruction, then, in the English language forms a necessary adjunct of any system of training; time must be

— as doubtless with proper arrangements it may be — found for the acquisition of this essential branch of knowledge ; and any higher culture would be dearly purchased at the expense of ignorance in this respect. Further, we are ready also to admit that the study of the English language may be made a useful instrument of mental discipline ; and, indeed, that in those cases, so common and almost universal among the lower grades of the middle and the lower classes of our population, where, in consequence of their too early removal from school, no other language can be mastered with sufficient accuracy and to a sufficient extent to exercise any appreciable disciplinary effect, it is perhaps the only medium through which that training, which the study of languages alone can give, can be effected.

But when we have granted thus much, we must, to enable us to decide the point at issue, take into account the following considerations :

1. To confine our language-studies to the vernacular is to narrow our range of thought and expression. " In learning Greek and Latin as boys," says Dr. Max Müller,[1] " we are learning more than a new language ; we are acquiring an entirely novel system of thought. The mind has to receive a grammatical training, and to be broken, so to say, to modes of thought and speech unknown to us from our own language."

2. Again, it is very difficult to arrive at a correct insight into the nature of language, its laws, forms, and analogies, and in a general way to attain to any great power or exactness in the use even of our own lan-

---

[1] Survey of Languages, p. 2.

guage, without acquiring some other one as well. For our mother tongue is so identified with our current modes of thought and expression, we use it with such facility, and with the exertion of so small an amount of reflection upon the meaning and force of the words and the structure of the sentences which we utter, that we fail to obtain from its study that knowledge of the principles of language and grammatical forms generally, and that force and accuracy in its own use, which we get from the acquisition of a language learned only by prolonged and laborious effort. And this absence of effort in the use of the vernacular seriously impairs, in other respects as well as in this, the value of its study regarded as a mental discipline.

3. Our own language would further appear to be inferior to the classical languages for the purposes of education for the following reason : it is singularly simple in the structure of its sentences, and in the arrangement of its words, while they are most varied in the collocation of their words, and most involved in the formation of their sentences ; and hence, to arrive at the meaning of a passage in a classical author requires a much greater exertion of the reflective and analytical faculties, and consequently involves a proportionately higher and more vigorous intellectual training.

4. Again, the English language, beautiful and expressive as it is, is not as perfect in its grammatical structure and forms as the languages of Greece and Rome, and accordingly cannot afford so good a specimen for the language studies of the student as they do. For example, it conveys by a cumbersome array of little

words what they convey by a change of inflection ; and
the abundant use of inflections in a language not only
makes it more terse and forcible in itself, but also renders it possible to arrange words in sentences in such a
way as to express ideas in the clearest and most striking manner ; while a deficiency of inflections often
renders it necessary, for the sake of making the meaning intelligible, to place the words so as to represent
the ideas much less appropriately and forcibly. The
inflection at once shows the proper position of a word
as regards the sense, wherever it may happen to be
placed in a sentence ; and thus, in Greek and Latin,
each idea can be arranged according to its relative importance, and where its expression will be most striking
to the mind, and we may add most euphonious to the
ear ; whereas in English a certain fixed order of
words and clauses must be for the most part observed,
or the sentence would become mere unintelligible
jargon.

5. Nor must it be forgotten that the classical languages lie at the foundation, and enter largely into the
structure, of our own language. Many of our words
are derived directly from them, and their meaning cannot be rightly appreciated without some classical attainments. "If," says the Edinburgh Reviewer,[1] "the
knowledge of Greek and Latin among our upper classes
were lost, it [our language] would become (as it un-
fortunately is to women, and to the mass of people
already) a strange collection of inexpressive symbols."
It is not, then, perhaps too much to say that an acquaint-

[1] July, 1864.

ance with Latin and Greek is almost indispensable for a precise and correct knowledge of our own language; at all events we may say, with Her Majesty's Public School Commissioners, that "the study of the classical languages is, or rather may be made, an instrument of the highest value for the purpose" of acquiring "a command of pure grammatical English." [1]

For all these reasons, we conclude that English is not fitted to take the place of Latin and Greek in our education.

II. But the question arises: If our own language will not answer the required purpose, and it be necessary to learn another one as well, why not choose, in preference to Latin and Greek, one or more of the modern languages, e.g. French or German, or both? for these are the ones whose claims have been especially urged.

The advocates of this view allege in defence of it the following assertions and arguments: Modern languages are as suitable for mental cultivation as the classical languages. Instruction in the principles, and training in the use, of language generally can be as well imparted through them as through Latin and Greek, to which they are not in themselves inferior. They, too, under the teaching of able men, can be made the vehicles of aesthetic culture and high philosophic discipline. They can be taught orally, as well as by the more laborious process of dictionary and grammar; and therefore, as well as through their being intrinsically less difficult, can be acquired more easily,

---

[1] Report, p. 83.

thoroughly, and in a shorter time. They are more useful when acquired, because of their being actually used by persons with whom, in the course of commerce, or in social intercourse, we frequently come into contact; and because they convey much valuable information on physical science, political economy, and other branches of knowledge, but imperfectly or erroneously understood by the writers of Greece and Rome. Thus, while they are indispensable to men in the higher walks of commercial life, to enable them to hold intercourse with foreign traders, they are equally so to men engaged in intellectual callings, because only through an acquaintance with these languages much knowledge connected with their respective pursuits is accessible. They are the key to the ideas of contemporary nations, and are — at least French and German are — the vehicles of literatures purer and more sublime than the classical; and these literatures contain much that is well fitted for the study, and calculated to rouse the sympathies, enlist the interests, and elevate the moral tone of youth, which the authors of Greece and Rome do not. They are, for these reasons, more attractive studies than the classical languages; and this is especially in their favor, because it is important that their studies should be attractive, not repulsive, to the young. Finally, as regards French and German, they are most valuable for the better understanding of our own language, because a large portion of it is derived from French and Teutonic sources. And on these grounds, it is maintained, the modern languages, and more particularly French and German,

3*

are preferable subjects of study to the classical, — at all events for those boys who are not intended for professions, and therefore not likely to require any knowledge of the Classics in their future life.

Such are some of the leading arguments advanced by those who advocate the use of the modern, *versus* the classical, languages. To all of them perhaps we must allow a certain, and to some of them very considerable, weight; at all events they prove indubitably that modern languages ought to occupy an important position in a liberal education. But, on the other side of the question, the following arguments must be taken into consideration :

1. The very fact that the modern languages can be so easily acquired, the very circumstance of their being living languages, and therefore capable of being learned orally by a mere exercise of memory, without the laborious process by which alone a dead ' nguage can be mastered, makes them less suitable and efficient instruments of intellectual discipline ; for intellectual development and culture are the results of intellectual effort, and, if you diminish the effort, you proportionately impede that development, and impair that culture.

2. On the other hand, the fact that the classical are " dead " languages, at the present time unused, and therefore unprogressive ; that, consequently, we are able to study them in every stage of their progress, from a comparatively imperfect state to their highest point of perfection, and through their subsequent decline ; and therefore there can be no difficulty in selecting from them the finest specimens of style, where

the language is found in the greatest perfection (a matter most difficult of decision in the case of any living language, which is ever changing, whether improving or deteriorating not being at any given time ascertainable) — renders them more serviceable models for the study of language.

3. Then, again, it must be borne in mind that Greek and Latin are in themselves more perfect languages, more logically accurate in the expression of ideas, with a more regular grammatical structure, and with grammatical details more easily traceable to general laws; and that, consequently, to adopt the conclusion of the Quarterly Review,[1] "Latin," to which we may add Greek in perhaps a greater degree, "though not well taught and less well remembered, leaves behind it more knowledge of general grammar and etymology than the study of any modern language can convey."

4. To this we may add that they afford a standard of the principles of language and of grammar common to the whole civilized world. Now it is manifest that, in the study of philology, it is important that there should be some common basis of proceeding, and some standard of reference agreed upon by all. It would be plainly inconvenient that each nation should take for its standard its own or some other modern tongue — e.g. that England should take French, Germany English, France German, or Italy any one of the three, or some other language; scholars could not thus compare their labors, and the variation in the point of view would probably produce hopeless discord as to the prin-

[1] July, 1864, p. 21.

ciples which are the ultimate object of research. Nor could it be expected that all modern nations would combine to elevate any one of their languages into the position of the one standard for them all. But Latin and Greek, being remote from national jealousies and the rivalries of modern life, standing out in the distant past, the common heritage of all, to which all are equally entitled, and all are equally, or nearly so, indebted, form a ground of study open to every civilized man, from which the fundamental principles of all language can be educed, and upon which the philologists of every nation can work together and compare the results of their labors.

5. And as they afford the most perfect specimens of language, so also they supply the finest literary models in poetry, history, and philosophy — models which have served as examples of thought and composition to all subsequent ages, and after the fashion of which all modern literature has taken its form. And, in addition to this fact, observing also that classical, as compared with modern literature, which is practically speaking boundless in extent, affords a limited area for study, containing a few recognized models, upon which all can agree, whereas, to make a selection from modern authors for the same purpose is almost impossible, — we conclude that the literatures of Greece and Rome, no less than their languages, are more suitable for educational purposes than those of modern nations.

6. Nor must this fact be forgotten. Modern literary productions abound in classical allusions, and in thoughts and sentiments either directly copied from the

Greek and Latin Classics, or framed on the model of similar passages in them. In evidence of this we may refer to the constant classical allusions in the speeches of our great statesmen — allusions which convey no meaning except to the classical scholar. And even in cases where this direct reference is not discernible, the Classics have exercised so vast an influence on modern thought, and so many of our current ideas are traceable to that influence, that much of our modern literature cannot be thoroughly understood and appreciated without some classical knowledge.

7. Another argument of considerable weight may be based on the circumstance that, in consequence of their remoteness from our own times, the classical authors are free from any reference to the controversies, religious, political, and social, which agitate ourselves, and with which it is exceedingly undesirable to disturb the minds of the young before they are thoroughly competent to think for themselves, to discriminate between what is true and what is false, and to settle their own principles on the conviction of disciplined reason, and under the influence of sound and well-trained judgment.

8. Further, it must be noted that the classical languages are, or at least Latin is, as it were, the key to many of the most important modern languages, and that the acquisition of the former makes the acquisition, whenever necessary or desirable, of the latter a comparatively easy task — a fact the converse of which is by no means true. Upon this point we quote the opin-

ion of Dr. Max Müller, who says: [1] " In Latin we have the key to Spanish, Portuguese, French, Italian. Any one who desires to learn the modern Romance languages — Italian, Spanish, and French — will find that he actually has to spend less time if he learns Latin first, than if he had studied each of these modern dialects separately, and without this foreknowledge of their common parent."

For all these reasons, we conclude that the modern languages, important as is the place which they ought to occupy in education, cannot be regarded as having the same educational value as those of Greece and Rome.

But if no other language and literature can rival those of Greece and Rome in educational value, it may be urged that they are surpassed, or at all events equalled, in this respect by some other subject; e.g. Mathematics, Natural Science, or history, for these are the branches of study whose claims have been especially, and with most force, insisted upon.

III. Are we, then, to regard Mathematics as better entitled than the Classics to occupy the central position spoken of?

Now, in attempting to give an answer to this question, we admit at once the very great importance of Mathematics; for without a knowledge of it some of the most important laws of the universe cannot be understood and explained; it forms one of the most potent instruments in promoting the progress of the natural sciences; and it is most valuable in the pursuit of some callings

[1] Survey of Languages, p. 16.

—e.g. that of engineering in all its branches—which conduce to the material comforts and advantages of life. Thus the practical utility of mathematical studies is undoubted.

But it must be borne in mind that we have now to regard the matter in an educational aspect; and that in the beginning of this inquiry, we enunciated it as a preliminary principle that the main object of education was not to impart knowledge which could be turned to direct account in the pursuits of after life, so much as to develop and invigorate the mental faculties, and generally to humanize and expand the intellect.

From this point of view, however, it must be allowed that the study of Mathematics exercises a most salutary and important influence on the cultivation of the mind; for it tends to fix the attention, and therefore cures the fault of mental distraction; it imparts the power of dwelling upon abstract ideas; it cultivates the habits of giving a definite form to vague notions, of collecting scattered details into fixed formulae, and afterwards applying those formulae to the production of new results; and while it sharpens the faculties generally, it trains the mind in the practice of close and consecutive reasoning, and thereby, in a special way, cultivates the faculty of reason.

We cannot, however, forget that this discipline has been denied to accrue from mathematical studies by so great a thinker as the late Sir W. Hamilton, and has been considered by that eminent philosopher and mathematician, Dr. Whewell, to result from the study of Geometry only, that of Analysis being almost useless,

if not actually injurious, for the proper development of the mind.[1]

Nor must we suppose that the mental discipline which Mathematics effects can be acomplished through its instrumentality alone. Indeed, many have doubted whether Mathematics is the best subject for training and developing the reason, and whether it is not inferior to Classics in this respect. For it has been urged against it, and with a great amount of force, that it is concerned only with number, quantity, and form, or the intuitions of time and space, and is thus limited to one sphere of existence, and therefore in no way applicable to the diversified phenomena of our intellectual life ; and that, inasmuch as it is concerned with *necessary* matter, it incapacitates, rather than trains, the reason for dealing correctly with *contingent* matter, and so for forming accurate and sound conclusions in questions of common life, and of moral, political, philosophical, or religious truth, where absolute certainty is unattainable, and probability, of greater or less degree of certainty, alone can be arrived at. But classical studies, they argue, while they are free from these defects as being engaged with *contingent* matter, and concerned with most of the problems which occupy the attention of the intellect, are yet a most effective means of cultivating the reason ; for the accurate syntax and complex structure of the classical languages require on the part of the student a great exercise of the logical powers, to enable him to comprehend the purport of the language used, to determine which he

---

[1] Whewell on Liberal Education, p. 56.

has to trace out the connection between clause and clause, and sentence and sentence, to weigh conflicting probabilities as to the exact meaning of words and phrases, to apply rules, and to form conclusions; and all this involves direct processes of syllogistic reasoning, rapidly and almost intuitively gone through, but no less real and valid on that account.

The fact upon which the foregoing argument is based seems to be by itself alone decisive of the question before us. Mathematics is concerned with a class of truths which have no relation to human affairs; it leads away the mind to a region of its own, quite remote from the sphere in which we live and think, and from our human interests and sympathies; whereas the study of the poets and orators, the historians and philosophers of classical antiquity, brings us into direct communion with human feelings and concerns, and the ordinary affairs of individual and political life. For this reason it would appear that education should have rather a literary, than a mathematical, or purely scientific, basis.

The conclusion at which we arrive is, that while Mathematics is an essential supplement of a classical, or indeed of any kind of liberal, education, yet that its proper position is an ancillary, and by no means that leading or central one which the Classics demand as their own.

IV. We next proceed to consider the claim which has been advanced on behalf of Natural Science, to fill the place from which, it is thought, the Classics ought to be dethroned.

4

The advocates of this claim urge in support of it, that the study of Natural Science must be preferable to that of language, on the broad principle that it is the study of things, rather than of words; that to study the latter before the former is indeed a reversal of Nature's order, according to which the observation of external nature precedes the use of language, and still more any intelligent comprehension of its forms and laws; that the acquisition in youth of a knowledge of external objects is of real use in the business of life, or at all events lays the foundation for profitable and interesting pastime in years to come; that many boys, who have not the slightest aptitude or taste for language and literature, may have great capability and inclination for the study of the facts of external nature; · that information of this kind is conveyed more easily and readily, and therefore more efficiently to an indolent student, than any other can be; and that any education is narrow, defective, and incomplete, which does not include within its course instruction in some portion at least of that vast store of facts and principles which modern science unfolds to its votaries. Then, again, it is maintained that the study of Natural Science exercises the mental faculties, and affords a real mental discipline. Thus Her Majesty's Public School Commissioners say:[1] "It quickens and cultivates directly the faculty of observation, which in very many persons lies almost dormant through life, the power of accurate and rapid generalization, and the mental habit of method and arrangement; it

[1] Report, p. 82.

accustoms young persons to trace the sequence of
cause and effect; it familiarizes them with a kind of
reasoning which interests them, and which they can
promptly comprehend; and it is perhaps the best corrective for that indolence which is the vice of half-
awakened minds, and which shrinks from any exertion
that is not, like an effort of memory, merely mechanical." And Mr. H. H. Vaughan, late Professor of
Modern History in the University of Oxford, asserts
that "the vital appropriation and application of"
knowledge of the physical sciences "involve acts of
memory, comprehension, comparison, imagination, deduction — the use of many and admirable faculties,
the exercise of which is a discipline truly noble."[1]

Now there is sufficient truth in all this, as we think,
to show, beyond the possibility of a reasonable doubt,
that the study of Natural Science, so far from being, as
one of the most distinguished of the Head Masters of
our Public Schools maintains it to be, "worthless" for
boys, is really valuable, not only for the sake of the information acquired, but also on account of its efficacy
in cultivating and developing certain powers of the
mind; and it makes out a strong case for the right of
this subject to occupy a recognized position in our education, establishing the dictum of the Report on the
Public Schools, that its exclusion from our education
"is a plain defect and a great practical evil."[2] It
must therefore be admitted that the too exclusive
possession of the educational field by the Classics, — a

[1] Oxford Reform and Oxford Professors, p. 26.
[2] Public Schools Commission Report, p. 32.

possession the commencement of which dates from a
time when the natural sciences were almost unknown,
and which was held by prescriptive right afterwards,
notwithstanding their vast expansion in modern times
— has kept those sciences too generally from occupying
that position as branches of instruction which is rightfully due to them.

But here again we must call attention to the fact,
that the question before us is, not whether they deserve
a place, but whether they ought to occupy the principal,
central place, in our system of education ; and this
question we must answer most decisively in the negative, both for the reasons already advanced in favor of
the right of language and literature in general, and
of those of Greece and Rome in particular, to this pre-
eminence ; and because we hold, that the study of
language and literature, as the study of the intellectual
and moral world, must be much higher than that of
the physical world, a truth expressed in the hackneyed
quotation — distorted indeed from its meaning as used
by its author, but none the less appropriate on that
account in its new application — " the proper study of
mankind is man."

Nor, again, must we forget that there is considerable
force in the arguments of those who maintain that the
mental discipline derivable from the study of Natural
Science arises chiefly from the investigation and contemplation of its more advanced, and not from the
study of its elementary, branches, with which alone for
the most part education is concerned. The advocates
of this view argue thus : the youthful mind is incapa-

ble of grasping the theories which are most disciplinary, and cannot get beyond the sensible facts of the subject, which exercise the observation and memory, and nothing more ; the elementary knowledge, then, which can be conveyed to the young, is for the most part made up of individual facts, and therefore only trains the minds to observe and remember, and affords but little scope for the exercise of those reflective faculties, which may, no doubt, be called into play in the generalizing of those facts into laws and principles.

The study of Natural Science, as concerned exclusively with the objects of the external world, would appear, indeed, in every case, to have a tendency to induce the neglect of the contemplation of the world within, and, therefore, of the cultivation of the reflective faculties ; and at the same time, from the nature of the subject-matter with which it is engaged, it affords little, if any, scope for the exercise of the imagination, and none at all for that of the moral judgment, which is perhaps of all our faculties the most valuable for the business of life ; in short, as occupied with the visible and tangible, it allows no opportunity for the development of those higher mental powers, which are employed upon the immaterial and unseen.

V. The claim of another subject, viz. History, or rather the history of the Middle Ages, to occupy the central position of our educational system, has been seriously urged, in a recent number of one of onr leading Reviews,[1] and now demands our attention, not so

---

[1] Westminster Review, July, 1864.

4 *

much from its intrinsic importance, as because of the gravity with which it is urged.

The writer of the article in question asserts that from the history of the Middle Ages we can "learn best our relation to the past and to one another;" that "it has a claim upon our principal attention which is superior to any other;" that it will be "admitted without hesitation," that History "can form a real centre, about which can be arranged all else that will have to be taught besides it;" and that to "early modern history" all other history, language, and literature, and even the physical sciences (which on this plan are to be "treated historically," and to "gain in importance" by being so handled), can naturally be subordinated. He further assumes that our present, i.e. the classical system of education does not attempt "the higher object of qualifying a man for citizenship in a state which is itself an integral part of the commonwealth of Western Europe," and "leaves the judgment untrained on the highest social and political questions, and does not fit a man, but rather unfits him, to feel his position, and to discharge his duty, as an Englishman and a European;" while by the proposed system, on the other hand, the mind would be trained to "the habit of viewing everything in strict relation to the one subject of highest human interest — the progress of the human race."

Now, in reply to this twofold assumption, we observe, in the first place, that even if it were true, we cannot regard the "qualifying a man for citizenship in a state of Western Europe," or the formation of "the habit of viewing everything in strict relation to the progress of the human race," as the primary object of intellectual education, which is, as we have before seen, to draw out, strengthen, and develop the mental faculties; and whatever best effects this is the most fitted to be the principal educational instrument, whether it "qualifies for citizenship," either in "Western Europe," or any other quarter of the globe — Asia, Africa, or America, — or not; whether it has any direct bearing upon "the progress of the human race," or not. The education of the individual is the primary object, that of the citizen a secondary and subordinate one; the latter cannot be well effected until the former has been well secured. And it may indeed be questioned, whether " the progress of the human race " be a matter of any, much less the " highest," interest to the young, or whether they can at all appreciate it; and even if they could, whether they would be best educated by " viewing everything in relation to " it : the idea itself is a somewhat abstract and shadowy one, ill calculated for the comprehension of youthful minds, and by no means such an important point of reference to the student as many others; for example, his future work in life, or his relation to his Creator, or his social relations to his fellow-men.

Then, again, with reference to the general question, we observe that history is but a part — an important one indeed, but still only a part — of a language and literature training ; from no course of literary education indeed could it be excluded; but to exalt it to a primary position is to exalt the part, which is necessarily subordinate, to a place of superiority over the other.

And further, we may ask : If the history of the Middle Ages is to be the great central subject of study, what authors are to be studied ? What Mediaeval historians are to fill the places of the great classical ones, Thucydides, Herodotus, and Xenophon, Tacitus, Livy, and Caesar, — not to mention such other authors as Homer and Virgil, Sophocles and Horace, Cicero and Demosthenes ? It would be difficult to find any suitable to educe the mental faculties of youth, or indeed at all comparable, in point of matter or style, to the great historians, and the other great writers, of Greece and Rome.

It must also be remembered that to the immature minds of the young, who have not yet the mental power, or the knowledge of life, to grasp its principles, history presents very little else than an assemblage of facts, the mastering of which is a mere exercise of memory, and nothing more; and the cultivation of the power of acquiring historical facts, or even of classifying them as well, can hardly be regarded as the principal object of education.

Nor, again, can we allow the claim of a subject to pre-eminence, which for its maintenance requires that physical science should be treated " historically; " physical science handled in such a way would soon cease to progress, and become a matter of history and nothing more ; so far from " gaining in importance " thereby, it would soon cease to have any importance at all ; thus studied, it could hardly be turned to any practical account in promoting the comfort, happiness, or advancement of man ; and those who are taught the subject on such principles may acquire some knowledge of the history of physical science indeed, but of the science itself, little, or rather no knowledge at all.

Lastly, as to the assertion that our present system does not qualify for forming a judgment on the highest social and political questions of the day, we should — with the example before us of men trained on that system, who as politicians, statesmen, and social philosophers have by their labors made the social and political condition of our country superior on the whole to that of any other country in the world — be disposed emphatically to deny. But whether this fact be recognized or not, so the classical system be in other respects the best mental discipline, its claim to superiority is fairly established.

For, after all, this is the question : Which is the best educational instrument? We have heard, no doubt, from the Reviewer all that can be said on behalf of the history of the Middle Ages ; we have already advanced in this essay arguments in favor of the right of language and literature, particularly of the languages and literatures of Greece and Rome, to fill the leading place in education ; which line of argument is the most weighty and conclusive can, we conceive, readily be decided.

We have thus at considerable length investigated the arguments which have been brought forward by their respective advocates, in support of the right of other leading branches of learning to occupy a high, or even a pre-eminent, position in our education ; we have considered in each case what may be said on the other side ; and we have thus been brought to the conclusion, on a survey of the whole matter, that while most, if not all, of the above-mentioned subjects should be included in any course of liberal instruction, yet that no one of them is as efficient an instrument of intellectual training, or as well fitted to occupy the centre of our educational system, as the Classics.

Besides the arguments which have been already brought forward in the preceding pages, there are others of considerable weight which next claim our attention.

1. The first of these is one, ably worked out by Dr. Whewell, in his work on " Liberal Education." The Classics are an indispensable part of our education course, because they connect us with the intellectual efforts of past ages ; they are stamped, as it were, upon the history of the civilized world, and their study preserves the traditions of moral and intellectual life ; and true nobility of intellect consists in the ability to trace the descent of ideas. To omit the study of the Classics, then, is to cut us off from the experience of the intellectual world, to make it impossible for us to investigate the progress of the thought of civilized man, and to destroy what may not inaptly be called the aristocratic element of human knowledge.

2. A second argument is based upon the great influence which the Greek and Roman mind has exercised in moulding our modern civilization. Mr. Gladstone [1]

1 Report of Public School Commissioners, Vol. ii. p. 43.

says : " The modern European civilization from the Middle Ages downwards is the compound of two great factors, the Christian religion for the spirit of man, the Greek (and in a secondary degree the Roman) discipline for his mind and intellect " ; and he even goes so far as to maintain, that " the materials of what we call classical training were prepared, and we have a right to say were advisedly and providentially prepared, in order that it might become not a mere adjunct, but in mathematical phrase the complement of Christianity, in its application to the culture of the human being, as a being formed both for this world and the world to come." And to the same effect Mr. J. S. Mill observes : [1] " The Jews jointly with them [the Greeks] have been the starting-point and main propelling agency of modern cultivation " — an observation endorsed by M. Guizot : [2] " Modern civilization is in effect derived from the Jews and from the Greeks. To the latter it is indebted for its human and intellectual, to the former for its Divine and moral, element." The civilized life of modern Europe generally is so impregnated by classical influences, — its human as apart from its Divine element is so entirely derived from classical sources, — that its nature and tendency cannot be rightly understood and duly estimated without an acquaintance with the mental productions, the civilization, and the national life of Greece and Rome.

3. Closely allied with the preceding is a third argument. The classical system has so long prevailed ; the

[1] Considerations on Representative Government, p. 43.
[2] Meditations on Christianity, p. 209.

intellectual life of our upper classes has been so completely, and that of our middle classes to so great an
extent, formed by it ; it is so intertwined with the ideas
of the educated, with our modes of thinking, and the
whole course of cultivated life among us, — that it
could not be departed from without giving a great
shock to our system of thought, and to our social culture. And though this consideration ought not to be
allowed to outweigh other and graver ones, which may
be urged against the pursuit of classical studies, yet it
is enough to render it imperative, on the part of an
opponent of them, to show very good reason why they
should be abandoned, and to advance very cogent arguments in favor of those studies which he proposes to
substitute in their stead.

4. Another argument is one, the force of which will
be generally recognized. For those preparing for the
learned professions, the work of legislation or of statesmanship, or indeed any high intellectual calling, the
knowledge of the classical languages is almost indispensable. In the profession of the Law, a knowledge
of Latin is necessary for the perusal of old legal documents, and the study of some of the greatest works on
Jurisprudence. In the Medical profession, without
some classical attainments the student cannot avail
himself of the ancient medical writers, e.g. Hippocrates,
Celsus, Galen ; nor can he fully understand the meaning of the technical terms used in his art. In the profession of Theology, no man who has not received a
thorough classical training, can attain to any except
the lowest standard of professional acquirements. For,

first of all, without a knowledge of Greek, it is impossible to acquire an exact and competent knowledge of the writings of the New Testament. Again, all the works of the great Fathers of the Church, nearly all the early Christian writings, all the productions of Mediaeval theologians, and many of the greatest works of comparatively modern divines, are written in the languages of Greece or Rome, and are therefore as sealed books to all who are not classical scholars. Add to this, that an accurate acquaintance with the manners, customs, institutions, and literatures of Greece and Rome is indispensable for the understanding and explaining of many allusions in the New Testament, and other ancient theological writings; and for tracing out the influence of Christianity upon the civilized races with which it first came into contact, and investigating the effect which through that influence it has exercised in modifying the elements of human society — reforming and renewing it. Nor is the utility of classical studies confined to the three learned professions. To the legislator and the statesman, a knowledge of the history, laws, and political institutions of Greece and Rome is almost essential, as a preparation for the discharge of their respective functions. For in the history of the States of Greece, and of the Republic and Empire of Rome, are to be discovered the elements of every national institution, the principles of national life, examples of the origin and progress of every political change, and illustrations of almost every possible form of government. And as a practical illustration of the value of this learning to the statesman, we may

5

refer to the well-known fact, that many of the most
distinguished statesmen of our time have been men
deeply versed in classical lore. The historian, the philosopher, and even the poet, cannot carry on their
respective pursuits without frequently finding an
acquaintance with the Classics most desirable for them;
while the scientific man can hardly fail in many cases
to recognize the value of some classical attainments, to
enable him to understand the nomenclature, and in
some instances to investigate the history and progress,
of his science. This argument goes far to prove the
absolute necessity of retaining the Classics in any system of liberal education.

5. A fifth argument is based on the intrinsic value
of the literature of Greece and Rome. It has been
truly said that that literature contains " some of the
noblest poetry, the finest eloquence, the deepest philosophy, the wisest historical writing." [1] And indeed,
without attempting to draw a comparison between the
respective excellences of classical and modern literature, no unprejudiced person can refuse to allow that
the languages in which the New Testament is written,
in which Homer and Virgil composed their poetry,
Demosthenes and Cicero gave utterance to their orations, and Thucydides and Tacitus wrote their histories,
are worthy of diligent study, for the sake of the literary
treasures to which they are the key. To Greek this argument applies with special force. In it were composed
the earliest specimens of epic and dramatic poetry, and
perhaps the most perfect and elaborate productions of

[1] Report of Public School Commissioners, p. 28.

the drama, which we possess; in it were written histories, not only the oldest in point of antiquity, if we except the sacred ones, which have been handed down to us, but also unsurpassed, perhaps unrivalled, by any of the histories of modern times; it was the language of the greatest orator which the world ever produced; in it wrote the masters of Logic, Metaphysics, Moral and Political Philosophy, to all succeeding generations; men unexcelled by their pupils, with all the extra experience of two thousand years; in it were composed the inspired records of Christianity — records which are the basis of the Christian faith, and the guide of the individual Christian in all that concerns his spiritual and eternal welfare.

Such is the train of reasoning by which the supremacy of the Classics in our educational course may be defended. Some of the arguments adduced may be applied, perhaps, on behalf of some other subject almost as appropriately, while others of them can be urged only in support of the Classics; some may be of greater, others of less weight; but their accumulative force is irresistable; at all events, until an equally strong case can be made out for some other branch of knowledge, which, as it appears to us, has not yet been, nor is very likely ever to be, done.

We now proceed to examine the objections which have been made against the use of the Classics in education. These are many. Some have been already in the course of our argument cursorily referred to; of the remaining ones we can only select a few, which are most common, or most important.

1. A first objection is based upon moral considerations. Classical literature is, as it is alleged, at once pagan and impure; much of it is of a demoralizing tendency, and calculated to debase rather than refine the mind and character of the student.

Now, that this charge can be to some extent sustained, as regards a portion of the surviving literature of Greece and Rome, may without hesitation be admitted, just as a similar accusation brought against some of our modern literature could not be controverted. And indeed we cannot but be conscious, that the fact of the works of Greek and Roman authors having been composed before the light of the Christian revelation enlightened the darkness of the human mind, and before the leaven of Christian principles interpenetrated and changed human society, must to some extent impair their educational value from a moral point of view.

We reply, however, first, that the objection is beside the question before us, which is, the value of the Classics as a means of educating the mind, and not as an instrument of moral culture. Still, we cannot for a moment deny that an immoral tendency, if it can be proved against any subject of study, is a fatal bar to its use in education; and therefore we rely rather upon the answer that the objection is only true in a very qualified sense, in fact, that it is substantially untrue; because the truth of the case is, that the classical writings contain much that is morally beautiful, indeed all that is best and noblest in thought and sentiment in the natural mind of man; that far more frequently than otherwise, vice is in them denounced as vice, and satirized, or condemned, accordingly; and, that even in those mythological fables to which perhaps the objection chiefly applies, that which is vicious lies only on the surface, while on a deeper investigation they are seen to embody ideas, often beautiful and profound in character, which an intelligent teacher may readily discern, and impress upon the students attention; and that, in short, their general tendency, so far from being demoralizing and debasing, is rather elevating and refining. And then, again, it must be remembered, that the fact of classical literature belonging to a bygone age, remote from our own, makes anything of an immoral tendency in it far less injurious than what is of a similar character in the literature of our own times; because it does not wear to our senses the same aspect of reality, and is not invested with the same personal interest to us.

2. Another objection, and perhaps the most common and frequently repeated of all, is, that classical studies are of no, or at all events of but little, practical utility — at least for the great majority of schoolboys, who are not destined for the learned professions, but intend to engage in commercial pursuits. And when it is objected that certain subjects of study are " not useful," what is meant is, that they have no direct bearing upon the student's future business, or calling; and an invidious contrast is drawn between them, and such subjects as arithmetic, writing, or our own and modern languages, which are of direct utility in the occupations of after life.

Now in meeting this objection we, in the first place, protest against the assumption therein involved, that

5 *

everything in education is to be regulated by the dictates of a vulgar utilitarianism. Surely there are other objects besides mere utility, such as the attainment of truth, the elevation of the moral nature, the culture of the intellect, which ought also to be kept in view. Thus intellectual cultivation is valuable as its own end, and has its own use quite independently of any subsequent results it may have upon our calling in life; in the words of a great thinker and writer, " health is a good in itself, though nothing came of it " ; and so " the culture of the intellect is a good in itself, and its own end." [1] And further, it may be remarked, that this objection is based upon a narrow and false idea of what is " the useful " in education. Knowledge has a twofold value, its value as knowledge, and its value as intellectual discipline ; and viewed as a preparation for life, it is often more important in the latter respect than it is in the former. So then a subject of study may be eminently " useful " in the highest, widest sense, without being of any direct use in the avocations of after life. If it has served to enlarge, sharpen, invigorate, or polish any one of the mental powers ; if it has imparted vigor and accuracy of reasoning ; if it has served to form a sound and correct judgment ; if it has trained the mind to a habit of close attention ; if it has enabled a man to to take larger, clearer, more accurate views of any subject which may be presented to him in the ordinary business of his every-day life ; if it has enabled him to express his thoughts with more clearness and power; if, in short, it has in any way made him wiser, better,

---

[1] Newman's Discourses on University Education, p. 236.

more able, or more refined, — then has that branch of knowledge been of the greatest " use " to him, though he has never had occasion to use the smallest iota thereof in the transaction of his business, or in the pursuits of his life. That knowledge, then, which may seem to a man profitless as regards its direct use, may, if he could only discern and estimate truly its results, have been to him indirectly of the greatest possible utility.

3. Thirdly, it is urged as an objection against classical studies, that they are appreciated only by a few; that boys generally do not see the use or the meaning of them; that most leave school knowing little or nothing of Greek and Latin, and that of the rest the larger number quickly give up the study of these languages altogether; and the conclusion drawn is, that studies so little appreciated, so distasteful, and so barren in results, are unfitted to occupy the attention of the young. And in support of this conclusion it is argued, with much plausibility, that it is absurd to suppose a disagreeable study to be more invigorating than one which is pleasant; that, on the contrary, the greater the interest taken in a subject, the more inclination must the student have to exercise his faculties upon it, and the more the faculties are exercised, the more are they expanded and invigorated; and that, indeed, a certain degree of interest in a subject is the motive power indicated by nature to support the will in the effort of sustained attention.

This objection may fairly be met by the following observations: First, the fact of classical studies not

being appreciated by the young is no proof of their un-
suitability for them; on the contrary, the circumstance
of their absolutely requiring exertion of mind and close
attention, which renders them unpopular, is just what
makes them most valuable. Every one practically
versed in education knows that boys and young men,
for the most part, like best what gives them mentally
least trouble, and requires the least exercise of their
intellectual faculties. And it is for the opponents of
classical studies to show that there are studies, equally
invigorating, which would be generally more accept-
able; and indeed that any studies, requiring laborious
effort, are likely to be agreeable to the majority of
young people. And then, as regards boys not seeing
the use of classical studies, it is not to be expected that
they should do so; boys have to learn, suffer, and do
much, the meaning and utility of which they cannot
possibly at the time comprehend; this is a necessary
condition of a state of pupilage. And lastly we reply,
that if but little has been learned, the learning of that
little may have been of the greatest value in training
the mind for its future work; and that even if these
studies have been quickly and altogether abandoned,
yet valuable results remain in the mental culture which
they have left behind.

4. A fourth objection assumes that since the classical
system of education was introduced before modern science and literature took their rise, therefore it cannot
possibly be the best; because, first, it cannot correspond with the spirit or meet the wants of the age; and
secondly, it takes no cognizance of the vast mass of new

facts, principles, and ideas which have been added to our stores of knowledge in modern times. And in particular it is said that, even if the poetry and eloquence of the ancients preserve their pre-eminence, yet their philosophy was neither the deepest nor the most true ; and their history lacks the enlarged views and enlightened wisdom with which centuries of additional experience have furnished mankind.

Now if this be urged merely to prove that the Classics ought not to have exclusive possession of our educational field, we have nothing to say in reply ; that the great discoveries of modern science, the great facts of modern history, and the great truths and ideas of modern literature ought not to be ignored in the education of our youth, is a matter upon which no one in our day can entertain a reasonable doubt.

But if more than this be meant, we reply, first, by calling attention to what we have already said with reference to the claim which the Classics rightfully make to occupy the central position in our education ; and, secondly, by referring to the fact before alluded to, that the very multiplicity of the objects presented to our attention by modern literature and science, and the vast extent of the field of study thus opened to us, seriously diminish their educational value, because there is the greatest difficulty in making a selection of what is most valuable and appropriate for the purpose of education, and there is no probability of educationists arriving at an agreement upon this point ; whereas the Classics present a limited number of authors, many of them in their kind models of thought and style ; and it is most desirable that we should have a common system, or at all events a common basis of our system, of education; while it is equally desirable, considering the limited nature of our faculties, and the shortness of the time into which the work of education must be compressed, that that basis should not be of too wide an extent.

5. A fifth objection is based upon the union in the classical system of the Greek and Latin languages. Why, it is asked, study Greek and Latin together? They are different in themselves, and are not necessarily connected. Why not make one of them the basis of our higher education, and not the two?

Now the validity of this objection must be conceded so far as this, that where education is cut short at the age at which boys intended for business usually leave school, one only of these languages should be studied. And as to which of the two has the first claim upon the student's attention is a question easily decided. For, notwithstanding the great superiority of the language and literature of Greece to those of Rome, when we consider that the Latin tongue enters so largely into the composition of our own and other modern languages; that it has done so much to mould our modern civilization, not only directly through its literature, but also indirectly through the influence which Latin modes of thought and expression had upon the ecclesiastical system and dogmas, and upon the social and political life of the Middle Ages; that its history is the basis of our modern history, and its jurisprudence, of our modern systems of law; that for so many ages it formed the common idiom of the professions and of the learned, and that, therefore, without it the thoughts of many generations are inaccessible, — when we consider all this we can hardly doubt that Latin should have the preference. In the case, then, of a large number of boys, those for example who are the objects of secondary or middle-class education, we allow that Latin only ought to be studied.

But in the case of those whose education is extended through a longer period, we maintain that it is desirable to learn another language as well, both for the sake of imparting to the mind a broader and more comprehensive view of things in general, and of the principles of language in particular. And Greek has, undoubtedly, after Latin, the next claim upon our attention, because in clearness and power, in philosophical precision of expression and grammatical structure, it is the most perfect of all languages; because it is from Greece that Rome borrowed her literature; because the productions of the Greek mind are the primary source of the literature, and a fundamental element in the civilization, of modern Europe; because, in short, Greece, by its language and literature, is the parent of intellectual efforts in poetry, eloquence, history, and philosophy, and thus possesses, as it were, the empire of the intellectual world, in all generations and throughout all time.

It would be tedious to go through and answer in detail all the various objections which have been raised against classical studies. Thus it has been said, that the early study of the Classics destroys the taste; that

classical literature has exercised a baneful influence on
art and on philosophy ; and that the best poets and
other writers of the present day owe nothing to the
Classics.　Now we may observe, in passing, with reference to the last mentioned assertion, that our higher
education hitherto has been so thoroughly and almost
exclusively classical, and that the intellectual atmosphere in which we live, and therefore every educated
mind, is impregnated to such an extent with classical
ideas and principles, as to render it quite impossible
to estimate how much our writers owe to the old Classics of Greece and Rome.　For the rest, we must content
ourselves with observing that such charges are easily
made against any studies ; but that, before they can
carry with them any weight, they must be established
by a wide and searching induction of particulars — a
task in this case most difficult of accomplishment, as we
venture to believe ; and that until they have been in
this way satisfactorily proved, any attempt to deal with
them would be futile.

With the question of the value of a classical education generally, there has often been mixed up another
question quite distinct from it, viz. the value of the
particular system of classical instruction pursued in
this country ; and arguments and objections which
properly belong only to the latter, have often been
imported into the former.

Sydney Smith, who was one of the earliest writers in
the present century to call attention to this subject,
drew a clear distinction between these inquiries, pro-
-nouncing an opinion as unfavorable in the latter case

as it was favorable in the former, to the study of the Classics. In his essay on " Professional Education," he observes : " That vast advantages may be derived from classical learning, there can be no doubt. The advantages which are derived from classical learning by the English mode of teaching, involve another and a very different question ; and we will venture to say that there never was a more complete instance in any country of such extravagant and overacted attachment to any branch of knowledge, as that which obtains in this country with regard to classical knowledge." He then goes on to complain of the exclusive position the Classics occupied in our course of instruction ; of the exaggerated estimate in which they were held, as proved by the conceit which attached the title of scholar to one versed in classical learning alone ; of the misfortune of scholars in England having come to regard the instrument rather than the end, e.g. not what may be read in Greek, but Greek itself; of the extraordinary perfection aimed at ; in short, that the then existing system of classical instruction " cultivated the imagination a great deal too much, and other habits of mind a great deal too little " ; and that it was " not making the most of life " to " constitute such an extensive and such a minute classical erudition an indispensable article in education."

To these objections it has been added by other writers, that the Classics are taught too early and too indiscriminately ; that boys would learn them better if they commenced them at a later period of their school course ; that other subjects, particularly those which, like the natural sciences, appeal to the outward senses, are the best for the earlier stages of education; that the custom of learning by rote certain forms of words, without any insight into their meaning, and without going through any process of intellectual digestion, is damaging even to the industrious student, while the parrot-repetition and sing-song knowledge of the idle and careless is destructive of the intellectual powers; and, to sum up all in one general statement, that our existing system of classical instruction is unsound in itself, and injurious in its results.

Now, while we trust that many of these objections apply to a state of things which has to some extent passed away, or at all events is passing away, yet we cannot deny that they carry with them considerable truth and force, although we do not admit them in their entirety. Making this general admission at the outset, let us proceed to state how far our own opinion coincides with the expressions of condemnation just referred to.

We have already granted that the Classics have no right to the exclusive position in education which they have so long held; that, however great may be their educational value, there are other subjects of study very efficacious for the exercise and development of the mind; that, though classical studies can do much, yet they cannot afford a complete mental discipline and culture. We are ready to allow, also, that in our country, in consequence of the exaggerated estimate formed of the Classics, other important branches of knowledge have been proportionately undervalued; and we are disposed to join in the protest of Sydney Smith against the unfairness of applying the title of " scholar " to those only who are acquainted with Greek and Latin.

Nor can it be denied that the subject-matter of the classical authors has been too often neglected in the great attention paid to their language, and that thus much of the advantage to be derived from their study has been lost. Still, after what we have said of the importance of the study of language as language, we cannot regard this as an evil unmixed with good. Indeed, the evil would probably have been greater, though of an opposite character, if, in paying more attention to the subject-matter, the critical and exact investigation of the language had been less cared for.

The question whether the Classics would be better learned if their study were commenced by the student at a later age than is at present usual, is one which probably admits of debate, and certainly cannot be satisfactorily decided except by a careful and extensive induction from experience ; and no experiments on a sufficiently large scale have yet been made to enable us to form a positive opinion upon the matter. It is asserted, indeed, in a recent number of the Westminster Review,[1] that, " if composition were wholly cut out of the curriculum, and boys were allowed to begin their Classics at a later age than they do now, and after a proper training, which they do not now receive, in English and French, or German, they might acquire in two years, or, in cases of exceptional stupidity, in three years, as much knowledge of Greek and

[1] July, 1864.

Latin as they do now after ten or twelve "; and, in
support of this statement, it is urged that in the
London Ladies' Colleges "young ladies, who leave
school at sixteen or seventeen, do learn Latin fairly"
in that time, studying simultaneously "a variety of
other subjects." Now, that they do learn something
of the subject is no doubt true, but how much, one
would be glad to know. Although, however, we
have no sufficient experience to guide us, we may
suggest a few points of much use in directing us
towards a tolerably accurate decision on the proposed
question. It is, we believe, a recognized fact that
students who take to classical studies after they have
passed the ordinary school-boy age rarely attain to
much proficiency in them, while, if they apply themselves to Mathematics, or many other branches of
learning, they often reach a high, or even the highest,
level of attainments. To this rule the exceptions are
very few ; and it would seem to indicate that classical
studies, if any useful amount of progress is to be made
in them, must be introduced at an early stage of the
educational course. It is not, however, decisive as to
the point whether the Classics are best mastered when
commenced by school-boys in their tenth or their
fourteenth year. It is undoubtedly true that studies
which involve external observation are most attractive
to the mind of a child, and that, therefore, in them
children at an early age are most likely to make rapid
progress. Still, it is highly probable that the mind
ought early to be directed to some extent, though not
excessively, to the study of language, with a view, not

so much to the acquiring a knowledge of the subject, as to the bending the faculties in the right direction, by way of preparation for the subsequent earnest and thorough pursuit of it. Thus young boys should spend a small, but only a small, portion of their time on their Latin, their attention being chiefly devoted to other more suitable, or practically useful, subjects. This time may gradually be extended as they progress in age and attainments. Nothing can be more indefensible than to devote in the case of young boys any considerable portion of their time to the Classics, when there are so many other branches of knowledge absolutely necessary for them to learn, in which they ought first to be well grounded, or which, at all events, they ought to be put in a fair way of acquiring in due course. To what has been already said upon this point, we may add, from our own experience, that we have known in one or two instances boys who, commencing classical studies at a late period of their school-boy career, have yet made considerable progress in them; but they have been boys of remarkable ability, and did not reach more than a respectable level of proficiency; and, after all, it is questionable whether from these studies, entered upon thus late, they have derived any very valuable discipline of the mind. And, again, it must be remembered that these instances are exceptional, and that in far the greater number of cases, when classics have been commenced late in the school course, our experience has proved that but a very small amount of knowledge of them has been acquired. Still, to those disposed to venture on the

6 *

experiment on a large scale, it is a matter at least worth a trial, whether the same or even a greater amount of classical proficiency may not be attained by commencing classical studies at a more advanced age. We can only say that in our judgment the result would not be found to justify the practice.

Lastly, with reference to what has been said in condemnation of rote-teaching, we are disposed to acquiesce in the opinion of the Edinburgh Reviewer,[1] that "to repeat with unfailing accuracy the old Eton and Westminster Grammars was an accomplishment, or rather a virtue, of which the value, intellectually speaking, was absolutely null." It cannot, indeed, be denied that in the method of teaching the Classics formerly, and perhaps to a great extent still, prevalent among us, too great importance has been attached to this mere *memoriter* acquisition of paradigms and rules; and thus the memory has been too much culti- vated, while other faculties have been neglected, and the general intelligence has been unawakened. It is, however, to be hoped that a more intelligent system of instruction is at all events beginning to prevail.

If we proceed to inquire into the remedies for the deficiencies of our system of classical instruction, by far the most important one at once presents itself. The truth is, that classical teachers, like all others, ought to be specially trained for their work. A young man may be an admirable classical scholar, and yet quite unfitted to impart classical instruction; and we believe that no really efficient method of teaching is

1 July, 1864, p. 170.

likely to prevail, until the teacher has been first taught
to teach, and so sent out thoroughly equipped and prepared for the work before him. The scholastic calling
ought to be elevated into the rank of a profession, like
that of the law or medicine, requiring a definite course
of preparatory professional training. We do not intrust
matters which concern our bodily health or the secur-
ity of our property to unskilled, untrained men. As
little should we intrust the equally or even more important task of disciplining the minds and forming
the characters of our children to men who have never
undergone any special preparation for so difficult and
momentous an employment. Our doctors and our
lawyers receive professional training, so should also
our schoolmasters ; and not only our elementary ones,
but still more those who undertake the education of
the upper and middle classes of the country ; for upon
their fitness for their work, much more than upon that
of the teachers of the lower orders, the well-being of
the nation depends, inasmuch as it is the upper and
middle classes who give the tone to, and impress their
form upon, the national character and life.

The whole question is one of pressing importance. For
the classical system cannot hold exclusive sway in our
schools ; with it the modern system must be combined ;
and the number of subjects thus required to be taught
make far too great a demand upon the limited time and
undeveloped faculties of the young ; the mind is
oppressed by the multiplicity of ideas presented to it,
none of which are sufficiently mastered ; and the result
is that it becomes enfeebled and stunted, instead of

being invigorated and developed. Thoroughness of
knowledge, no matter in how limited a sphere, is an
essential of true mental training ; with it there is intellectual development, small it may be, but still development ; without it there is none. The attempt to teach
too many things is the great evil which educationists
have at present to contend against, — an evil, which is
marring the beneficial effects of our education, and will,
unless countervailed, we fear, manifest itself fatally
in the lowered tone and diminished vigor of the minds
of the next generation. One way of averting this fatal
defect alone presents itself, and that is, the introduction of some more speedy and effectual mode than that
at present in vogue of teaching classics ; for until this
is done, " there is very little room," as the *Quarterly
Review*[1] well says, " for any fresh studies " ; to which
it adds, " if the fresh studies are pursued with no better
method than the old, it matters little whether they are
introduced or not." Unless this can be done, one thing
seems certain, viz. that the days of the classical system
are numbered ; it must wane and finally perish beneath
the pressing exigencies of business and common life,
which will always give to the opposing modern system
great and ever increasing weight.

In conclusion we will briefly state a few of the practical results to which we have been led by the foregoing
considerations.

For the purpose of thorough mental training, and the
culture of the higher intellectual faculties, the study of
the Classics is indispensable ; or at all events no substi-

[1] July, 1864, p. 204.

tute for it, equally efficacious, has been, or, so far as we can see, is ever likely to be, found. In any system of education which aims at anything more than elementary instruction, or imparting the mechanical information necessary for engaging in ordinary commercial pursuits, — i.e. in any system of education above the lowest, — the Classics have a right to occupy the central position, as the principal subject of study.

Yet classical studies manifestly cannot be forced upon all. For instance, they are, of course, out of the question in Primary education, for those who remain at school only long enough to acquire the bare elements of knowledge—Reading, Writing, and Arithmetic. Nor can they with any great advantage find a place in the lower kind of Secondary education, viz. that intended for those who from the exigencies of their position are obliged to go out at an early age (say about thirteen years old) to their trade, or business; for they have not time to acquire, together with such information as is absolutely necessary to fit them for the mere routine performance of their future duties, a sufficient amount of classical knowledge to be of any practical value, as a discipline, or otherwise, to them; for them such an exact and critical knowledge, as is within their power to attain, of the English language must be made to supply partially — for it can only do so partially — what the Classics effect for more fortunate students, who can prolong the period of their education. For the latter, who are or ought to be the recipients of the upper kind of Secondary, or of the Higher education, i.e. for those who are being educated in the true sense of the term, the study of Latin, and then, if time and the state of progress of the student permit, that of Greek super-added, cannot without injury be dispensed with.

As regards the period of school-life at which classical studies should be commenced, we believe that those who are designed to pursue them at all should enter upon them at an early age, devoting, however, a smaller portion of their time and attention to them at first than subsequently; the object in view being, as we have before observed, to habituate them early to the frame of mind required for carrying on effectually such studies, and so prepare them for their earnest pursuit at a later period.

Lastly, while we have no sympathy with the vulgar outcry against the Classics on the score of their in-utility — an outcry which we have shewn to arise from a complete misunderstanding of what "the useful" in education really is, — we are constrained to admit, that in our English educational system too much time has been hitherto devoted to them; that in consequence many important branches of study have been neglected; and that the result has been, that large numbers in successive generations of students have been, and are still turned out of our leading seminaries of learning, ignorant of what every educated man ought to know, and in fact not educated, in any true and sufficient sense of the term. For we must recall to recollection what has been before urged in this paper, that high in-tellectual culture, which is at once the aim and the result of all true education, consists in the harmonious development and action of all the intellectual faculties;

and that this can be secured, not by an exclusive attention to any one subject, not by the study of language
alone; or of mathematics alone, or of physical science
alone, but by acquiring a knowledge of all these subjects,—more perhaps of one, and less of another, but
a competent knowledge of them all,—the knowledge
of one not existing independently of that of another,
but all arranged and consolidated around a common
centre of attainments, forming a fixed and certain possession of the mind. We must remember, in short,
that the perfect education of man can only be obtained
by an accurate and complete study of all the objects
which fall within the sphere of the cognizance of man's
intelligence. This universality of knowledge, then,
should be the ultimate point of our educational aim
and aspiration; though we may never forget that, in
consequence of the finite nature of our faculties, and
the limited extent of our existing opportunities, we
cannot do more in the present stage of our being than
approximate to this goal of perfection, which can be
reached by us only in that state of existence, where we
shall " know," not " in part " as now, but with a knowledge, universal in its range, and perfectly accurate in
its grasp, " even as we are known."

II.

WERE the nations of classical antiquity entirely disconnected with us, had they no influence over us, or were their influence prejudicial to our interests, then it would be unwise to put their literary productions into the hands of the young. In that case, we should come to the same result, though in a different way, as the emperor Julian did, who excluded the classic writers from Christian schools, in order to exclude learning and influence from Christian society. But this whole view springs from an arbitrary distinction, and rests upon no better foundation than a plausible error. To what extent the works of the ancients are intelligible to us, and fitted to act upon our minds, may be learned from the fact that the productions of the oldest Greek bard, the Iliad and the Odyssey of Homer, notwithstanding their foreign air, are more popular, even among those who do not understand Greek, than any modern, or even German epic.

If a man of a vigorous and sound mind cannot attain to a true knowledge and just appreciation of the greatness and excellence of the immortal productions of the ancients, whence comes the honest admiration which '

This Essay is from the "Learned Schools" of Professor Frederic Thiersch, translated from the German by Rev. Barnas Sears, D.D., and published by him in the fifth volume of the Christian Review, of which he was Editor.

has always been cherished for them, even in times less enlightened than ours, by the noblest spirits of our race? True, indeed, these relics of ancient genius have to us a foreign air; but this peculiarity relates to the form more than to the spirit, and it is as necessary to rise above that in the study of Cervantes as of Sophocles, of Dante as of Homer. Beneath this form, there is, in the best writers of antiquity, an almost divine simplicity, springing directly from the justness of their views and the truth of their pictures of real life.

The *foreign air* of classical literature, and the consequent *difficulty* of mastering its forms and imbibing its spirit, are sometimes urged as objections to making it the basis of education. But *these very difficulties* — the mental activity and labor which it costs to overcome them — furnish to learned schools the best means of intellectual discipline and culture. It is with the mind of the youth as it is with his body. "This," says an ancient writer, "cannot be trained in the *palaestra* by merely promenading its groves, and witnessing the exercises, the strength, the skill, the perseverance of others, nor by a mere study of the rules. The youth himself must struggle and contend, as well as others; must exercise himself in running, in leaping, and throwing the discus and the spear; must oppose power to power, and skill to skill; must call forth and exert to the utmost every energy, and by an unyielding determination to conquer, sustain his exhausted and sinking powers, that, by protracted struggles and hardships, he may develop his full strength, and thereby secure the victory which shall one day crown his efforts at Olympia." It is equally true that the mind cannot be strengthened and disciplined by being conducted through the field of literature, and entertained with its flowery attractions, as on an excursion of pleasure. Let a teacher try the experiment. Let a young man be taught, if he can be, to find pleasure in studying the Adventures of Telemachus, or in Tasso, in the Andromache and Phoedra of the French, or the Clytemnestra and Merope of the Italian theatre; let him entertain himself with the history of Rollin or the tales of Florian, or satiate his desires with the most elegant productions of our own literature. It will be but a passive process of education, an excitement of the fancy, an inactive surrender to a charm, perhaps an ecstasy, a mere admiration of the glowing images that have been presented. But, for the solid material of a scientific education, the discipline and *gymnastic* exercise of the mind, and consequent intellectual power, nothing will have been gained. On the contrary, there is in such a procedure great danger of quenching the natural pleasure of mental activity, and of destroying all intellectual energy. The inevitable result of such a training will be the raising up of a class of young men unaccustomed to hardship, impatient of earnest application, flippant in counsel, incapable of the serious responsibilities of life, unable to meet the demands of science, or to discharge the duties of official stations, competent, perhaps, to increase the amount of our sunken literature, and to sit in judgment on its shadowy images.

All instruction for the education of a young man must aim at the discipline of his entire spiritual nature;

and the *gymnasium* must be for the *gymnastic* exercise of the mind, as it was anciently for that of the body. This demand is met in no way so effectually as by the earnest, thorough, well-directed and well-sustained study of the classic productions of ancient Greece and Rome. The very difficulties which the young mind has to overcome in mastering the wonderful inflections and constructions of the ancient languages call into action its undeveloped energies more than any other study. The intellectual struggles, which cannot be so great nor so protracted in the study of modern languages where, in order to an introduction to their entire literature, nothing but grammatical difficulties are to be contended with, must, in the ancient languages, be repeated in each new department of literature, as in passing from the poets to the historians, to the philosophers, and to the orators.

To the difficulties already mentioned must be added those of acquiring a thorough knowledge of the mythology, the antiquities, the history, laws, and customs of the Greeks and Romans. All this compels the student to muster every power of his mind in seizing, combining, and comprehending his materials, so that by extending his knowledge in every direction, by associating and properly adjusting what belongs together, by deducing from the known the unknown, he may be able to penetrate the sanctuary of genius, and become master of its perfection, as though it were his own.

As such an exercise puts all the intellectual powers of the student in motion and gives them greater expansion, it tends directly to improve the *judgment* and to form the *taste*. In a perfect model, ever fresh and glowing before him in spite of its antiquity, be it a strain of Homer or of Virgil, an oration of Demosthenes or of Cicero, a book of Thucydides or of Sallust, he sees, if all its parts have with careful study been duly inspected, the whole art of just arrangement and skilful execution distinctly exemplified. He will, under the guidance of a competent teacher, learn from one such great example how a subject ought to be treated, how arranged and divided, to what place each part should be assigned, with what it should be interwoven, what is to be adopted and what rejected, and how the inferior parts should be subordinated to the rest, and the more important held up conspicuously to observation. Thus he learns to comprehend in the work of a master the difficult art of invention, division, arrangement, and combination, and is in a fair way to be able himself to practise the art. Besides this internal economy, which is the soul and spirit of a production, the student will learn to appreciate and ultimately acquire the exterior excellences of representation, itself the token of a good training. He will discover the secret of a right distribution of the members of a sentence, the mutual relation of its parts, the harmonious play of its rising and falling undulations, its variety of detail and general equipoise, all of which is thrown around the idea like graceful drapery. In poetical works the incomparable perfection of the rythmical and musical form awakens first a sensibility to its charm, and then creates a taste for harmonious and just representation. The mind thus disciplined feels, at length, spontaneously a similar in-

7 *

spiration, and gradually acquires a command of harmonious proportions. From such a power the beauties of style naturally put forth like buds and blossoms from a tree ; for the style is but the blossom of the mind, or, as a celebrated writer has observed, "the style is the man." It can be fresh and vigorous and fair only where the mind possesses internal elasticity and power. So the bud opens into a flower, the rains swell it, the vernal breezes fan it, and the sunbeam brings forth its beautiful form to the eye.

But there are those who maintain the direct contrary of all this. "You torment the youth," say they, "with difficulties beyond their powers, and thereby weaken their courage and fill them with disgust, and, in the end, destroy all disposition and all ability to study." It is possible that instruction in classical literature may have all these ill effects ; it is probable and even undeniable where the teacher is injudicious and his method confused, dry, and spiritless. But such a man would ruin any cause that should be committed to him. If he should not seriously injure the mind of the youth, it would be only because the study itself, by its own good tendencies, would have power to repair the damage.

The complaint that there is necessarily too great difficulty in the study of the classics, comes either from those who have no knowledge on these subjects, or from unfortunate individuals who have suffered the evils of bad training, and who ought to find fault with their teachers rather than with the study.

If the teacher is worthy of his trust, he will, as may be observed in every good school, soon show his pupils how to overcome the difficulties, which do indeed exist, but which readily yield to enterprise and skill. He will teach them the shortest way (and the most thorough is invariably the shortest) through these difficulties to their object; he will raise their hopes, he will call into exercise their courage, so that as the result of their toil they shall feel conscious of the reward of increased power and knowledge, the best fruit of instruction, the surest pledge of ultimate success, and the rejoicing of every well-disciplined youthful mind. Nothing but the consciousness of misspent time and consequent mental imbecility, can create that disgust frequently witnessed in a poor school, the grave of all scientific culture, and the hot-bed of unrestrained insolence and vulgarity.

The school where the classics are successfully studied is pre-eminently a place of youthful enterprise and joy, the natural consequence of well-directed study and conscious advancement in knowledge.

It is absurd to suppose that straining the powers of the mind will injure it, just as if it were a mechanical instrument. Overstraining the mind is, indeed, attended with great evil ; and we have a right to expect of every teacher that he acquaint himself with the measure of his pupil's ability, and never overcharge it. Vigorous effort, if kept within the limits of one's capacities, is always the parent of strength. The mind that is kept in continual exercise, like the arm accustomed to wielding the sword, will thereby accumulate strength and greatly increase its power of rapid execution.

We come now to speak of the influence which classical study has upon practical education, both in relation to subsequent study in the university, and to the active duties of life. The young man whose mind has been well disciplined by classical study has greatly increased his intellectual power, and his ability to apprehend and manage scientific subjects in general. Already accustomed to the same kind of difficulties which, in a new form only, will meet him in his university course, practised in forming new mental combinations and in exercising the judgment, and inured to strenuous effort in grasping and mastering a wide range of thought, he finds in the scientific method of his advanced course of study nothing but the application and extension of those principles which, in their elementary character, occupied his youth. Thus qualified to enter upon the higher pursuits of learning, he will soon be able to acquire a mastery over the new materials presented to him, and, by an independent exercise of his own expanding mind, to make a right disposal of them, and to move directly onward without embarrassment to still higher attainments. He only who comes to the university with such a preparation is on the way to distinction. Without that preparation the student, notwithstanding his swelling manuscripts of copied lectures, and the wisdom which he carries about with him in black and white, however much he may hurry from lecture-room to lecture-room, will, after all, always continue to be in his minority. Should he sooner or later discover his error, he will find that the object of his education and perhaps of his whole life, is irreparably lost. Inquire of the professor of law, of medicine, or of theology, and he will point you to the student who has been well-trained in the classics as the one who bears with most strength and ease the weight of his new labors. Even mathematicians find that students from a good gymnasium make better progress than those who come from practical high schools where the classics are excluded.

Not less directly does such an education prepare one for the business of life. I mean not that petty business which barely administers to our immediate necessities, but that comprehensive business, to the prompt and energetic performance of which, enlarged views, great principles, wisdom in deliberation, power in execution, and an indomitable and enterprising spirit, trained to severities and hardships, and stimulated by the recollection of noble examples, are indispensable. No nation · is destitute of lofty sentiment or of noble examples, which, if sufficiently known might serve to stimulate other nations. Many are as rich in these as were the Greeks and Romans. But with none are greatness, magnanimity, heroism, practical wisdom, and all the public virtues, so fully exhibited and so perpetuated in immortal works of poetry, history, eloquence, politics, and philosophy, as with these two ancient nations. Many a hero, not only before Agamemnon, as Horace says, but after him, has fallen into oblivion unwept, for having no sacred bard or gifted chronicler to immortalize his deeds. Only that representation of greatness in which the deed itself, the sentiment, and the virtue exercised, shine forth in their full splendor, acts with effect upon the youthful mind, and moulds it with a plastic power. Such rich repositories of counsels and examples, of sound views and just principles, of confidence in action and fortitude in suffering, have a mighty power in forming the character of the young. What Cicero says of Caesar, viz. that he acted and wrote in the same spirit, is true to a greater or less extent of other ancient writers. They were mostly men, formed in active life, in the very midst of its events, practised in managing great interests; and their wisdom and experience passed directly over from their actions to their writings.

By abandoning Greek literature, as some propose, and in limiting the schools to the study of the Roman authors, we exclude our youth from the fairer portion of ancient learning. We limit them not only to what is derived from the Greek and is far inferior to it in originality and freshness, but to that which cannot even be comprehended without the other. The Latin writers are continually referring us back to the Greek fountains,—to the sentiments and forms of expression from which their own were borrowed, and, for the most part, in such a way that the copy cannot be understood without a comparison of the original.

Furthermore, the happy effects of a classical education, as above described, depend on the joint study of both languages. Far be it from us to affirm, that a long and close intimacy with the noblest productions of the Roman authors, with the works of Cicero, Sallust, Tacitus, Virgil, and others, will not secure discipline. But what we would say is, that a study of classical literature which shall embrace all antiquity, presents a much wider scope of mental culture, and crowns the labors of the student with more than a twofold harvest.

Here, at least, the half is not better than the whole. Hence Horace, in training the young Piso, does not refer him to his own writings nor to those of the older Roman authors, but to those of the Greeks :

" Vos exemplaria Graeca
Nocturna versate manu, versate diurna."

If it be said that the study of the Greek consumes the time that ought to be devoted to more useful studies, and that it infringes upon the Latin, we reply, that there are schools enough where the study of both languages has been prosecuted with success to refute the charge. But the assertion that the study of the Latin is injured by that of the Greek, is contradicted by all experience. For a period of nearly twenty years, during which I have been a teacher in public schools, not a single case has occurred where the pupil who distinguished himself in Greek was not a good master of the Latin, and vice versa ; but where one has failed in Greek, it has been no better with him in Latin. All the teachers whom I have questioned on this point have confirmed my own observation. This sure test of manifold experience, all leading to the same result, is an incontestible proof that when the pupil fails in the Latin the cause does not lie in the study of the Greek, but in his own incapacity or want of application. And yet no opinion is more prevalent than the one just noticed.

But, on the other hand, a regard for the Greek, for the beauty of the language, for the rich variety and perfection of its works, must not be allowed to mislead us as it has many schools, to make the study of that language the basis of education, and to give the Latin a subordinate rank. The whole fabric of our education and learning has a Latin foundation. Besides, the Latin language, notwithstanding the extent to which modern languages have taken its place, is still the common language of the learned. It is suitable, therefore, that the student be trained to write in it according to the best models. But the Greek is remoter from daily use, and therefore the same kind of mastery in it is not indispensable. It is not so important to be able to express one's thoughts in Attic Greek as it is to write pure Latin. The object of education is not to be able to write Greek poetry, but to understand accurately the productions of the Greek poets, to perceive all their excellences and feel their power. Nor does this imply that translations into Greek are to be banished from our schools; on the contrary, these are the very best means of arriving at a nice acquaintance with the language, and the only sure proof of having made the attainment. If the Latin be made the basis of education, it will facilitate instruction in the Greek, for it will accustom the student to the same kind of study that is requisite in the latter. To this may be added another facility in the acquisition of the Greek, originating in the greater regularity, and if properly treated, greater simplicity, of the Greek grammar. The Latin, therefore, should be commenced earlier than the Greek, and, through the whole course, have the larger portion of time allotted to it.

The study of the two ancient languages, their literature and the circle of knowledge necessary to a comprehension of them, as well as the other studies of the gymnasium, furnish the only sure foundation of the continued existence and progress of literature and science in general.

In naming the three learned professions,[1] we have made no direct allusion to other branches of a liberal education, such as intellectual philosophy, history, eloquence, and poetry. The first of these as well as the rest has its foundation in the writings of antiquity. Greek literature contains not only the beginnings but the fairer portion, nay the most essential part, of mental philosophy. Whatever changes and modifications particular doctrines have, in the processes of modern criticism, undergone, the great problems of philosophy were there comprehended, and solved, and laid down in works, not only with the freshness of new discovery and originality, but with a method of treatment which excites the admiration of later ages, and still serves as a model for imitation. Here a wide field has been laid open for observation by recent investigation respecting the doctrines of the Ionic, the Eleatic, the Pythagorean and the Platonic schools; and the new results which are hereby gained shed a clearer and broader light over the whole range of philosophic inquiry. Without going back to those original fountains of philosophy, it will be impossible for us to take a wide survey of its entire history, and learn our own true position. As no one can pretend to be a scientific theologian who is not

[1] The author's illustrations of the aid which these professions derive from the study of the Classics are omitted here.

8

master of the original scriptures, so can no one be regarded as a learned philosopher who must inquire of
others, be they translators or commentators, in order
to know what Plato or Aristotle taught.

The historian finds himself sustaining a similar relation to classical literature. Whether it be his object to
trace out the history of the nations of antiquity and
unfold their peculiarities, or to familiarize himself with
models of historical composition, his first study must
be the classics. So also is it with the geographer, the
chronologist, the mythologist, and the antiquary. No
one of them can dispense with a knowledge of the ancient languages. He who is preparing for any one of
these departments without such knowledge, will find
his education a failure.

Not less inseparably connected with the study of
antiquity is elegant literature. Our poetry made a
noble beginning in narrative verse and in the songs
of the *Minne*, but soon declined. Again the Silesian
poetry, partly in modern style, flourished for a time,
but passed away without effect. After several successful attempts in the first half of the last century,
Klopstock raised our poetry to a manly character, and
his strong mind, imbued with the spirit of Zion's sacred
bard, and with Pindar's lofty strain, shows, especially
in his odes, how the study of the ancient classics can
mould a noble genius without destroying its peculiarities, and elevate it to a style of poetry which will remind
one of those ancient masters, and at the same time
breathe a truly national spirit, elsewhere scarcely to be
found. With what success Goethe, and after him Schil-

ler, drank in the Greek tragedy, and thereby refined and elevated their own powers, the former has shown in his Iphigenia, the latter in his Wallenstein and still more in the Bride of Messina. No sooner was our literature brought by exalted genius into contact with the best classical productions, as by Herder in the anthology, and Voss in the Homeric epos and the idyll, than works of a kindred spirit, and still peculiarly national, appeared as the fruit, and we had an abundance of the most touching elegies and epigrams and epic songs, as the Louise of Voss and the Hermann and Dorothea of Goethe.

We have imitated our neighbors, at one time the French, then the Italians or Spanish, and finally ourselves; and what is the consequence? Miserable flowers without fragrance or beauty, which have withered like the mown grass, whereas the works mentioned above are still in full bloom, having an indigenous growth and constituting the true ornaments of our literature, and such they will remain as long as the language shall endure. Is this difference accidental? Impossible.

Cease, then, ye graceless, spiritless poets; ye shadows of those lofty German geniuses who drank deeply at the Castalian fountains; ye admirers of our gray antiquity, who discern not its productive elements; ye historians, with ponderous tomes of chaotic learning, and words upon words without soul or spirit, cease to malign the mother which has nourished the greatest and best of our native poets, and which proffers the same nutriment and fostering influence to the intellect and heart of every gifted youth who will subject himself to her discipline. He will, if he follow in the tracks of his great predecessors, find himself on the true road to distinction, and will be able to sustain the honor and the fresh vigor of our national literature.

To sum up these remarks in a few words, modern civilized nations have not become what they are through themselves. Our religion, laws, science, and refinement have descended to us from antiquity, and are inseparably connected with it. Classical literature is not only the necessary medium through which this connection is to be kept, but is in itself the direct instrument for upholding and perfecting all the sciences and all the culture that grows out of them. As the direct object of education, the formation of the intellectual character, is best attained by this means, so also the foundations and pillars of the whole fabric of our culture are thus most securely fixed, and those who would remove this study from its present prominent position in our learned schools, would, so far as in them lies, obscure the light which has blessed the world. The consequence of such an outrage against the highest interests of humanity would be the relapse of science, and the loss of that vigor which the revival of letters gave to Europe.

III.

L'AVARICE, says La Rochefoucault,.est plus opposée à l'économie que la libéralité. We have the same answer to make to those, who, in the matter of education, would sacrifice what is really useful to their own narrow or perverse theory of utility, and, out of sheer abhorrence of the luxuries and prodigality of learning, would indulge the neophyte in a very scanty allowance of its bare necessaries. They who apply to literature this radical levelling, degrading *cui bono* test, who estimate genius and taste by their value in exchange, and weigh the results of science in the scales of the money-changer, may be wiser in their generation than the disinterested votaries of knowledge; but they have, assuredly, made no provision in their system for the noblest purposes of our being. The same thing may be said of those who are for sacrificing what are rather ambiguously called the ornamental to what are just as absurdly considered as *par excellence* the useful parts of education. According to this theory, a boy should be taught mathematics, chemistry, mineralogy, metaphysics, and the metaphysical part of moral philosophy, and be allowed, from his most tender years, we suppose,

This Chapter is from the Collected Works of Hon. Hugh S. Legaré, of Charleston, South Carolina, and is a part of the first Article in the Southern Review, to which Mr. Legaré was the chief contributor.

to dabble *ad libitum* in politics, speculative and practical
— in other words, he is to be brought up in studies,
which, although they lead to far more important results,
are, as a mere discipline for youth with a view to future
usefulness in life, we really think, not a great deal better
than the dry thorny dialectics of the schoolmen,—while
no object should be suffered to approach him that may
speak to his taste, his imagination, or his heart. Our
youth are to be trained up as if they were all destined
to be druggists and apothecaries, or navigators and
mechanists, or, if it sounds better, they are to be deeply
versed in the economy of the universe, and the most
recondite and shadowy subtleties of transcendental
geometry, or transcendent psychology — but what, after
all, ought to be the capital object of education, to form
the moral character, not by teaching what to think but
persuading to act well ; not by loading the memory
with cold and barren precepts, but forming the sensibility by the habitual, fervid, and rapturous contemplation of high and heroical models of excellence ; not by
definitions of virtue and speculations about the principle
of obligation, but by making us love the one and feel
the sacredness of the other — would, in such a system
of discipline, be sadly neglected. This is a radical and
an incurable defect in the *cui bono* theory. If we compare different aeras of history with each other, and
inquire what it is that distinguishes the flourishing and
pure from the degenerate and declining state of commonwealths, we shall seldom find that it is any falling
off in mere speculative knowledge, or even in the mass
of talent and ability displayed at any one time.

We really cannot, with a clear conscience, undertake to promise that Greek and Latin will make better artisans and manufacturers, or more thrifty economists; or, in short, more useful and skilful men in the ordinary routine of life, or its mere mechanical offices and avocations. We should still refer a young student of law, aspiring to an insight into the mere craft and mystery of special pleading, to Saunders's Reports rather than to Cicero's Topics; the itinerant field-preacher would, doubtless, find abundantly greater edification, and for his purposes, more profitable doctrine, in honest John Bunyan, than in all the speculations of the lyceum and the academies; and we do conscientiously believe, that not a single case, more or less, of yellow fever, would be cured by the faculty in this city, for all that Hippocrates and Celsus have said, or that has been ever said or sung of Chiron and Aesculapius. It is true, their peculiar studies would not be hurt, and might occasionally even be very much helped and facilitated, by a familiar acquaintance with these languages; and what would they not gain as enlightened and accomplished men! But it is not fair to consider the subject in that light only. It is from this false state of the controversy that the argument of Mr. Grimké derives all its plausibility. We on the contrary, take it for granted in our reasonings, that the American people are to aim at doing something more than "to draw existence, propagate, and rot." We suppose it to be our common ambition to become a cultivated and a literary nation. Upon this assumption, what we contend for, is, that the study of the classics is and ought to be, an essential part of a liberal education — that education of which the object is to make accomplished, elegant, and learned men : to chasten and to discipline genius, to refine the taste, to quicken the perceptions of decorum and propriety, to purify and exalt the moral sentiments, to fill the soul with a deep love of the beautiful both in moral and material nature, to lift up the aspirations of man to objects that are worthy of his noble faculties and his immortal destiny; in a word, to raise him as far as possible above those selfish and sensual propensities, and those grovelling pursuits, and that mental blindness and coarseness and apathy, which degrade the savage and the boor to a condition but a little higher than that of the brutes that perish. We refer to that education and to those improvements which draw the broad line between civilized and barbarous nations, which have crowned some chosen spots with glory and immortality, and covered them all over with a magnificence, that, even in its mutilated and mouldering remains, draws together pilgrims of every tongue and of every clime, and which have caused their names to fall like a " breathed spell " upon the ear of the generations that come into existence, long after the tides of conquest and violence have swept over them, and left them desolate and fallen. It is such studies we mean, as make that vast difference in the eyes of a scholar between Athens, their seat and shrine, and even Sparta with all her civil wisdom and military renown, and have (hitherto at least) fixed the gaze and the thoughts of all men with curiosity and wonder, upon the barren little peninsula between Mount Cithaeron and Cape Sunium, and the islands and the shores around it, as they stand out in lonely brightness and dazzling relief, amidst the barbarism of the West on the one hand, and the dark and silent and lifeless wastes of Oriental despotism on the other. Certainly we do not mean to say that in any system of intellectual discipline, poetry ought to be preferred to the severe sciences. On the contrary, we consider every scheme of merely elementary education as defective, unless it develop and bring out all the faculties of the mind as far as possible into equal and harmonious action. But, surely, we may be allowed to argue from the analogy of things, and the goodness that has clothed all nature in beauty, and filled it with music and with fragrance, and that has at the same time bestowed upon us such vast and refined capacities of enjoyment, that nothing can be more extravagant than this notion of a day of philosophical illumination and didactic soberness being at hand, when men shall be thoroughly disabused of their silly love for poetry and the arts. For what is poetry? It is but an abridged name for the sublime and beautiful, and for high wrought pathos. It is, as Coleridge quaintly, yet, we think, felicitously, expresses it, "the blossom and the fragrance of all human knowledge." It appears not only in those combinations of creative genius of which the *beau ideal* is the professed object, but in others that might seem at first sight but little allied to it. It is spread over the whole face of nature: it is in the glories of the heavens and in the wonders of the great deep, in the voice of the cataract and of the coming storm, in Alpine precipices and solitudes, in the balmy gales and sweet bloom and freshness of spring. It is in every heroic achievement, in every lofty sentiment, in every deep passion, in every bright vision of fancy, in every vehement affection of gladness or of grief, of pleasure or of pain. It is, in short, the feeling — the deep, the strictly moral feeling, which, when it is affected by chance or change in human life, as at a tragedy, we call sympathy; but as it appears in the still more mysterious connection between the heart of man and the forms and beauties of inanimate nature, as if they were instinct with a soul and a sensibility like our own, has no appropriate appellation in our language, but is not the less real or the less familiar to our experience on that account. It is these feelings, whether utterance be given to them, or they be only nursed in the smitten bosom; whether they be couched in metre, or poured out with wild disorder and irrepressible rapture, that constitute the true spirit and essence of poetry, which is, therefore, necessarily connected with the grandest conceptions and the most touching and intense emotions, with the fondest aspirations and the most awful concerns of mankind.

We have enlarged the more upon this head because we have uniformly observed that those who question the utility of classical learning, are at bottom, equally unfavorable to all elegant studies. They set out, it is true, in a high-flown strain, and talk largely about the superiority of modern genius. But the secret is sure to be out at last. When they have been dislodged, one by one, from all their literary positions, they never fail to take refuge in this cold and desolate region of utility.

They begin by discoursing magnificently of orators, poets, and philosophers, and the best discipline for forming them; and end by citing the examples of A the broker, or B the attorney, or C and D members of Congress, and what not, who have all got along in the world without the least assistance from Latin and Greek. Just as if our supposed great men had troubled their heads any more about the exact sciences and modern literature, than about the Classics, or were not quite as little indebted to Newton, to Milton, or to Tasso, as Virgil and Tully; and just as if an argument which proves so much were good for anything at all.

We now approach the second question: How far it is worth our while to study the writings of the ancients as models, and to make them a regular part of an academic course.

And first, it is, independently of all regard to their excellence, a most important consideration, that our whole literature, in every part and parcel of it, has immediate and constant reference to these writings. This is so true, that no one who is not a scholar can even understand, without the aid of labored scholia, which, after all, can never afford a just, much less a lively, idea of the beauties of the text, thousands of the finest passages, both in prose and poetry. Let any one who doubts this, open Milton where he pleases, and read ten pages together, and we think he will confess that our opinion is well founded. Indeed, a knowledge of Latin and Greek is almost as much presupposed in our literature as that of the alphabet, and the facts or the fictions of ancient history and mythology are as familiarly alluded to in the learned circles of England, as any of the laws or phenomena in nature. They form a sort of conventional world, with which it is as necessary for an educated man to be familiar as with the real. Now, if there is no sort of knowledge which is not desirable, and scarcely any that is not useful; if it is worth the while of a man of leisure to become versed in the Chinese characters or the Sanscrit, or to be able to decipher the Egyptian hieroglyphics, what shall we say of that branch of learning which was the great fountain of all European literature — which has left its impress upon every part of it, of which we are every moment reminded by its beauties, and without which much that is most interesting in it is altogether enigmatical? It is vain to say that good translations are at hand which supersede the necessity of studying the originals. Works of taste it is impossible to translate; and we do not believe there is any such thing in the world as a faithful version that approaches to the excellence of the original work. They are casts in plaster of Paris, of the Apollo or the Venus, and, indeed, not near so good, inasmuch as eloquence and poetry are far less simple and more difficult of imitation than the forms of sculpture and statuary. There remains nothing but the body — and even that not unfrequently so altered in its very lineaments, that its author would scarcely recognize it — while all " the vital grace is wanting, the native sweetness is gone, the color of primeval beauty is faded and decayed." It will not be so easily admitted that the same objection holds in works of which utility, merely, is considered

as the object, such as histories, etc. Yet it certainly
does. The wonderful, the magical power of certain expressions cannot by any art of composition be transfused
from one language into another. The associations connected with particular words and phrases must be
acquired by long acquaintance with the language as it
came warm from the hearts of those who spoke it, or
they are frigid and even unmeaning. What translation
can give any idea to the English reader of the bitter
and contemptuous emphasis, and the powerful effect
with which Demosthenes pronounces his $Μακεδὼν\ ἀνήρ$,
or of the force of that eloquent horror and astonishment
with which Cicero exclaims against the crucifixion of a
Roman citizen?

In this connection we would insist upon the stores of
knowledge which are sealed up to all who are not conversant with the learned languages. This is a trite
topic, but not the less important on that account. By
far the most serious and engrossing concern of man —
revealed religion, is built upon this foundation. The
meaning of the scriptures, which it is so important to
understand, can be explained only by scholars, and the
controversies of the present day turn almost exclusively
upon points of biblical criticism, etc. How can a divine
whose circumstances allow him any leisure, sit down
in ignorance of such things? How can he consent to
take the awful information which he imparts to the
multitudes committed to his care, at second hand?
Surely here, if anywhere, it may emphatically be said :
tardi ingenii est consectari rivulos, fontes rerum non
videre. Indeed, this single consideration is weighty.

9

enough to maintain the learned languages in their places in all the universities of Christendom.

But it is not to theologians only that this branch of study is of great importance. How is the jurist to have access to the *corpus juris civilis*, of which Mr. Grimké expresses so exalted an opinion ? We agree with him in this opinion ; and while we have a mysterious reverence for our old and excellent common law, uncodified as it is, still we would have our lawyers to be deeply versed in the juridical wisdom of antiquity. Why ? For the very same reason that we think it desirable that a literary man should be master of various languages, viz. to make him distinguish what is essentially, universally, and eternally good and true from what is the result of accident, of local circumstances, or the fleeting opinions of a day. That most invaluable of intellectual qualities — which ought to be the object of all discipline, as it is the perfection of all reason — a sound judgment, can be acquired only by such diversified and comprehensive comparisons. All other systems rear up bigots and pedants, instead of liberal and enlightened philosophers. Besides, every school has its mannerism and its mania, for which there is no cure but intercourse with those who are free from them, and constant access to the models of perfect and immutable excellence which other ages have produced, and all ages have acknowledged. To point the previous observations, which are of very general application, more particularly to a topic touched upon before ; even admitting that modern literature were as widely different from the ancient as the enemies of the latter contend, yet that would be no reason for neglecting the study of the Classics, but just the contrary. Human nature being the same in all ages, we may be sure that men agree in more points than they disagree in, and the best corrective of the extravagances into which their peculiarities betray them, is to contrast them with the opposite peculiarities of others. If the tendency, therefore, of the modern or romantic style is to mysticism, irregularity, and exaggeration, and that of the classical, to an excess of precision and severity, he would be least liable to fall into the excesses of either who was equally versed in the excellences of both. Certainly a critic who has studied both Shakspeare and Sophocles must have a juster notion of the true excellence of dramatic composition, than he who has only studied one of them. Where they agreed he would be sure they were both right; where they happened, as they frequently do, to differ, he would at once be led to reflect much before he awarded the preference to either, and to have a care lest in indulging that preference, he should overstep the bounds of propriety and " the modesty of nature." It is thus, we repeat it, and only thus, that sound critics, sound philosophers, sound legislators, and lawyers worthy of their noble profession can be formed.

There are other kinds of knowledge besides what is interesting to divines and jurists locked up in the learned languages. Whole branches of history and miscellaneous literature, of themselves extensive enough to occupy the study of a life. Look into Du Cange, Muratori, Fabricius, etc. In short we pronounce, without

fear of contradiction, that no man can make any pre-
tentions to erudition who is not versed in Greek and
Latin. He must be forever at a loss, and unable to
help himself to what he wants in many departments of
knowledge, even supposing him to have the curiosity to
cultivate them, which is hardly to be expected of one
who will not be at the pains of acquiring the proper
means to do so with success. For we have always
thought, and still think, that those who refuse to study
a branch of learning so fundamental and so universally
held in veneration as the Classics, have forgotten " the
know thyself," when they prattle about profound erudition. In addition to all this, we venture to affirm
that the shortest way to the knowledge of the history,
antiquities, philosophy, etc., of all those ages, whose
opinions and doings have been recorded in Greek and
Latin, even supposing English writers to have gone
over the same ground, is through the originals. Compare the knowledge which a scholar acquires, not only
of the policy and the *res gestae* of the Roman emperors,
but of the minutest shades and inmost recesses of their
character, and that of the times in which they reigned,
from the living pictures of Tacitus and Suetonius, with
the cold, general, feeble, and what is worse, far from
just and precise idea of the same thing, communicated
by modern authors. The difference is incalculable. It
is that between the true Homeric Achilles, and the
Monsieur or Monseigneur Achille of the Théatre Fran-
çais, at the beginning of the last century, with his bob
wig and small sword. When we read of those times in
English, we attach modern meanings to ancient words,

and associate the ideas of our own age and country
with objects altogether foreign from them. In this
point of view, as in every other, the cause of the Classics
is that of all sound learning.

We mention as another important consideration, that
the knowledge of these languages brings us acquainted,
familiarly, minutely, and impressively, with a state of
society altogether unlike anything that we see in modern times. When we read a foreign author of our own
day, we occasionally, indeed, remark differences in
taste, in character, and customs; but in general we find
ourselves *en pays de connaissance*. Modern civilization,
of which one most important element is a common
religion, is pretty uniform. But the moment we open
a Greek book we are struck with the change. We are
in quite a new world, combining all that is wonderful
in fiction with all that is instructive in truth. Manners
and customs, education, religion, national character,
everything is original and peculiar. Consider the priest
and the temple, the altar and the sacrifice, the chorus
and the festal pomp, the gymnastic exercises, and those
Olympic games, whither universal Greece repaired with
all her wealth, her strength, her genius and taste;
where the greatest cities and kings, and the other first
men of their day, partook with an enthusiastic rivalry
scarcely conceivable to us, in the interest of the occasion, whether it was a race, a boxing-match, a contest
of musicians, or an oration, or a noble history to be
read to the mingled throng; and where the horse and
the rider, the chariot and the charioteer, were consecrated by the honors of the crown and the renown of

9 *

the triumphal ode. Look into the theatres where "the lofty grave tragedians" contend, in their turn, for the favor of the same cultivated people, and where Aristophanes, in verses which by the confession of all critics were never surpassed in energy and spirit, in Attic purity and the most exquisite modulations of harmony, is holding up Socrates, the wisest of mankind, to the contempt and ridicule of the mob, if that Athenian Demus that could only be successfully courted with such verses does not disdain the appellation. Next go to the schools, or rather "the shady spaces" of philosophy; single one object out of the interesting group — let it be the most prominent, he, in short, who for the same reason was made to play so conspicuous a part in the "Clouds." Consider the habits of this hero of Greek philosophy, according to Xenophon's account of them; now unlike anything we have heard among the moderns, passing his whole life abroad and in public, early in the morning visited the gymnasia and the most frequented walks, and about the time that the market-place was getting full resorting thither, and all the rest of the day presenting himself wheresoever the greatest concourse of people was to be found, offering to answer any question in philosophy which might be propounded to him by the inquisitive. Above all, contemplate the fierce democracy in the popular assembly, listening to the harangues of orators, at once, with the jealousy of a tyrant and the fastidiousness of the most sensitive critics, and sometimes with the levity, the simplicity, and the wayward passions of childhood. Read their orations — above all, his, whose incredible

pains to prepare himself for the perilous post of a
demagogue, and whose triumphant success in it everybody has heard of — how dramatic, how mighty, how
sublime! Think of the face of the country itself, its
monumental art, its cities adorned with whatever is
most perfect and most magnificent in architecture; its
public places peopled with the forms of ideal beauty;
the pure air, the warm and cloudless sky, the whole
earth covered with the trophies of genius, and the very
atmosphere seeming to shed over all the selectest influences, and to breathe, if we may hazard the expression,
of that native Ionian elegance which was in every object
it enveloped.

It is impossible to contemplate the annals of Greek
literature and art, without being struck with them as
by far the most extraordinary and brilliant phenomenon
in the history of the human mind. The very language,
even in its primitive simplicity, as it came down from
the rhapsodists who celebrated the exploits of Hercules
and Theseus, was as great a wonder as any it records.
All the other tongues that civilized man have spoken
are poor and feeble and barbarous in comparison of it.
Its compass and flexibility, its riches and its powers,
are altogether unlimited. It not only expresses with
precision all that is thought or known at any given
period, but it enlarges itself naturally with the progress
of science, and affords, as if without an effort, a new
phrase or a systematic nomenclature whenever one is
called for. It is equally adapted to every variety of
style and subject, to the most shadowy subtlety of distinction, and the utmost exactness of definition, as well

as to the energy and pathos of popular eloquence, to the majesty, the elevation, the variety of the epic, and the boldest license of the dithyrambic, no less than to the sweetness of the elegy, the simplicity of the pastoral, or the heedless gaiety and delicate characterization of comedy. Above all, what is an unspeakable charm, a sort of *naiveté* is peculiar to it, which appears in all those various styles, and is quite as becoming and agreeable in a historian or a philosopher — Xenophon for instance — as in the light and jocund numbers of Anacreon. Indeed, were there no other object in learning Greek but to see to what perfection language is capable of being carried, not only as a medium of communication, but as an instrument of thought, we see not why the time of a young man would not be just as well bestowed in acquiring a knowledge of it — for all the purposes, at least, of a liberal or elementary education — as in learning algebra, another specimen of a language or arrangement of signs perfect in its kind. But this wonderful idiom happens to have been spoken, as was hinted in the preceding paragraph, by a race as wonderful. The very first monument of their genius, the most ancient relic of letters in the Western world, stands to this day altogether unrivalled in the exalted class to which it belongs. What was the history of this immortal poem and of its great fellow? Was it a single individual, and who was he, that composed them? Had he any master or model? What had been his education; and what was the state of society in which he lived? These questions are full of interest to a philosophical inquirer into the intellectual history of the species, but they are especially important with a view to the subject of the present discussion. Whatever causes account for the matchless excellence of these primitive poems, and for that of the language in which they are written, will go far to explain the extraordinary circumstance, that the same favored people left nothing unattempted in philosophy, in letters and in arts, and attempted nothing without signal, and in some cases unrivalled, success. Winkelman undertakes to assign some reasons for this astonishing superiority of the Greeks, and talks very learnedly about a fine climate, delicate organs, exquisite susceptibility, the full development of the human form by gymnastic exercises, etc. For our own part, we are content to explain the phenomenon after the manner of the Scottish school of metaphysicians, in which we learned the little that we profess to know of that department of philosophy, by resolving it at once in an original law of nature; in other words, by substantially but decently confessing it to be inexplicable. But whether it was idiosyncrasy or discipline, or whatever was the cause, it is enough for the purposes of the present discussion, that the *fact* is unquestionable.

We shall now add the last consideration which our limits will permit us to suggest on this part of the subject.

In discussing the very important question whether boys ought to be made to study the Classics, as a regular part of education, the innovators put the case in the strongest possible manner against the present system, by arguing as if the young pupil under this discipline was to learn nothing else but language itself. We admit that this notion has received some sort of countenance from the excessive attention paid in the English schools to prosody, and the fact that their great scholars have been, perhaps (with many exceptions to be sure) more distinguished by the refinement of their scholarship than the extent and profoundness of their erudition. But the grand advantage of a classical education consists far less in acquiring a language or two, which, as languages, are to serve for use or for ornament in future life, than in the things that are learned in making that acquisition, and yet more in the manner of learning those things. It is a wild conceit to suppose that the branches of knowledge which are most rich and extensive, and most deserve to engage the researches of a mature mind, are, therefore, the best for training a young one. Metaphysics, for instance, as we have already intimated, though in the last degree unprofitable as a science, is a suitable and excellent, perhaps a necessary part of the intellectual discipline of youth. On the contrary, international law is extremely important to be known by publicists and statesmen, but it would be absurd to put Vattel into the hands of a lad of fifteen or sixteen. We will admit, therefore, what has been roundly asserted at hazard, and without rhyme or reason, that classical scholars discontinue these studies after they are grown wise enough to know their futility, and only read as much Greek and Latin as is necessary to keep up their knowledge of them, or rather to save appearances and gull credulous people ; yet we maintain that the concession

does not affect the result of this controversy in the
least. We regard the whole period of childhood and
of youth, up to the age of sixteen or seventeen, and
perhaps longer, as one allotted by nature to growth
and improvement in the strictest sense of those words.
The flexible powers are to be trained rather than tasked,
to be carefully and continually practised in the preparatory exercises, but not to be loaded with burdens that
may crush them, or be broken down by overstrained
efforts of the race. It is in youth that Montaigne's
maxim, always excellent, is especially applicable — that
the important question is, not who is most learned, but
who has learned the best. Now, we confess we have
no faith at all in young prodigies, in your philosophers
in teens. We have generally found these precocious
imatterers sink in a few years into barrenness and imbecility, and that as they begin by being men when
they ought to be boys, so they end in being boys when
they ought to be men. If we would have good fruit
we must wait until it is in season. Nature herself has
pointed out, too clearly to be misunderstood, the proper
studies of childhood and youth. The senses are first
developed, observation and memory follow, then imagination begins to dream and to create, afterwards
ratiocination, or the dialectical propensity and faculty
shoots up with great rankness, and last of all, the
crowning perfection of intellect, sound judgment and
solid reason, which, by much experience in life, at
length ripen into wisdom. The vicissitudes of the sea-
sons, and the consequent changes in the face of nature,
and the cares and occupations of the husbandman, are

not more clearly distinguished or more unalterably ordained. To break in upon this harmonious order, to attempt to anticipate these pre-established periods, what is it, as Cicero had it, but after the manner of the Giants, to war against the laws of the universe and the wisdom that created it? And why do so? Is not the space in human life, between the eighth and twentieth year, quite large enough for acquiring *every* branch of liberal knowledge, as well as is needed, or indeed can be acquired in youth? For instance, we cite the opinion of Condorcet, repeatedly quoted with approbation by Dugald Stewart, and if we mistake not by Professor Playfair too (each of them the highest authority on such a subject), that any one may, under competent teachers, acquire all that Newton or La Place knew in two years. The same observation, of course, applies *a fortiori* to any other branch of science. As for the modern languages, the study of French ought to be begun early for the sake of the pronunciation, and continued through the whole course, as it may be, without the smallest inconvenience. Of German we say nothing, because we cannot speak of our own knowledge ; but for Italian and Spanish, however difficult they may be, especially their poetry, to a mere English scholar, they are so easy of acquisition to any one who understands Latin, that it is not worth while even to notice them in our scheme. All that we ask then, is, that a boy should be thoroughly taught the ancient languages from his eighth to his sixteenth year or thereabouts, in which time he will have his taste formed, his love of letters completely, perhaps enthusiastically awakened, his knowledge of the principles of universal grammar perfected, his memory stored with the history, the geography, and the chronology of all antiquity, and with a vast fund of miscellaneous literature besides, and his imagination kindled with the most beautiful and glowing passages of Greek and Roman poetry and eloquence; all the rules of criticism familiar to him, the sayings of sages and the achievements of heroes indelibly impressed upon his heart. He will have his curiosity fired for further acquisition, and find himself in possession of the golden keys which open all the recesses where the stores of knowledge have ever been laid up by civilized man. The consciousness of strength will give him confidence, and he will go to the rich treasures themselves and take what he wants, instead of picking up eleemosynary scraps from those whom, in spite of himself, he will regard as his betters in literature. He will be let into that great communion of scholars throughout all ages and all nations — like that more awful communion of saints in the holy church universal — and feel a sympathy with departed genius and with the enlightened and the gifted minds of other countries, as they appear before him in the transports of a sort of Vision Beatific, bowing down at the same shrines and glowing with the same holy love of whatever is most pure and fair and exalted and divine in human nature. Above all, our American youth will learn that liberty, which is sweet to all men, but which is the passion of proud minds that cannot stoop to less, has been the nurse of all that is sublime in character and genius. They will see her form and feel her

10

influence in everything that antiquity has left for our
admiration, that bards consecrated their harps to her,
that she spoke from the lips of the mighty orators, that
she fought and conquered acted and suffered with the
heroes whom she had formed and inspired. Our young
student will find his devotion to his country — his free
country — become at once more fervid and more enlightened, and think scorn of the wretched creatures
who have scoffed at the sublime simplicity of her institutions, and " esteem it," as one expresses it, who
learned to be a republican in the schools of antiquity,
much better to imitate the old and elegant humanity
of Greece than the barbaric pride of a Norwegian or
Hunnish stateliness; and, let us add, will come much
more to despise that slavish and nauseating subservi-
ency to rank and title with which all European literature is steeped through and through. If Americans
are to study any foreign literature at all, it ought,
undoubtedly, to be the classical, and especially the
Greek

IV.

It is one of the characteristics of the present time, alarming to many persons, but, if we use the occasion well, a blessing rather than an evil, that doctrines which have hitherto passed unquestioned, and on which the frame of the institutions of European states is founded, are unscrupulously and rudely assailed. The propriety of the use of what are called the learned languages (Greek and Latin), among the main instruments of education, is a doctrine of this kind. And the question whether in modern education these languages are to retain their ancient supremacy, or whether, on the contrary, the languages and literature of modern Europe are to be placed by their side or before them, has been recently discussed with reference to educational institutions, both in this and other countries. In France, for example, this has been the subject of animated debates in the Chamber of Deputies; and that distinguished man of science, M. Arago, is reported on such an occasion to have expressed himself to the following effect:

" I ask for *classical* studies; I require them; I consider them as indispensable; but I do not think that they must necessarily be Greek and Latin. I wish that

This Chapter is from "The Principles of English University Education," by Rev. Dr. William Whewell, of Trinity College, Cambridge.

111

in certain schools these studies should be replaced, at the pleasure of the municipal councils, by a thorough study of our own tongue. I wish that in each college it should be permitted to put, in the place of Greek and of Latin, the study of a living language."

In opposition to the opinion thus expressed, I maintain that Greek and Latin are peculiar and indispensable elements of a liberal education ; and it is my business to show that the study of the modern authors just enumerated, and of others, however admirable their works may be, does not produce that kind of culture of the mind which is the true object of a liberal education.

This culture of the mind consists in sharing in the best influences of the progressive intellectual refinement of man. The present age is not independent of those which have preceded it. On the contrary, it is the heir of all the past. Its wealth, intellectual and material, may have been improved in the hands of the present holders, but the value of what we have added is small, compared with the amount of what we found already accumulated. In thought and language, as well as in arts and the products of art, we inherit an inestimable fortune from a long line of ancestors. In literature we are the children of the early Greeks :

Κάδμου τοῦ πάλαι νέα τροφή.

But thoughts can be inherited, and words, in all their force, transmitted, only by those who are connected with their ancestors in the line of thought and understanding, as well as in the mere succession of time.

And how is this connection of generations, thus requisite to the transmission and augmentation of mental wealth to be kept up ?

The cultivated world, up to the present day, has been bound together, and each generation bound to the preceding, by living upon a common intellectual estate. They have shared in a common development of thought because they have understood each other. Their standard examples of poetry, eloquence, history, criticism, grammar, etymology, have been a universal bond of sympathy, however diverse might be the opinions which prevailed respecting any of these examples. All the civilized world has been one intellectual nation ; and it is this which has made it so great and prosperous a nation. All the countries of lettered Europe have been one body, because the same nutriment, the literature of the ancient world, was conveyed to all, by the organization of their institutions of education. The authors of Greece and Rome, familiar to the child, admired and dwelt on by the aged, were the common language, by the possession of which each man felt himself a denizen of the community of general civilization, free of all the privileges with which it had been gifted from the dawn of Greek literature up to the present time.

What can the best authors of modern days do in the way of filling such an office ? Even if their language were universally familiar in cultured Europe, how do they connect us with the past? How do they enable us to read the impress which was stamped upon thought and language in the days of Plato and Aristotle, in virtue of which it is still current? How do they

10 *

enable us to understand the process by which the language of Rome conveyed the culture, the philosophy, the legislation of the ancient civilized world into the modern? How do they enable us to understand the thoughts and feelings to which they themselves appeal? If the Greek and Latin languages were to lose their familiar place among us, Montesquieu and Bossuet, Corneille and Racine, would lose their force and their charm. Those who read and admire these authors constantly make a reference in their minds to the works of the ancients, which they know immediately or through a few steps of derivation. If this knowledge were taken away, many of the strings would be broken in the instrument on which those artists played. And though, so long as a liberal education continues what it has been, the well-educated diffuse to others a general admiration of the " classical authors " of their own language; if Greek and Latin were to cease to be parts of general culture, the admiration of the classical authors of England and France would become faint and unintelligible, and, in a few generations, would vanish.

The same may be said of language. The languages of ancient Greece and Rome have, through the whole history of civilization, been the means of giving distinctness to men's ideas of the analogy of language, which distinctness, as we have seen, is one main element of intellectual cultivation. The forms and processes of general grammar have been conveyed to all men's minds by the use of common models and common examples. To all the nations of modern Europe, whether speaking a Romance language or not, the

Latin grammar is a standard of comparison, by reference to which speculative views of grammar become plain and familiar.

And then, as to the derivation of the modern European languages: Those who are familiar with Greek and Latin cannot but feel, in every sentence they read and write, that the whole history of the civilized world is stamped upon the expressions they use. The progress of thought and of institutions, the most successful labors of the poet, the philosopher, the legislator, have, in thousands of cases, operated to give a meaning to one little word. Those who feel this, have a view of the language which they speak, far more intelligent, far more refined, than those who gather the force of words from blind usage, without seeing any connection or any reason. What does intellectual culture mean, if it does not mean something more than this? What does it mean but that insight, that distinctness of thought with regard to the terms we employ, which saves us from solecisms, not by habit, but by principle, which shows us analogy where others see only accident, and which makes language itself a chain connecting us with the intellectual progress of all ages.

In what a condition should we be if our connection with the past were snapped; if Greek and Latin were forgotten? What should we then think of our own languages? They would appear a mere mass of incoherent caprice and wanton lawlessness. The several nations of Europe would be, in this respect at least, like those tribes of savages who occupy a vast continent, speaking a set of jargons, in which scarcely any resemblance can be traced between any two, or any consistency in any one. The various European languages appear to us obviously connected, mainly because we hold the Latin thread which runs through them; if that were broken the pearls would soon roll asunder. And the mental connection of the present nations with each other, as well as with the past, would thus be destroyed. What would this be but a retrograde movement in civilization?

In nations as in men, in intellect as in social condition, true nobility consists in inheriting what is best in the possessions and character of a line of ancestry. Those who can trace the descent of their own ideas and their own language through the race of cultivated nations; who can show that those whom they represent or reverence as their parents have everywhere been foremost in the fields of thought and intellectual progress — those are the true nobility of the world of mind; the persons who have received true culture; and such it should be the business of a liberal education to make men.

With these views I cannot conceive it possible that any well-constituted system of University teaching, in any European nation, can do otherwise than make the study of the best classical authors of Greece and Rome one of its indispensable and cardinal elements.

V.

To comment upon the course of education at the Scottish Universities is to pass in review every essential department of general culture. The best use, then, which I am able to make of the present occasion, is to offer a few remarks on each of those departments, considered in its relation to human cultivation at large; adverting to the nature of the claims which each has to a place in liberal education; in what special manner they each-conduce to the improvement of the individual mind and the benefit of the race; and how they all conspire to the common end, the strengthening, exalting, purifying, and beautifying of our common nature, and the fitting out of mankind with the necessary mental implements for the work they have to perform through life.

Let me first say a few words on the great controversy of the present day with regard to the higher education, the difference which most broadly divides educational reformers and conservatives; the vexed question between the ancient languages and the modern sciences and arts; whether general education should be classical — let me use a wider expression and say literary — or scientific. A dispute as endlessly and often as fruit-

This Chapter is from the Inaugural Address delivered to the University of St. Andrews, by John Stuart Mill, Rector of the University.

lessly agitated as that old controversy which it resembles, made memorable by the names of Swift and Sir William Temple in England and Fontenelle in France — the contest for superiority between the ancients and the moderns. This question, whether we should be taught the classics or the sciences, seems to me, I confess, very like a dispute whether painters should cultivate drawing or coloring, or, to use a more homely illustration, whether a tailor should make coats or trousers. I can only reply by the question : Why not both ? Can anything deserve the name of a good education which does not include literature and science too ? If there were no more to be said than that scientific education teaches us to think, and literary education to express our thoughts, do we not require both ? and is not any one a poor, maimed, lopsided fragment of humanity who is deficient in either? We are not obliged to ask ourselves whether it is more important to know the languages or the sciences. Short as life is, and shorter still as we make it by the time we waste on things which are neither business nor meditation nor pleasure, we are not so badly off that our scholars need be ignorant of the laws and properties of the world they live in, or our scientific men destitute of poetic feeling and artistic cultivation. I am amazed at the limited conception which many educational reformers have formed to themselves of a human being's power of acquisition. The study of science, they truly say, is indispensable ; our present education neglects it ; there is truth in this too, though it is not all truth ; and they think it impossible to find room for the studies which they desire to encourage, but by turning out, at least from general education, those which are now chiefly cultivated. How absurd, they say, that the whole of boyhood should be taken up in acquiring an imperfect knowledge of two dead languages! Absurd indeed; but is the human mind's capacity to learn measured by that of Eton and Westminster to teach? I should prefer to see these reformers pointing their attacks against the shameful inefficiency of the schools, public and private, which pretend to teach these two languages and do not. I should like to hear them denounce the wretched methods of teaching, and the criminal idleness and supineness which waste the entire boyhood of the pupils without really giving to most of them more than a smattering, if even that, of the only kind of knowledge which is even pretended to be cared for. Let us try what conscientious and intelligent teaching can do, before we presume to decide what cannot be done.

Scotland has on the whole, in this respect, been considerably more fortunate than England. Scotch youths have never found it impossible to leave school or the university having learned somewhat of other things besides Greek and Latin; and why? Because Greek and Latin have been better taught. A beginning of classical instruction has all along been made in the common schools; and the common schools of Scotland, like her universities, have never been the mere shams that the English universities were during the last century, and the greater part of the English classical schools still are. The only tolerable Latin grammars for school purposes that I know of, which had been produced in these islands until very lately, were written by Scotchmen. Reason, indeed, is beginning to find its way by gradual infiltration even into English schools, and to maintain a contest, though as yet a very unequal one, against routine. A few practical reformers of school tuition, of whom Arnold was the most eminent, have made a beginning of amendment in many things; but reforms, worthy of the name, are always slow, and reform even of governments and churches is not so slow as that of schools, for there is the great preliminary difficulty of fashioning the instruments, of teaching the teachers. If all the improvements in the mode of teaching languages which are already sanctioned by experience, were adopted into our classical schools, we should soon cease to hear of Latin and Greek as studies which must engross the school years, and render impossible any other acquirements. If a boy learned Greek and Latin on the same principle on which a mere child learns with such ease and rapidity any modern language, namely by acquiring some familiarity with the vocabulary by practice and repetition, before being troubled with grammatical rules — those rules being acquired with tenfold greater facility when the cases to which they apply are already familiar to the mind; an average schoolboy, long before the age at which schooling terminates, would be able to read fluently and with intelligent interest any ordinary Latin or Greek author in prose or verse, would have a competent knowledge of the grammatical structure of both languages, and have had time besides for an ample amount of scientific instruction. I might go much

further, but I am as unwilling to speak out all that I
think practicable in this matter, as George Stephenson
was about railways, when he calculated the average
speed of a train at ten miles an hour, because if he
had estimated it higher, the practical men would have
turned a deaf ear to him, as that most unsafe character
in their estimation, an enthusiast and a visionary. The
results have shown in that case who was the real practical man. What the results would show in the other
case, I will not attempt to anticipate. But I will say
confidently, that if the two classical languages were
properly taught, there would be no need whatever for
ejecting them from the school course, in order to have
sufficient time for everything else that need be included
therein.

Let me say a few words more on this strangely limited estimate of what it is possible for human beings
to learn, resting on a tacit assumption that they are
already as efficiently taught as they ever can be. So
narrow a conception not only vitiates our idea of education, but actually, if we receive it, darkens our antici-
pations as to the future progress of mankind. For if
the inexorable conditions of human life make it useless
for one man to attempt to know more than one thing,
what is to become of the human intellect as facts accumulate? In every generation, and now more rapidly
than ever, the things which it is necessary that somebody
should know are more and more multiplied. Every
department of knowledge becomes so loaded with details, that one who endeavors to know it with minute
accuracy must confine himself to a smaller and smaller

portion of the whole extent; every science and art must be cut up into subdivisions, until each man's portion, the district which he thoroughly knows, bears about the same ratio to the whole range of useful knowledge that the art of putting on a pin's head does to the field of human industry. Now, if in order to know that little completely, it is necessary to remain wholly ignorant of all the rest, what will soon be the worth of a man for any human purpose except his own infinitesimal fraction of human wants and requirements? His state will be even worse than that of simple igno-rance. Experience proves that there is no one study or pursuit, which, practised to the exclusion of all others, does not narrow and pervert the mind; breed-ing in it a class of prejudices special to that pursuit, besides a general prejudice, common to all narrow specialities against large views, from an incapacity to take in and appreciate the grounds of them. We should have to expect that human nature would be more and more dwarfed and unfitted for great things by its very proficiency in small ones. But matters are not so bad with us; there is no ground for so dreary an anticipation. It is not the utmost limit of human acquirement to know only one thing, but to combine a minute knowledge of one or a few things with a general knowledge of many things. By a general knowledge I do not mean a few vague impressions. An eminent man, one of whose writings is part of the course of this university, Archbishop Whately, has well discriminated between a general knowledge and a superficial knowl-edge. To have a general knowledge of a subject is to know only its leading truths, but to know these not superficially but thoroughly, so as to have a true conception of the subject in its great features; leaving the minor details to those who require them for the purposes of their special pursuit. There is no incompatibility between knowing a wide range of subjects up to this point, and some one subject with the completeness required by those who make it their principal occupation. It is this combination which gives an enlightened public; a body of cultivated intellects, each taught by its attainments in its own province what real knowledge is, and knowing enough of other subjects to be able to discern who are those that know them better. The amount of knowledge is not to be lightly estimated, which qualifies us for judging to whom we may have recourse for more. The elements of the more important studies being widely diffused, those who have reached the higher summits find a public capable of appreciating their superiority, and prepared to follow their lead. It is thus too that minds are formed capable of guiding and improving public opinion on the greater concerns of practical life. Government and civil society are the most complicated of all subjects accessible to the human mind; and he who would deal competently with them as a thinker, and not as a blind follower of party, requires not only a general knowledge of the leading facts of life both moral and material, but an understanding exercised and disciplined in the principles and rules of sound thinking, up to a point which neither the experience of life nor any one science or branch of knowledge affords. Let us understand, then,

that it should be our aim in learning, not merely to
know the one thing which is to be our principal occupation, as well as it can be known, but to do this and
also to know something of the great subjects of human
interest, taking care to know that something accurately,
marking well the dividing line between what we know
accurately and what we do not, and remembering that
our object should be to obtain a ·true view of nature
and life in their broad outline, and that it is idle to
throw away time upon the details of anything which
is to form no part of the occupation of our practical
energies.

It by no means follows, however, that every useful
branch of general, as distinct from professional, knowledge should be included in the curriculum of school
or university studies. There are things which are
better learned out of school, or when the school years,
and even those usually passed in a Scottish university,
are over. I do not agree with those reformers who
would give a regular and prominent place in the school
or university course to modern languages. This is not
because I attach small importance to the knowledge
of them. No one can in our age be esteemed a well-
instructed person who is not familiar with at least the
French language so as to read French books with ease;
and there is great use in cultivating a familiarity with
German. But living languages are so much more
easily acquired by intercourse with those who use them
in daily life; a few months in the country itself, if
properly employed, go so much further than as many
years of school lessons, that it is really waste of time

for those to whom that easier mode is attainable, to labor at them with no help but that of books and masters ; and it will in time be made attainable through international schools and colleges to many more than at present. Universities do enough to facilitate the study of modern languages, if they give a mastery over that ancient language which is the foundation of most of them, and the possession of which makes it easier to learn four or five of the continental languages than it is to learn one of them without it. Again, it has always seemed to me a great absurdity that history and geography should be taught in schools, except in elementary schools for the children of the laboring classes, whose subsequent access to books is limited. Who ever really learned history and geography except by private reading ? and what an utter failure a system of education must be if it has not given the pupil a sufficient taste for reading to seek for himself those most attractive and easily intelligible of all kinds of knowledge ? Besides, such history and geography as can be taught in schools exercise none of the faculties of the intelligence except the memory. A university is indeed the place where the student should be introduced to the philosophy of history, where Professors who not merely know the facts but have exercised their minds on them, should initiate him into the causes and explanation, so far as within our reach, of the past life of mankind in its principal features. Historical criticism also — the tests of historical truth — are a subject to which his attention may well be drawn in this stage of his education. But of the mere facts of history, as

11 *

commonly accepted, what educated youth of any mental activity does not learn as much as is necessary if he is simply turned loose into an historical library? What he needs on this and on most other matters of common information, is, not that he should be taught it in boyhood, but that abundance of books should be accessible to him.

The only languages, then, and the only literature, to which I would allow a place in the ordinary curriculum are those of the Greeks and Romans; and to these I would preserve the position in it which they at present occupy. That position is justified by the great value in education of knowing well some other cultivated language and literature than one's own, and by the peculiar value of those particular languages and literatures.

There is one purely intellectual benefit from a knowledge of languages which I am specially desirous to dwell on. Those who have seriously reflected on the causes of human error, have been deeply impressed with the tendency of mankind to mistake words for things. Without entering into the metaphysics of the subject, we know how common it is to use words glibly and with apparent propriety, and to accept them confidently when used by others, without ever having any distinct conception of the things denoted by them. To quote again from Archbishop Whately, it is the habit of mankind to mistake familiarity for accurate knowledge. As we seldom think of asking the meaning of what we see every day, so when our ears are used to the sound of a word or a phrase, we do not suspect that it con-

veys no clear idea to our minds, and that we should
have the utmost difficulty in defining it, or expressing
in any other words what we think we understand by it.
Now it is obvious in what manner this bad habit tends
to be corrected by the practice of translating with accuracy from one language to another, and hunting out
the meanings expressed in a vocabulary with which we
have not grown familiar by early and constant use. I
hardly know any greater proof of the extraordinary
genius of the Greeks, than that they were able to make
such brilliant achievements in abstract thought, knowing, as they generally did, no language but their own.
But the Greeks did not escape the effects of this deficiency. Their greatest intellects, those who laid the
foundation of philosophy and of all our intellectual
culture, Plato and Aristotle, are continually led away
by words; mistaking the accidents of language for real
relations in nature, and supposing that things which
have the same name in the Greek tongue must be the
same in their own essence. There is a well-known
saying of Hobbes, the far-reaching significance of which
you will more and more appreciate in proportion to
the growth of your own intellect: " Words are the
counters of wise men, but the money of fools." With
the wise man a word stands for the fact which it represents; to the fool it is itself the fact. To carry on
Hobbes's metaphor, the counter is far more likely to be
taken for merely what it is by those who are in the
habit of using many different kinds of counters. But
besides the advantage of possessing another cultivated
language, there is a further consideration equally im-

portant. Without knowing the language of a people, we never really know their thoughts, their feelings, and their type of character; and unless we do possess this knowledge of some other people than ourselves, we remain, to the hour of our death, with our intellects only half expanded. Look at a youth who has never been out of his family circle; he never dreams of any other opinions or ways of thinking than those he has been bred up in ; or, if he has heard of any such, attributes them to some moral defect, or inferiority of nature or education. If his family are Tory, he cannot conceive the possibility of being a Liberal ; if Liberal, of being a Tory. What the notions and habits of a single family are to a boy who has had no intercourse beyond it, the notions and habits of his own country are to him who is ignorant of every other. Those notions and habits are to him human nature itself; whatever varies from them is an unaccountable aberration which he cannot mentally realize ; the idea that any other ways can be right, or as near an approach to right as some of his own, is inconceivable to him. This does not merely close his eyes to the many things which every country still has to learn from others ; it hinders every country from reaching the improvement which it could otherwise attain by itself. We are not likely to correct any of our opinions or mend any of our ways, unless we begin by conceiving that they are capable of amendment ; but merely to know that foreigners think differently from ourselves, without understanding why they do so, or what they really do think, does but confirm us in our self-conceit, and connect our national vanity with the preservation of our own peculiarities. Improvement consists in bringing our opinions into nearer agreement with facts; and we shall not be likely to do this while we look at facts only through glasses colored by those very opinions. But since we cannot divest ourselves of preconceived notions, there is no known means of eliminating their influence but by frequently using the differently colored glasses of other people; and those of other nations, as the most different, are the best.

But if it is so useful on this account to know the language and literature of any other cultivated and civilized people, the most valuable of all to us in this respect are the languages and literature of the ancients. No nations of modern and civilized Europe are so unlike one another as the Greeks and Romans are unlike all of us; yet without being, as some remote Orientals are, so totally dissimilar that the labor of a life is required to enable us to understand them. Were this the only gain to be derived from the knowledge of the ancients, it would already place the study of them in a high rank among enlightening and liberalizing pursuits. It is of no use saying that we may know them through modern writings. We may know something of them in that way, which is much better than knowing nothing. But modern books do not teach us ancient thought; they teach us some modern writer's notion of ancient thought. Modern books do not show us the Greeks and Romans, they tell us some modern writer's opinions about the Greeks and Romans. Translations are scarcely better. When we want really to know what a

person thinks or says, we seek it at first hand from
himself. We do not trust to another person's impression of his meaning, given in another person's words;
we refer to his own. Much more is it necessary to do
so when his words are in one language, and those of
his reporter in another. Modern phraseology never
conveys the exact meaning of a Greek writer; it cannot
do so, except by a diffuse explanatory circumlocution
which no translator dares use. We must be able, in a
certain degree, to think in Greek, if we would represent
to ourselves how a Greek thought; and this not only
in the abstruse region of metaphysics, but about the
political, religious, and even domestic concerns of life.
I will mention a further aspect of this question, which,
though I have not the merit of originating it, I do not
remember to have seen noticed in any book. There is
no part of our knowledge which it is more useful to
obtain at first hand — to go to the fountain head for —
than our knowledge of history. Yet this, in most cases,
we hardly ever do. Our conception of the past is not
drawn from its own records, but from books written
about it, containing not the facts, but a view of the
facts which has shaped itself in the mind of somebody
of our own or a very recent time. Such books are very
instructive and valuable; they help us to understand
history, to interpret history, to draw just conclusions
from it; at the worst, they set us the example of trying
to do all this; but they are not themselves history.
The knowledge they give is upon trust, and even when
they have done their best, it is not only incomplete but
partial, because confined to what a few modern writers

have seen in the materials, and have thought worth picking out from among them. How little we learn of our own ancestors from Hume or Hallam or Macaulay, compared with what we know if we add to what these tell us even a little reading of contemporary authors and documents! The most recent historians are so well aware of this, that they fill their pages with extracts from the original materials, feeling that these extracts are the real history, and their comments and thread of narrative are only helps towards understanding it. Now it is part of the great worth to us of our Greek and Latin studies, that in them we do read history in the original sources. We are in actual contact with contemporary minds; we are not dependent on hearsay; we have something by which we can test and check the representations and theories of modern historians. It may be asked : Why then not study the original materials of modern history ? I answer, it is highly desirable to do so ; and let me remark by the way, that even this requires a dead language ; nearly all the documents prior to the Reformation, and many subsequent to it being written in Latin. But the exploration of these documents, though a most useful pursuit, cannot be a branch of education. Not to speak of their vast extent, and the fragmentary nature of each, the strongest reason is, that in learning the spirit of our own past ages, until a comparatively recent period, from contemporary writers, we learn hardly anything else. Those authors, with a few exceptions, are little worth reading on their own account. While, in studying the great writers of antiquity, we are not only

learning to understand the ancient mind, but laying in
a stock of wise thought and observation still valuable
to ourselves, and at the same time making ourselves
familiar with a number of the most perfect and finished
literary compositions which the human mind has produced — compositions which, from the altered conditions
of human life, are likely to be seldom paralleled in their
sustained excellence by the times to come.

Even as mere languages, no modern European language is so valuable a discipline to the intellect as those
of Greece and Rome, on account of their regular and
complicated structure. Consider for a moment what
grammar is. It is the most elementary part of logic.
It is the beginning of the analysis of the thinking process. The principles and rules of grammar are the
means by which the forms of language are made to
correspond with the universal forms of thought. The
distinctions between the various parts of speech, between the cases of nouns, the moods and tenses of verbs,
the functions of particles, are distinctions in thought,
not merely in words. Single nouns and verbs express
objects and events, many of which can be cognized by
the senses ; but the modes of putting nouns and verbs
together, express the relations of objects and events,
which can be cognized only by the intellect, and each
different mode corresponds to a different relation.
The structure of every sentence is a lesson in logic.
The various rules of syntax oblige us to distinguish
between the subject and predicate of a proposition, between the agent, the action, and the thing acted upon ;
to mark when an idea is intended to modify or qualify,

or merely to unite with, some other idea; what assertions are categorical, what only conditional; whether the intention is to express similarity or contrast, to make a plurality of assertions conjunctively or disjunctively; what portions of a sentence, though grammatically complete within themselves, are mere members or subordinate parts of the assertion made by the entire sentence. Such things form the subject-matter of universal grammar; and the languages which teach it best are those which have the most definite rules, and which provide distinct forms for the greatest number of distinctions in thought, so that if we fail to attend precisely and accurately to any of these, we cannot avoid committing a solecism in language. In these qualities the classical languages have an incomparable superiority over every modern language, and over all languages, dead or living, which have a literature worth being generally studied.

But the superiority of the literature itself, for purposes of education, is still more marked and decisive. Even in the substantial value of the matter of which it is the vehicle, it is very far from having been superseded. The discoveries of the ancients in science have been greatly surpassed, and as much of them as is still valuable loses nothing by being incorporated in modern treatises; but what does not so well admit of being transferred bodily, and has been very imperfectly carried off even piecemeal, is the treasure which they accumulated of what may be called the wisdom of life; the rich store of experience of human nature and conduct, which the acute and observing minds of those ages, aided in their observations by the greater simplicity of manners and life, consigned to their writings, and most of which retains all its value. The speeches in Thucydides, the Rhetoric, Ethics, and Politics of Aristotle, the Dialogues of Plato, the Orations of Demosthenes, the Satires, and especially the Epistles of Horace, all the writings of Tacitus, the great work of Quintilian, a repertory of the best thoughts of the ancient world on all subjects connected with education; and, in a less formal manner, all that is left to us of the ancient historians, orators, philosophers, and even dramatists, are replete with remarks and maxims of singular good sense and penetration, applicable both to political and to private life; and the actual truths we find in them are even surpassed in value by the encouragement and help they give us in the pursuit of truth. Human invention has never produced anything so valuable in the way both of stimulation and of discipline to the inquiring intellect, as the dialectics of the ancients, of which many of the works of Aristotle illustrate the theory, and those of Plato exhibit the practice. No modern writings come near to these in teaching, both by precept and example, the way to investigate truth on those subjects, so vastly important to us, which remain matters of controversy from the difficulty or impossibility of bringing them to a directly experimental test. To question all things; never to turn away from any difficulty; to accept no doctrine either from ourselves or from other people without a rigid scrutiny by negative criticism, letting no fallacy or incoherence or confusion of thought slip by unperceived; above all, to insist upon having the meaning of a word clearly understood before using it, and the meaning of a proposition before assenting to it; these are the lessons we learn from the ancient dialecticians. With all this vigorous management of the negative element, they inspire no scepticism about the reality of truth, or indifference to its pursuit. The noblest enthusiasm, both for the search after truth and for applying it to its highest uses, pervades these writers, Aristotle no less than Plato, though Plato has incomparably the greater power of imparting those feelings to others. In cultivating, therefore, the ancient languages as our best literary education, we are all the while laying an admirable foundation for ethical and philosophical culture. In purely literary excellence — in perfection of form — the pre-eminence of the ancients is not disputed. In every department which they attempted, and they attempted almost all, their composition, like their sculpture, has been to the greatest modern artists an example to be looked up to with hopeless admiration, but of inappreciable value as a light on high guiding their own endeavors. In prose and in poetry, in epic, lyric, or dramatic, as in historical, philosophical, and oratorical art, the pinnacle on which they stand is equally eminent. I am now speaking of the form, the artistic perfection of treatment; for, as regards substance, I consider modern poetry to be superior to ancient, in the same manner, though in a less degree, as modern science; it enters deeper into nature. The feelings of the modern mind are more various, more complex and manifold, than those of the ancients ever were. The modern mind is, what the ancient mind was not, brooding and self-conscious; and its meditative self-consciousness has discovered depths in the human soul which the Greeks and Romans did not dream of and would not have understood. But what they had got to express they expressed in a manner which few even of the greatest moderns have seriously attempted to rival. It must be remembered that they had more time, and that they wrote chiefly for a select class possessed of leisure. To us who write in a hurry for people who read in a hurry, the attempt to give an equal degree of finish would be loss of time. But to be familiar with perfect models is not the less important to us because the element in which we work precludes even the effort to equal them. They show us at least what excellence is, and make us desire it and strive to get as near to it as is within our reach. And this is the value to us of the ancient writers, all the more emphatically because their excellence does not admit of being copied or directly imitated. It does not consist in a trick which can be learned, but in the perfect adaptation of means to ends. The secret of the style of the great Greek and Roman authors, is that it is the perfection of good sense. In the first place, they never use a word without a meaning, or a word which adds nothing to the meaning. They always (to begin with) had a meaning; they knew what they wanted to say, and their whole purpose was to say it with the highest degree of exactness and completeness, and bring it home to the mind with the greatest possible clearness and vividness. It never entered into their thoughts to

conceive of a piece of writing as beautiful in itself,
abstractedly from what it had to express; its beauty
must all be subservient to the most perfect expression
of the sense. The *curiosa felicitas* which their critics
ascribed in a pre-eminent degree to Horace, expresses
the standard at which they all aimed. Their style is
exactly described by Swift's definition, "the right words
in the right places." Look at an oration of Demosthenes; there is nothing in it which calls attention to itself
as style at all; it is only after a close examination we
perceive that every word is what it should be, and where
it should be, to lead the hearer smoothly and impercep-
tibly into the state of mind which the orator wishes to
produce. The perfection of the workmanship is only
visible in the total absence of any blemish or fault, and
of anything which checks the flow of thought and feeling, anything which even momentarily distracts the
mind from the main purpose. But then (as has been
well said) it was not the object of Demosthenes to make
the Athenians cry out, "What a splendid speaker!"
but to make them say, "Let us march against Philip!"
It was only in the decline of ancient literature that
ornament began to be cultivated merely as ornament.
In the time of its maturity not the merest epithet was
put in because it was thought beautiful in itself, nor
even for a merely descriptive purpose; for epithets
purely descriptive were one of the corruptions of style
which abound in Lucan, for example; the word had no
business there unless it brought out some feature which
was wanted, and helped to place the object in the light
which the purpose of the composition required. These

12 *

conditions being complied with, then indeed the intrinsic beauty of the means used was a source of additional
effect, of which it behooved them to avail themselves,
like rhythm and melody of versification. But these
great writers knew that ornament for the sake of ornament, ornament which attracts attention to itself and
shines by its own beauties, only does so by calling off
the mind from the main object, and thus not only interferes with the higher purpose of human discourse,
which ought, and generally professes, to have some
matter to communicate apart from the mere excitement
of the moment, but also spoils the perfection of the
composition as a piece of fine art, by destroying the
unity of effect. This, then, is the first great lesson in
composition to be learned from the classical authors.
The second is, not to be prolix. In a single paragraph
Thucydides can give a clear and vivid representation
of a battle, such as a reader who has once taken it into
his mind can seldom forget. The most powerful and
affecting piece of narrative, perhaps, in all historical
literature, is the account of the Sicilian catastrophe, in
his seventh book; yet how few pages does it fill! The
ancients were concise because of the extreme pains they
took with their compositions; almost all moderns are
prolix because they do not. The great ancients could
express a thought so perfectly in a few words or sentences, that they did not need to add any more; the
moderns, because they cannot bring it out clearly and
completely at once, return again and again, heaping ·
sentence upon sentence, each adding a little more
elucidation, in hopes that though no single sentence

expresses the full meaning, the whole together may give a sufficient notion of it. In this respect I am afraid we are growing worse, instead of better, for want of time and patience, and from the necessity we are in of addressing almost all writings to a busy and imperfectly prepared public. The demands of modern life are such, the work to be done, the mass to be worked upon, are so vast, that those who have anything particular to say, who have, as the phrase goes, any message to deliver, cannot afford to devote their time to the production of masterpieces. But they would do far worse than they do if there had never been masterpieces, or if they had never known them. Early familiarity with the perfect makes our most imperfect production far less bad than it otherwise would be. To have a high standard of excellence often makes the whole difference of rendering our work good when it would otherwise be mediocre.

For all these reasons I think it important to retain these two languages and literatures in the place they occupy as a part of liberal education, that is, of the education of all who are not obliged by their circumstances to discontinue their scholastic studies at a very early age. But the same reasons which vindicate the place of classical studies in general education, show also the proper limitation of them. They should be carried as far as is sufficient to enable the pupil, in after life, to read the great works of ancient literature with case. Those who have leisure and inclination to make scholarship or ancient history or general philology their pursuit, of course require much more; but there is no room for more in general education. The laborious idleness in which the school-time is wasted away in the English classical schools. deserves the severest reprehension. To what purpose should the most precious years of early life be irreparably squandered in learning to write bad Latin and Greek verses? I do not see that we are much the better even for those who end by writing good ones. I am often tempted to ask the favorites of nature and fortune whether all the serious and important work of the world is done, that their time and energy can be spared for these *nugae difficiles?* I am not blind to the utility of composing in a language as a means of learning it accurately. I hardly know any other means equally effectual. But why should not prose composition suffice? What need is there of original composition at all? if that can be called original which unfortunate schoolboys, without any thoughts to express, hammer out on compulsion from mere memory, acquiring the pernicious habit which a teacher should consider it one of his first duties to repress, that of merely stringing together borrowed phrases? The exercise in composition most suitable to the requirements of learners, is that most valuable one of retranslating from translated passages of a good author; and to this might be added what still exists in many continental places of education, occasional practice in talking Latin. There would be something to be said for the time spent in the manufacture of verses if such practice were necessary for the enjoyment of ancient poetry; though it would be better to lose that enjoyment than to purchase it at so extravagant a price.

But the beauties of a great poet would be a far poorer thing than they are, if they only impressed us through a knowledge of the technicalities of his art. The poet needed those technicalities; they are not necessary to us. They are essential for criticizing a poem, but not for enjoying it. All that is wanted is sufficient familiarity with the language for its meaning to reach us without any sense of effort, and clothed with the associations on which the poet counted for producing his effect. Whoever has this familiarity and a practised ear, can have as keen a relish of the music of Virgil and Horace, as of Gray or Burns or Shelley, though he know not the metrical rules of a common Sapphic or Alcaic. I do not say that these rules ought not to be taught, but I would have a class apart for them, and would make the appropriate exercises an optional, not a compulsory, part of the school teaching.

VI.

THE American colleges from the first and uniformly, have been schools of classical study and learning. A knowledge of the elements of the Greek and Latin languages has been required for admission, and the study of the two has been enforced upon all as the condition of receiving the Bachelor's degree. This has been universally true, the few exceptions being too inconsiderable to deserve attention. The enforced study of these languages upon all the students, and for the most of the undergraduate course, is a ground of complaint, and its advocates are required to give anew the reasons for adhering to it. The trustees of the Cornell University, while they shrink from the charge of abandoning or depreciating the study of the classics, have distinctly taken the position, that for the purposes of discipline and culture the study of the French and German classics is as efficient as the study of the Greek and Latin, and that an equivalent knowledge of either two should entitle the student to the same college honors. The doctrine is also very extensively taught that it is questionable whether the study of language is better fitted to train and discipline the mind in early life than the study of physics or history; and, granting that it is,

This Chapter is an Extract from an Article in the New Englander, — "The American Colleges and the American Public," — for January, 1869, by Professor Noah Porter, of Yale College.

that it does not follow that the study of Greek or Latin is essentially to be preferred to that of German or French. In short, the mind of our tribunal, " the American public," is at present undecided and disturbed by the question whether the colleges do not commit a grievous wrong in enforcing classical studies upon all their students, and in giving to these studies especial honor.

We contend not only that the colleges have judged rightly in giving to the study of language the prominence which it receives, and that the Greek and Latin deserve the special pre-eminence which has been assigned them, but that there are peculiar reasons why they should be even more thoroughly and earnestly cultivated than they have been.

Our first position is, that for the years appropriated to school and college training, there is no study which is so well adapted to mental discipline as the study of language. We argue this from the fact that language is the chief instrument of intelligence. It is thought made visible and clear, not merely to the person to whom thoughts are to be conveyed, but to the person who thinks for and by himself. The earliest discriminations and memories to which we are tasked by nature are those which are involved in the mastery of our mother tongue. It is true the observation of nature, in the education of the eye and the ear, and in the control and discipline of the body, involves a multitude of " object lessons," and imposes much " object teaching," but it can scarcely be contended that the discipline of the senses requires either the culture or the discipline of the intellect, in the same sense as does that attention to language which is required in learning to speak and write the language that is first acquired. We assume, because it is not necessary to prove, that the most conspicuously intellectual of the various intellectual acts of infancy and childhood are exercised with language. The slowness and difficulty with which some children learn to use language is taken as an infallible sign of some defect or late development of intellectual power. The most important part of the knowledge which we acquire is gained through words spoken or written, and the study of nature itself must mainly be prosecuted through books. Natural history, with its curious facts and nice discriminations; geography with its descriptions of distant and unseen lands, of mountains and rivers; and romance with its fairy tales, so exciting and so dear to the child, all presuppose and exercise this same knowledge. The world of words is, in its way, as important and as real to the child as the world of things; and most of the intellectual relations of either things or thoughts can only be discerned by an attention to and apprehension of the relations of words.

As school life advances the intellect is tasked and disciplined by special classes of studies, the object of which is to train the rational powers, and to furnish them with facts and truths. The mind is constrained to reflection and analysis. From acquisition, observation, and memory it proceeds to be trained to the independent judgments of science. What shall be the subject-matter upon which its essays are employed?

13

Nature directs, and the experience of many generations
has confirmed the wisdom of her intimations, that
language is the appropriate sphere of these essays.
The mind is not sufficiently matured to study nature
in a scientific way. Of natural history the mind at
this period is capable, but not of the sciences of nature.
The facts of natural history, the experiments of physics
and chemistry, do not discipline the mind enough ; the
science of these facts involves a training and position
which the intellect has not yet attained. The mathematics present a most important field, but the field is
peculiar and unique. For the sphere and materials of
what we call intellectual training we are shut up to the
study of language; not exclusively, indeed, for, as we
shall show in its place, facts and imaginations should
both instruct and relieve the excessive and one-sided
strain which the discipline of language involves ; but if
there is to be discipline in the eminent sense, it must be
effected by means of the study of language. Whatever
substitute be devised, it will fail of imparting that peculiar intellectual facility and power which this study
secures.

Assuming that the study of language is the most
efficient instrument of discipline, we assert that the
study of the classical languages should be universally
preferred to any other as a means of discipline in every
course of liberal education, and should continue to be
made prominent and necessary in the American colleges. When we assert this, we do not assert it as a
self-evident or as an unquestioned proposition. It is
a fair question to ask, and a reasonable one to be an-

swered: " Why is not French as efficient an instrument
of discipline and culture as the Latin, and why may
not German be substitued for the Greek, provided
each be thoroughly and scientifically studied?" This
question is fair and reasonable to answer and discuss,
because the *prima facie* evidence is that the one is as
good as the other. But this *prima facie* probability is,
in our opinion, far from being the self-evident certainty
which it seems to be in the judgment of our accomplished and admirable friend President White, when
he says: " It is impossible to find a reason why a man
should be made Bachelor of Arts for good studies in
Cicero and Tacitus and Thucydides and Sophocles,
which does not equally prove that he ought to have
the same distinction for good studies in Montesquieu
and Corneille, and Goethe and Schiller, and Dante and
Shakspeare."[1] With all due respect to the President,
we think that it is not only easy to find one such reason, but that many very readily suggest themselves.
First of all, it is obvious, we think, that the student
who makes " good studies " in Cicero and Thucydides
will be likely, in the present state of society in this
country, also to make " good studies " in Montesquieu,
Goethe, etc., etc. We cannot take so narrow a view
of the nature and operation of a literary education as
for a moment to think of it as limited to a four years'
course. The classical student who is zealous enough
to do well, will not, in the present state of knowledge,
and with the facilities which he enjoys, be likely to fail
to learn one or two of the modern languages also. If

[1] Letter to the New York Tribune.

he does not do this in college, should he have special
occasion to use them for the purposes of study, travel,
or business, he will have acquired the power to learn
them with comparative ease and rapidity. If he is to
acquire several Romanic languages, the thorough study
of Latin will even be a positive gain in their acquisition,
so far as time is concerned. Mr. John Stuart Mill goes
so far as to assert that the mastery of Latin " makes it
easier to learn four or five of the continental languages
than it is to learn one of them without it." Mr. Mill
would make little or no provision for the study of the
modern languages in the university, for the reason that
it is to be supposed that a man who is bred a scholar
will study some things after he leaves college, and
especially such of the modern tongues as he has occasion to use.

They are trite sayings that all modern literature goes
back to these languages for its germs and beginnings,
and cannot be thoroughly understood without a knowledge of the languages and the life which they reveal ;
that not only the roots of the languages of modern
Europe are to be found in them, but the roots and
germs of modern literature are in their literature as
well ; that much of what we call learning is written in
Latin and Greek ; that Greek is the original language
of the New Testament which records the beginning of
the history of the Christian Church, and the great truths
which the church has received ; that modern science
has constructed its most refined and complicated ter-
minology out of materials derived freshly from both
languages, and the Greek in particular. But to all

these considerations we shall be met with the reply, that the majority of the men who are educated at college will never become scholars at all, and do not require the education which is fundamental to a scholar's knowledge. We answer that, if this is so, the majority of such persons have even the greater need, and will be likely to make a more efficient use of the power and discipline and scholarship which classical study will give them than of the more or less of German and French which they may study in its place. The manifold relations by which a knowledge of the ancient languages and of ancient life are connected with the history they read, the literature which they enjoy, and the institutions under which they live, makes even a scanty knowledge of both to be of constant use and application.

The student of Corneille and Goethe is also mainly conversant with modern ideas and modern civilization. However exquisite the diction or masterly the genius of his writer, the sentiments and passions are all modern. But the student of Virgil and of Homer cannot painfully translate a few books of the Aeneid or the Odyssey, without entering into the thoughts and sympathizing with the feelings, and living somewhat of the life of human beings greatly unlike those whom he has ever known or imagined. Their thoughts and feelings do not repel him by their strangeness so much as they attract him by their dignity and truth, and open to him a new world of sentiment and emotion. The people, into whose life he very imperfectly learns to enter, though in many respects so unlike the men of present

13 *

times, are yet closely connected with them by the civilization, the arts, the literature, the institutions, the manners, and the laws which the ancients perfected and transmitted. We do not say that to receive such impressions as an imperfect scholarship may impart, is worth all the painstaking which the study of Greek and Latin involves, but we do assert that if these impressions can be superadded to the advantages which come from the discipline which the grammatical study of two languages requires, then this is a sufficient reason why Greek and Latin should be preferred to French and German.

We contend, moreover, and it is generally conceded, that in disciplinary influence the study of the classics is far superior to that of the modern tongues, not excepting the German, which is most nearly akin to the Greek. The regularity and fixedness of the structure, the variety of the inflections, the distinctness of the articulations, the refinement of the combinations, the objective utterances to the mental ear, and the graphic painting to the imagination when coupled with the wealth of thought and feeling, which verb and adjective, which noun and particle, enshrine in words and sentences, all combine to give the classic tongues a supremacy over the languages of modern civilization, which all candid and competent judges have confessed. It is not pertinent to claim that one complicated and artistic language is of itself equally efficient with another for discipline, especially in the beginning of one's school studies. It cannot be soberly urged that one dialect, if it be African or Semitic, is as good as another, provided it leads the mind to analyze and reflect. The discipline which is required for higher education is not a simple gymnastic to the intellect, it is not the training of the curious philologist, or the sharp logician, but it is a discipline which prepares for culture and thought, and which gradually lifts the mind from the hard and dry paradigms of the pedagogue and the enforced syntax of the class-room to the comparative judgment and the aesthetic culture of the critic and philosopher.

We find, then, the following reasons why what are called " good studies " in French and German should not entitle a person to the Bachelor's degree ; and why these studies, however " good " they may be for certain purposes, cannot be as good for the commanding objects for which language and the languages are studied in a course of education.

They are not as good to teach attention to the structure of language and all which such attention involves, and thus to train the student to the intelligent and facile use of English, or to the criticism of the same. They are not as good to prepare the mind to learn other languages than themselves with rapidity, intelligence, and retention. They are not as good to prepare for the comparative judgment of the languages which one may learn. The exercise of such a judgment, whether it is employed for the remoter ends of the philologist, or the more general aims of the reflective thinker, is one of the most instructive employments of the educated man. No man can be a linguist in the best and most intellectual sense of the word, who is not a classical scholar, because these languages are the best

material with or upon which to study language. The ·
student, who has mastered the elements of Greek and
Latin, has gone much further in the way to the intelligent knowledge of language generally, than one who has
made greater advances in the elements of French and
German. This is explained by the fact already adverted
to, that the structure of the classical tongues is so complicated yet clear, ramified yet regular, artificial yet
symmetrical, objective yet artistic, and that in all these
features these languages are pre-eminent above the
modern tongues. Some philologists do not confess this,
we know. They persuade themselves that an Englishman can be trained as successfully to the reflective
study of language by the use of his own and one or two
modern languages, as by the aid of the classic tongues.
But we think such persons, being always themselves
classicists, mistake their own insight and science of
such relations for the insight and science which they
imagine their pupils might or do attain. In short, they
imagine their pupils see with an eye and reflect with a
mind that have been enriched and disciplined by classical study.

Again, such studies cannot be as good for the discipline of the intellect. (The study of languages so
characterized must be a better training for the intellect
than the study of the languages which task the intellect less, from the greater simplicity of their structure
and their greater similarity to the mother tongue.) We
of course assume that the two kinds of languages are
taught equally well, and are pursued with equal zeal
and spirit. This, we think, is possible.

Studies in the modern languages are not as good as studies in the ancient, for the knowledge of man which they directly and indirectly impart. The man of the ancient world is a different being from the man of modern life. Stately, artificial, decided, clear in his opinions, positive and outspoken in his aims, objective in his life, positive and sharp in his diction, impetuous in his impulses, grand in his connection with the state, heroic in his virtues and almost in his vices, he stands out in a striking contrast with the man of modern times — the self-cultured Pagan against the self-denying Christian, the self-cultured against the self-sacrificing, the idolater of country and the state against the worshipper of the Father and Redeemer of man. He is always intellectual, impressive, and intelligible, because he is the perfection of the natural and earthly in its purest and noblest manifestations. The man of modern life is weakened and divided, it may be, by the strife of the natural with the spiritual, of passion with duty, of selfishness with love. And yet the classic humanity is not so strange that it repels or overawes us. It moves our common sympathies, while it enlarges our conceptions of what man may become. All that is good in it is the more impressive from its very exaggerated and one-sided character. It also conveys what it has learned or experienced by means of the clear, beautiful, and positive diction which it always employs. It corrects our special defects of thought, of sentiment, and of action, by the clear rationalism, the simple emotion, the manly behavior which it always sets forth. It even preserves us against its own peculiar errors by the very

distinctness with which it avows them, and the consist-
ent energy with which it acts them out. The student
of modern literature is always conversant with men,
thinking, feeling, and acting like himself. The student
of ancient literature is confronted with human beings
and a human life, which are in some most important
particulars unlike what he has experienced or even
conjectured; and yet they were a positive and potent
reality.

The modern languages are not as good as the ancient
to prepare for the intelligent study of modern history.
Modern history and modern literature have their roots
in ancient institutions and in ancient life. Modern
poetry, philosophy, and art were, at the first, inspired
by the poetry, philosophy, and art of Greece. Modern
polity and law were derived from Rome. Modern religion came from Judea through Grecian and Roman
society. To understand the beginning and trace the
progress of the new developments which these prime
elements of modern history have undergone, we must
go back to the beginning and understand the society
and life in which they were first rooted and germinated.
We cannot successfully penetrate into the spirit of
ancient life without mastering the languages and appreciating the literature in which the ancients have
enshrined and perpetuated this life. Our modern educational reformers make much of the study of history
and of the philosophy of history. But what can the
teacher of history accomplish with classes who are
practically incapable of appreciating the spirit and life
of antiquity ? How can *they* judge of his assertions or

follow his analyses, to whom the most important elements with which he deals are substantially unknown, and must remain forever unappreciated ?

The last reason which we give why studies in the modern are not as good as studies in the ancient languages is, that they do not as efficiently further the intellectual and aesthetic culture of the student. The evidence for this has been furnished in the considerations already adduced. If modern history is rooted in the ancient, much more obviously are modern thought and modern culture rooted in ancient thought and ancient culture. Its speculation was born of ancient speculation, and still recognizes its parentage, as it agrees with or dissents from the doctrines of Plato and Aristotle. The modern materialists scarcely more than illustrate and enforce from modern physics the ancient metaphysics of the Atomists and Epicureans. The modern spiritualists give greater definiteness and authority to the mythical constructions of Plato and the masterly analyses of Aristotle.. The images of the Iliad and the Odyssey are as fresh and as quickening as ever, and their rhythm as musical and inspiring as they have been in all the generations since the birth of modern poetry. They have not been superseded by the subjective tendencies of the modern muse. The Greek tragedies are still pregnant with mystery to the most subjective and questioning of the moderns, who brood over the seeming perplexities of fate and Providence. Allusions to classical images, scenes, events, and personages, are woven into the tissue of all modern writing. Classical art, with its outlines as sharply cut as the

faces of a crystal, and yet as graceful as the undulations
of the moving waters, has not ceased to be the model
of beauty and grace to modern art, because its products
have been animated by the living spirit. of Christian
love, or warmed and elevated by the spiritual graces
of Christian faith and hope.

The student who makes " good studies " in modern
thought and literature, cannot fail, indeed, of a quickening influence and guidance; but the student who has
made good studies in ancient thought, has made himself ready to occupy his life with a far more intelligent
and refined appreciation of modern thought and culture.
As in the order of the culture of the race, the severe
discipline of ancient institutions first prepared the way
for the more genial influences of Christian and modern
thought and feeling, so in the training of the individual
on the most generous scale, the pedagogical period is
most profitably spent in the ancient schools, before the
pupil enters upon the second stage of thought and
conception in which he is to live and act, but which is
none the less truly educating, because the process goes
on in the wider school of life.

The modern educators, who claim to themselves the
merit and name of being especially broad and enlightened, take, in fact, the narrowest and most limited
views of education and of living. They forget that as
soon as the student steps forth into life, modern thinking, modern literature, and modern culture will take
him almost exclusively into their possession, and will
assert supreme control over his education. Under the
fair pretence of preparing him for the fields of thought

and action on which he is to enter, they confine him from the first to the same round in which he is to walk through life, forgetting that the most efficient preparation for a sphere of action is not always made in that sphere, but that to be prepared most efficiently for the intellectual and aesthetical activity in which we are to be employed, we must be conversant with their germinant forces and their controlling principles.

Against these views it will be urged, that though they are plausible in the ideal, they are impracticable in the real — that it is impossible to bring all the members of a college class to study the classics with sufficient interest and zeal to make them eminently profitable; that while a third of the earnest men will study them with zeal, the remaining two-thirds will study them with reluctance. Or, as President White says: "When I was a student in one of the largest New England colleges, there were over a hundred in my class. Of these twenty or thirty loved classical studies, and could have made them a noble means of culture; but these were held back by perhaps seventy, who dreamed or lounged or 'ponied' or 'smouged' through, sadly to the detriment of their minds and morals. Consequently the classical professors — as good as ever blessed any college — were obliged to give their main labor to stirring up the dullards, to whipping in the laggards, in short, not to the thirty who loved their particular studies, but to the seventy who loathed them." The Cornell University will not have things so ordered; it will "indulge in no tirades against the classics." "It will have the best classical professors it can secure, it will equip

14

their departments thoroughly, it will not thwart them
by forcing into their lecture-rooms a mass of students
who, while reciting Greek, are thinking of German,
etc., etc." That is, President White would have us to
infer that in his opinion, and we believe there are many
who agree with him, that " the dullards " and " the
laggards," the men who " ponied " and " smouged " in
the classics, would have neither been nor done either
if they had been allowed to study German instead of
Greek, and that the majority of every college class
would study the languages with alacrity and zeal, if
only they were allowed to study German or French.
We do not believe this opinion to be correct, and we
think it effectually disproved by the indisputable fact
that the men who are dull and who lag in Greek and
Latin, are almost invariably " dullards " and " laggards " in German and French, in these very same
college classes and class-rooms. The few exceptions
are explained by the greater maturity of mind and of
character with which the study of the modern languages
is begun, and pre-eminently by the better elementary
instruction with which it is introduced to the mind, to
say nothing of the advantage which has been gained by
even an imperfect study of the classics.

Moreover, what was true of the class of President
White in respect to the classics was true *eminentiori
sensu* in respect to the mathematics; and yet we do not
observe that in the scheme of the Cornell University it
is proposed to dispense with a thorough study of the
mathematics in the several courses, which are different
ways to the same degree. Nor is the principle to be

admitted that those who are dull in the mathematics
are to be excused from studying them because they
long for the classics or long for history, or it may be,
long for the lecture courses to the exclusion of recitations. We do not deny that the evils complained of
by President White in fact exist. But they are not
peculiar to any course of study. We do not despair
of a partial remedy of these evils, but are confident that
the remedy is not to be found in the substitution of the
modern for the ancient languages.

It should always be remembered that the question
with which we are concerned relates to the best theo-
retical selection of studies, and cannot always be decided
by the practical results in particular cases. What is
best in theory will be best in practice only when it
is thoroughly and wisely administered, provided the
circumstances are equally favorable. Among these
circumstances are to be enumerated — adequate preparation, by previous study and training, the best methods
of teaching and discipline, sufficient time to bring the
prescribed course to its completion, and a warm faith
in, and enthusiasm for, the value of a study in pupils
and students. In some of these respects there is room
for great improvement, and this improvement, as we
shall show, is to be desired and hoped for in the American colleges. At present we are concerned with the
theory of the selection and distribution of the studies.

It may be contended, again, that if the modern cannot
altogether take the place of the ancient languages they
may share an equal portion of time and of honor with
them. It being conceded that a knowledge of two or

three modern languages is indispensable to the scholar who is truly educated, it is urged that the college ought to provide instruction in these languages as a part of its curriculum. In accordance with this view the modern languages have been provided for, more or less definitely and completely, in many of the colleges, and instruction in them is given either in the regular or the optional courses. The advantages are obvious. The student passes from a dead to a living language, as from a Pompeiian to a modern dwelling. The first is artistic and ornate, but its associations are with the past ; the second is fresh and fragrant with modern elegances and comforts. The sense of a certain or possible utility in the language learned awakens a peculiar interest, especially if the student has advanced several stages from school life and school-boy associations and if the interests and responsibilities of manhood have begun to awaken and sober him. The mingling of the ancient and modern in grammatical analysis and in etymological research and literary criticism, is in every respect happy in its influence.

On the other hand, it is to be feared that the time for classical study will in this way be seriously diminished, that the interest in, and estimate of, classical culture will be so far weakened, that the high academical tone will be injuriously lowered, and the most important ends of academical discipline will be in a measure thwarted.

VII.

THE writer has attempted to show that science teaches better, that is, more directly and soundly, than any other study, how to observe, how to arrange and classify, how to connect causes with effects, how to comprehend details under general laws, how to estimate the practical value of facts. Having, however, dealt out this measure of justice to science, he maintains that the difficulties which lie in the way of the attainment of these valuable results, by means of school education, have not yet been overcome ; and that even if they were and science were fully admitted into the curriculum — which ought to be the case — that the classical and literary training is better adapted to the development of the whole man than the scientific, and should therefore take the lead. In pursuing this argument he has been led specially to deal with two fallacies, which, under a variety of forms, are extensively prevalent at present, and, by their evil influence, tend very much to hinder the cause which they are apparently designed to promote. The first is, that because there is so much to know in the world, we are bound to try

This Chapter is from a Pamphlet containing the substance of two Lectures,— "The Curriculum of Modern Education, and the respective Claims of Classics and Science "— delivered at the monthly meetings of the College of Preceptors, London, 1866, by Joseph Payne, late of Leatherhead; Fellow, and one of the Vice Presidents, of the College of Preceptors, etc.

to make our children learn it all. The second is, that because there is so much to do in the world, we ought to force all kinds of business upon children's attention beforehand, by way of preparation for it. — *Preface.*

The object we have in view is to discuss the curriculum of modern education as far as the middle classes of society are concerned — excluding, on the one hand, those whose instruction must, from circumstances, be limited to the barest elements of learning; and those, on the other hand, whose course is intended to terminate in a university career. The question then is — considering the age in which we live, with its immense accumulation and wonderful applications of knowledge; considering too that the longest life is too short for securing for the individual man any large portion of this, which constitutes the treasury of the race; and that the immature faculties of the child can grasp only a very limited portion of that which is ultimately attained by the man — whether we do wisely in giving up any considerable portion of the small space of time available for acquisition, to the attainment of a kind of knowledge which appears, in comparison with scientific and general information, to be only slightly demanded by the wants and the wishes of the age. If it is necessary, or even important and desirable, that we should all attempt to know all things, this question is at once settled by the exigencies of the case. Every moment of the time devoted to instruction must, on that assumption, be given up to the earnest and unremitting pursuit of the " things that lie about in daily life ";

and everything which impedes or interferes with that pursuit must be regarded as impertinent. It is, however, perfectly clear that the attempt to force the individual man to keep up with the intellectual march of the human race, must end in utter disappointment, and, moreover, involves a fatal misconception of the object which all true education should have in view. It cannot be too frequently repeated, that development and training, and not the acquisition of knowledge, however valuable in itself, is the true and proper end of elementary education, nor too strongly insisted on that he who grasps too much holds feebly, or as the French pithily express it, *qui trop embrasse mal étreint.* The fact that there is a vast store of knowledge in the world is no more a reason why I should acquire it all, than the fact that there is an immense store of food is a reason why I should eat it all. We may mourn over the limitation of our powers, but as our fate in this respect is quite inevitable, it is our duty, as rational creatures, to submit to it, and to be satisfied with doing, if not all that we fondly wish, yet all that we can, and, what is more important, as well as we can.

I have already suggested that development and training, not the acquisition of knowledge, however valuable in itself, is the true and proper end of elementary education. In a general way it may be asserted that the former is the main tenet of the old or conservative, the latter of the new or reforming, school. We shall have to dwell at some length on this point, that we may be prepared to recognize the respective claims of various subjects to be admitted into the curriculum. It is

perfectly true that neither view, of necessity, excludes
the other.   Any subject, however suitable in itself for
the discipline of the pupil, may be so taught as to involve no good training; and a subject presumptively
unsuitable may, by the skill of the teacher, be made to
yield the happiest fruits.   Still the prominence given
to these respective features in theory must materially
affect the practice founded on them.   I need not refer
to the very etymology of the word "education" to
support the more old-fashioned view of the case.   All
will allow that it means training or development; but
I would dwell for a moment on the meaning of the
cognate term "instruction," in support of the same
argument, and also to show that a real and judicious
teaching of science, not a random gathering together
of scraps of "useful knowledge," does indeed involve
a genuine discipline of the mind.   The original meaning of *instruere* is to heap up, or pile up, or put together
in a heap generally, and seems somewhat to countenance the chrestomathic notion; but the secondary
meaning, and that with which we are more concerned,
is "to put together in order, to build or construct";
so that instruction is the orderly arrangement and disposition of knowledge, a branch of mental discipline
which all must acknowledge to be of great importance
and value.   But heaping bricks together, and building
a house with them are two very different things.   The
orderly arrangement of facts in the mind implies a
knowledge of their relation to each other; and, if carried out to a certain extent, furnishes the groundwork
for the establishment of those general laws which con-

stitute what is properly called science. The knowledge, however, of these mutual relations is gained by quiet, earnest brooding over facts, viewing them in every kind of light, comparing them carefully together for the detection of resemblances and differences, classifying them, experimenting upon them and so on. Allowing, then, to science, properly so called, all that can be claimed for it as a constituent of the curriculum — and of its immense value in education I shall have to speak presently — we must explode, definitely and finally, the notion that these valuable results can be elicited by frittering away the powers of the mind on a great variety of subjects. Nor must we be led away by the frequently meaningless clamor for " useful knowledge." Knowledge which may be unquestionably useful to some persons may not be useful at all to others; therefore, although education is to be a preparation for after life, yet it is to be a general, not a professional preparation, and cannot provide for minute and special contingencies. The object of education is to form the man, not the baker — the man, not the lawyer — the man, not the civil engineer.

What then, we may now inquire, should be the main features of a training, as distinguished from an accumulating, system of instruction? It should, I conceive, aim at quickening and strengthening the powers of observation and memory, and forming habits of careful and persevering attention; it should habituate the pupil to distinguish points of difference and recognize those of resemblance, to analyse and investigate, to arrange and classify. It should awaken and invigorate the understanding, mature the reason, chasten while it kindles the imagination, exercise the judgment and refine the taste. It should cultivate habits of order and precision, and of spontaneous, independent, and long-continued application. It should, in short, be a species of mental gymnastics, fitted to draw forth, exercise, invigorate, and mature all the faculties, so as to exhibit them in that harmonious combination which is at once the index and the result of manly growth. In order to gain the ends I have specified, or indeed any considerable number of them, it is essential that the studies embraced in the training course should be few. We cannot hope to have, in the early stage of life, both quantity and quality. In giving a preference to the latter we do but consult the exigencies of the case. At the same time it may be hoped that, because the aim is to enrich and prepare the soil, the ultimate harvest will be proportionately bountiful.

I have said that the subjects to be studied in the training course should be few. But I proceed further and maintain that for the purpose of real discipline it is advisable, nay, even necessary, to concentrate the energies for a long period together on some one general subject, and make that for a time the leading feature, the central study. of the course — keeping others in subordination to it. By giving this degree of prominence to some particular branch of instruction, we may hope to have it studied to such an extent, so closely, so accurately, so soundly, so completely, that it may become a real possession to the pupil — a source of vital power which the mind " will not willingly let die."

The concentration of mind and range of research necessary for this purpose obviously involve many of the advantages I have recently enumerated. In this way, too, the pupil will become fully conscious of the difference between knowing a thing and knowing something about it, and will be forcibly impressed with the superiority of the former kind of knowledge. This conviction is of no small importance; for it gives him a clear, experimental appreciation of the agency — the measure and kind of intellectual effort — by which the complete and accurate knowledge was gained, and thus can hardly fail to exercise a valuable influence upon his character. He who has learned by experience the difficulty of obtaining a thorough mastery of a subject has made no trifling advance in the knowledge of himself. He has tested his power of struggling with difficulties, and acquired in the contest that command over his faculties, and that habit of sustained and vigorous application which will ensure success in any undertaking. He who has only begun a study, or advanced but little in it, is a stranger to that consciousness of strength and range of mental vision which are involved in the cultivation of it to a high point. The knowledge, thus thoroughly acquired and possessed as a familiar instrument by the pupil, becomes not only a powerful auxiliary to his further attainments, but a high standard to which he may continually refer them.

One of the chief reasons why the study of one thing, one subject, or one book, is so valuable a discipline, is that the matter thus submitted to the mind's action forms a whole, and by degrees reacts on the mind itself,

and creates within it the idea of unity and harmony.
Suppose, for instance, that we read a book with the
view of thoroughly studying and mastering it. We
find, as a consequence of the unity of thought and
expression pervading it, that one part explains another,
that what is hinted at in one page is amplified in the
next, that the matter of the first few sentences is the
nucleus (the oak in the acorn, as it were) of the entir
work. Thus the beginning of the book throws ligh.
upon the end, which the end in its turn reflects upon
the beginning. He who studies in this way must carefully weigh each word and estimate its value in the
sentence of which it is a part, and its bearing on those
which have preceded it; he must also keep it in r ꞏit
lection, that he may observe its connection with wl ꞏ
follows. When he encounters difficulties which
cannot at the moment solve, he must retain ther ꞏi
mind until the clue to their solution is gained. ꞏ
must often retrace his steps with the experience he 1 ꞏ
acquired in advancing, and then advance again witu
the added knowledge gained in his retrogression. It
is only by thus wrestling—agonizing, as it were—with
a subject, that we eventually subdue it, and make it
ours and a part of us. By such or analogous processes
constantly and patiently pursued, we rise at last to
the highest generalizations; so that a knowledge of tr
phenomena of the material world is digested into science, a knowledge of the facts and matter of language
is elaborated into learning, and a knowledge and intimate appreciation of the facts of human life ripens into
wisdom. Every one will bear me out in the remark,

that it is from those few books that we read most carefully; that we "chew and digest," to use Bacon's
words; that we peruse again and again with still
increasing interest; that we take to our bosom as
friends and counsellors, — it is from these that we are
conscious of deriving real nourishment for the mind.
Nor is it perhaps rash to assert that the general ten-
.ency, in our day, to dissipate the attention on all sorts
.f books, on all sorts of subjects, which just flash before
the mind, excite it for a moment, leave a vague impression, and are gone, is stamping a character upon the
age which will render nugatory the well-meant efforts
which have of late been made for the enlightenment of
 ̨ popular mind, and the extension of useful knowl-
̨e. It is, I say, characteristic of the age, that we
̨sculate and enfeeble our powers by the vain attempt
 ̨ow everything which everybody else knows; and
 ̨n in conformity to the fashion of the times, even to
 ̨ it as a reproach that we have not " dipped into,"
 ̨ " skimmed over," or " glanced at " (very significant
phrases) all the articles in all the newspapers, maga-
zines, and reviews of the day. We indolently allow
ourselves to be carried on in spite of our silent protest,
against our real convictions, with the shallow tide
which is sweeping over the land; and, inasmuch as we
 ̨ so, are neutralizing the real interests of the cause
we profess to be advocating, and preventing the formation of valuable and useful judgments on any subject
whatever.

It is not, perhaps, too much to assert, that concentration of mind on a few subjects is, and ever has been,

the only passport to excellence. All the great literary
and scientific men of all ages, whose opinions we value,
whose judgments are received as the dictates of wisdom
and authority, have acted on the conviction that the
powers of the mind are strengthened by concentration,
and weakened by dissipation.

The practical inference from the foregoing remarks
is, that in order to train the mind usefully, concentration, and not accumulation, must be our guiding
principle; in other words, we must direct the most
strenuous efforts of our pupils to the complete and full
comprehension of some one subject as an instrument of
intellectual discipline.

The next consideration then, is, what the subject submitted to this accurate and complete study ought to be.

If science is to constitute a real discipline for the
mind, much, nay everything, will depend on the manner
in which it is studied. In the first place, it is to be remembered that the pupil is about to study things, not
words; and therefore treatises on science are not to
be in the first instance placed before him. He must
commence with the accurate examination of the objects
and phenomena themselves, not of descriptions of them
prepared by others. By this means not only will his
attention be excited, the power of observation previously
awakened, much strengthened, and the senses exercised
and disciplined, but the very important habit of doing
homage to the authority of facts rather than to the authority of men be initiated. These different objects
and phenomena may be placed and viewed together, and
thus the mental faculties of comparison and discrimi-

nation usefully practised. They may, in the next place, be methodically arranged and classified, and thus the mind may become accustomed to an orderly arrangement of its knowledge. Then the accidental may be distinguished from the essential, the common from the special, and so the habit of generalization may be acquired; and lastly, advancing from effects to causes, or conversely from principles to their necessary conclusions, the pupil becomes acquainted with induction and deduction — processes of the highest value and importance. Every one will allow that such a course as this, faithfully carried out, must prove to be a very valuable training. It would not, indeed, discipline the mind so closely as pure mathematics, yet its range is wider, and it is more closely connected with human interests and feelings. It is no small advantage, too, that it affords, both in its pursuit and in its results — both in the chase and the capture — a very large amount of legitimate and generous mental pleasure, and of a kind which the pupil will probably be desirous of renewing for himself after he has left school. After all, however, it will be observed that, while the study of the physical sciences tends to give power over the material forces of the universe, it leaves untouched the greater forces of the human heart; it makes a botanist, a geologist, an electrician, an architect, an engineer, but it does not make a man. The hopes, the fears, the hatreds and the loves, the emotions which stir us to heroic action, the reverence which bows in the presence of the inexpressibly good and great; the sensitive moral taste which shrinks from vice and approves virtue; the sen-

sitive mental taste, which appreciates the sublime and
beautiful in art, and sheds delicious tears over the immortal works of genius — all this wonderful world of
sensation and emotion lies outside that world which is
especially cultivated by the physical sciences. This is
no argument, of course, against their forming a proper,
nay an essential, part of the curriculum, but it is an
argument against their taking the first place. They
are intimately connected, of course, with our daily
wants and conveniences. The study of them cultivates
in the best way the faculties of observation, and leads
naturally to the formation, in the mind, of the idea of
natural law, and so ultimately to investigations and
suggestions of a very high order, in the pursuit of which
it is sought to define the shadowy boundary between
mind and matter, or to reveal to present time the long
buried secrets of the past. But in order to attain at
last these eminent heights of science, the preliminary
training must be rigorous and exact. It must embrace
the difficult as well as the pleasing and amusing — that
which requires close and long-continued attention as
well as that which only ministers to a transient curiosity. It must be based on the " firm ground of experiment," and be independent of mere book study, which
it has been well observed is in relation to science, only
as valuable, in the absence of the facts, as a commentary on the Iliad would be to him who had never read
the poem.

We may assent, then, on the whole, without hesitation, to the wise and careful judgment passed on the
study of physical science as a part of the curriculum by

the Public School Commissioners in their Report. " It quickens," they say, "and cultivates directly the faculty of observation, which in very many persons lies almost dormant through life, the power of accurate and rapid generalization, and the mental habit of method and arrangement; it accustoms young persons to trace the sequence of cause and effect; it familiarizes them with a kind of reasoning which interests them, and which they can promptly comprehend; and it is perhaps the best corrective for that indolence which is the vice of half-awakened minds, and which shrinks from any exertion that is not, like an effort of memory, merely mechanical." In spite, then, of Dr. Moberly's denunciation of such studies as " worthless," and as " giving no power " in education, I maintain that it is utterly impossible to exclude a subject with pretensions like these from our curriculum. They must and will occupy a considerable space in it—they deserve to do so. For reasons however, already stated, I would not give them the post of the highest distinction, which ought to be reserved for the studies which exercise, not special faculties, but the whole man; not the man as a professional and with a utilitarian end in view, but as a citizen of the world, as one who is to meet his fellow-men and to influence their decisions upon the difficult and complicated problems of society.

Some think that pure mathematics should occupy this central post of honor, A moment's consideration, however, will show that the study of algebra, geometry, the calculus, etc., not only does not embrace those topics of common interest which are essential for our

15 *

purpose ; but has a special and limited office to perform
— I mean, of course, independently of their practical
applications. Lord Bacon has judiciously summed up
their special functions. " They do," he says, " remedy
and cure many defects in the wit and faculties intellectual ; for if the wit be too dull they sharpen it ; if too
wandering, they fix it ; if too inherent in the sense
they abstract it. So that as tennis is a game of no use
of itself, but of great use in respect it maketh a quick
eye, and a body ready to put itself into all postures ;
so with mathematics, that use which is collateral and
intervenient is no less worthy than that which is principal and intended." These words aptly characterize
the advantages of the study of mathematics, and point
out their proper office in education. They cannot,
from their very nature, exercise a formative power over
the whole mind ; but they are very profitably employed
in correcting certain defects, and in teaching, as scarcely
anything else can teach, habits of accuracy. They call
into play but few of the faculties ; but these they exercise rigorously, and therefore usefully. It has been
objected to them that when pursued to any considerable
extent, without the counterpoise of more general studies,
they become particularly exclusive and mechanical in
their influence ; but this perhaps can hardly be considered as an essential characteristic. On the whole, however, it can scarcely be maintained that mathematics
will serve as the basis we require for our educational
operations, though no education can be considered as
complete which excludes them.

Having, then, shown that, notwithstanding the great

value both of physics and of mathematics in education, they are too special in their application to serve as the central subject in our curriculum, we turn once more to language, and especially to the Latin language, which I should propose as the exercising ground best adapted for the intellectual drilling of our young soldier. Greek, in the case of those whose school education is to terminate at sixteen years of age, must, I think, be displaced in favor of the practical claims of German. And it is the less necessary to contest this point, as nearly all the disciplinary advantages which so eminently characterize the study of the classical languages may be gained from the study of Latin alone. It may, then, I conceive, be fairly maintained that the place which classical instruction holds in the curriculum of English education is not due to prejudice, as some believe; nor to ignorance of what is going on in society around us, as others pretend; but to a well-judged estimate of its importance and value as a discipline for the youthful mind, and as an element of the highest rank among the civilizing influences of the world.

This study may be considered under two aspects, the language itself and its literature.

My first proposition is that the study of the Latin language itself does eminently discipline the faculties, and secure, to a greater degree than that of the other subjects we have discussed, the formation and growth of those mental qualities which are the best preparatives for the business of life, whether that business is to consist in making fresh mental acquisitions or in directing the powers thus strengthened and matured to professional or other pursuits.

Written language consists of sentences, and sentences of words. In commencing the study of a language we may consider these words as things which we have to investigate and analyze. They possess many qualities in common with natural objects, and may be therefore treated in a somewhat similar way. They have material qualities; they can be seen, they can be named (their sound is their name), they can be compared together; their resemblances and differences discriminated, and arrangements or classifications of them made in accordance with observed similarity or difference in form. The memory, too, is practically and systematically exercised. The paradigms of inflections must be accurately learned by heart, and so familiarly known that the constant comparison between them as standards, and the varying forms which arise for interpretation, may be spontaneous and easy. And these acts of comparison are themselves of great value, and tend to cultivate accuracy of judgment; the very blunders made are instructive; the half-perception induced by indolence must be corrected by increased labor. The attempt at evasion ends in a more complete reception; hence a moral as well as a mental lesson. Thus, acts of attention, observation, memory, and judgment are called forth; and these acts, by being performed numberless times, grow into habits. Again, these words can be analyzed, separated into their component parts, and these parts severally examined and their functions ascertained. Conversely, we may employ the synthetic process. We may fashion these elements in conformity with some given model, and thus adapt them to some given end. By closer investigation and comparison, affinities before unperceived are traced and appreciated, the transformation of letters detected, and the foundation laid for the science of philology. It should be observed that all these operations or experiments (for so they may be called) are performed on facts, on objects (a word is as much an object as a flower) directly exposed to observation ; that they are at the same time simple in their nature, and though requiring minute attention, and so forming the habit of accuracy, are evidently within the comprehension of a child. It is no small advantage that the means of training the mind to such habits are always within reach, and available to an unlimited extent; and not, as is often the case with respect to physical objects, adapted to elicit somewhat similar exertions obtained with difficulty, and therefore, perhaps, only heard of, and not seen.

But the attention of the pupil, at times necessarily occupied with the accidents or inflections — the characteristic point of difference between his own and the Latin language — is at others directed especially to what we may call the *being* of each word, the idea which it is intended to convey or suggest. And now these words, lately treated as simply material, inanimate, and dead—anatomical " subjects," are to be considered as invested with a kind of physiological interest, and as exhibiting phenomena of life, whose nature it becomes important to study. Our pupil's interest in them, viewed under this aspect, cannot but be much augmented. Words are now no longer things merely, but significant symbols of ideas. These little organisms, in one sense mere torpid aggregations of matter, are in another, when placed in juxtaposition with words of our language, or when viewed in connection with cognates of their own, capable of affording vivid illustrations of the methods and artifices by which languages are formed. Hence arise exercises in derivation, or tracing of words up to their roots, and in analysis, or breaking up the compounds into their several components. These exercises in derivation cultivate moreover, when properly carried out, the habit of deducing the secondary and figurative senses of words from the primary and literal. Such an exercise leads the pupil beyond the boundaries of mere language. In pursuing it he learns to study the mode in which the early stages of society formed their conceptions, and to notice how, as civilization advanced, the language too bore evidence of the change. Thus the word *gubernare* primarily means to pilot a vessel; secondarily, to direct the vessel of the state, to govern.

But words, in themselves vital organisms, though frequently the life is rather latent than visible, are also to be considered in their combination in sentences Their vitality now becomes intensified. The origina author, speaking to men of his own nation, and aptly employing the resources of his craft, had by a kind of intellectual magnetism converted the neutral and indif ferent into the active and significant, and constrained all to co-operate in effecting his great purpose of speak ing out to other minds. And there before the eyes of our pupil is the result. But it does not speak out to him. That sentence, beginning with a capital and ending with a full stop, is a body with a soul in it, with which he has to communicate. But how to do this? His eye passes over it. It looks unattractive, dark, and cold. Soon, however, something is seen in the words or their inflections which he recognizes, by a kind of momentary flash as significant. The soul within begins to speak to him, and he catches some faint conception of what it would reveal. As he still gives heed, other points show symptoms of life, and the lately brute and torpid mass becomes vocal and articulate. One after another the words kindle into expression; clause after clause is disentangled from its connection with the main body of the sentence, and appreciated both separately and in combination, until at length a thrill of intelligence pervades the whole, and the passage, before dark, inanimate, and unmeaning, becomes instinct with light and life.

By these and similar processes, which it is needless to specify, the pupil learns to apprehend his author's meaning, though perhaps at first only obscurely. The next stage in his training is to find words and phrases in his native tongue suited to express it. To do this adequately, he must not only ascertain the meaning of each term, but conceive fully and correctly all the propositions that constitute a complete sentence, in their natural connection and interdependence; he must observe the bearing of the previous sentences on the one under consideration, and the ultimate point to which all are tending. Now, in order to convey perfectly to others the meaning which he has himself laboriously acquired, he must not only have made an

exact logical analysis of the sentence, so as to see what
he has to say, but must exercise his judgment and taste
(not to say knowledge) on the choice of words and
phrases which will best answer the purpose, and truly
represent the clearness, energy, or eloquence of the author. To do this faultlessly requires of course the
matured judgment and refined taste of the accomplished
scholar; but the very effort involved in the attempt to
grasp the spirit of the author, to rise to the elevation
of his thoughts, and to gain the sympathy of others for
them by an adequate and worthy representation of
them in his native language, cannot but elevate his own
mental stature. " We strive to ascend, and we ascend
in our striving."

The advantages of such a course as I have now
sketched must be acknowledged to be very great, although only the language is as yet under consideration.
But there are two or three other points that must not
be omitted. The first of these is the value of the strict
grammatical analysis required. The process of eliciting
light out of darkness, before described, can only be
accomplished by one who is armed with grammatical
power. Without this, the efforts made to communicate
with the soul of the author must be feeble and ineffect-
ual. It is one of the special objects of the course I am
advocating, to cultivate this faculty, because in doing
so we are in fact cultivating to a high degree the reasoning powers of the pupil. The construction of words
in a sentence does not depend upon arbitrary laws, but
upon right reason, upon the exact correspondence between expression and thought, and therefore " good

grammar," as has been well observed, "is neither more nor less than good sense."

A wise teacher, one who wishes to quicken, and is anxious not to deaden, his pupil's mind, will not, of course, force upon him those indigestible boluses, the technical rules and definitions of syntax, before training him to observe the facts on which the rules are founded; but will accustom him to the habit of reasoning only in the presence of facts, which is so valuable at all times. The habit of reasoning on the construction, the syntax, of one language is, of course, generally applicable to others; and its practice in connection with Latin tends by an amount of experience which countervails all theory, to prepare the pupil for learning his own language thoroughly.

In addition to the grammatical advantage just named, there are two others I would mention, which prove that learning Latin is a good preparation for the better knowledge of the mother tongue. The one is, that as so large a part of the vocabulary of the English language is derived from the Latin, either directly or indirectly through the French, no accurate study of the former can be accomplished without a fundamental knowledge of Latin. According to Archbishop Trench, thirty per cent of the vocabulary actually used by our authors is derived from the Latin; and the proportion is still greater if we analyze the columns of our English diotionary, where the words are, what is called, "at rest." Indeed, to so great a degree have we admitted these aliens into our language, that·we have learned to attach Latin prefixes and suffixes to pure English roots,

16

so as to form new and hybrid compounds. But further — and this point is less obvious than that just adduced — as almost all our greatest authors were trained in the classical school, both their vocabulary and phraseology, their language and their thoughts, bear a characteristic stamp upon them which can only be fully appreciated by those who have undergone a similar training. It is not too much to say that many exquisite graces, both of thought and expression, in the works of Bacon, Milton, Sir T. Brown, Jeremy Taylor, Sir W. Temple, Gray, Young, Cowper, and others, must elude the notice — and so far fail in their object — of a reader not qualified to meet the authors as it were on their own ground. And may I add that as far as my own observation goes, by far the most enthusiastic lovers of our own language and literature are the votaries of classical learning. They love more because they can appreciate better.

But it will be thought that I have sufficiently pleaded the cause of Latin, as far as the language is concerned. I must therefore devote a few words to its literature. In a course such as I have proposed, and which I would commence at twelve, with the idea of carrying it on up to the age of sixteen, and employing in it half the hours of every school-day, and which would comprehend, besides the study of the language, such cultivation of geography, history, archaeology, etc., as would be required for the elucidation of the text, and also the parallel study of English literature, we could not hope to read many authors. Indeed, faithful to the principle, *multum non multa*, I would not even attempt it.

A selection of the best might be made, to be studied on the principle that they were to be actually known, not merely "gone through," by means of which not only would the pupil profit by the invigorating discipline I have described, but be subjected to the enlarging and refining influence which would place him in communion with some of the master spirits of antiquity, and therefore give him an introduction to those great authors of all modern times whose labors have tended to form the civilization of Europe. In no other way can he so well be introduced to the commonwealth of letters, and be made free to avail himself of its privileges. The fact that these finished works of literary art still survive amongst us, as real substantial powers whose influence cannot be gainsaid, is a wondrous proof of their merit as models of composition. They present us with histories which still enlighten and instruct men in the art of government, with oratory which still speaks in trumpet tones to the human heart, with poetry still " musical as is Apollo's lute " ; in short, with matter which however now disparaged, has served in successive ages both to furnish men with thoughts, and to teach them how to think; so that in truth, though styled dead, hey are, in the highest sense, ever living; having (to use Hobbe's eloquent expression) " put off flesh and blood, and put on immortality."

VIII.

A THREE years' course of study in the preparatory school ought to be insisted on in all ordinary cases. Every moment of this period may be filled up to the best advantage. The parent or guardian who abridges it, in order to save expense, or because his son or ward is somewhat advanced in life, may commit an irreparable injury. Imperfect preparation for college often operates as a serious discouragement throughout the course, and occasions embarrassment and mortification in all subsequent life. The number of studies which are required for admission to college cannot be well mastered in less than three years. The principles and details of the two classical languages are to be fixed in the memory for life. The thorough study of the elements of these languages is necessarily a slow process. Repetition is the only road to success. Frequent and searching reviews are indispensable. Many points in topography and geography are to be ascertained. Maps and drawings are to be freely canvassed, and all the appliances of modern classical erudition are to be brought into requisition. The details of prosody and versification must now be investigated. In short, the forms, the syntactical laws, the outward history and

This Chapter is from the January Number of the Bibliotheca Sacra, 1851, — "Collegiate Education: Mathematical and Classical Study," — by Professor B. B. Edwards, one of the Editors.

the inward structure of these noble languages are to become familiar to the ingenuous youth as household words, so that when he enters upon his college course, he may enjoy the beauty of the landscape. The urudgery of the ascent should be ended. He should now be ready to take in the wide horizon, and grasp those forms of everlasting beauty which shine around him. In other words, he may now *enjoy* Tacitus and Demosthenes. He can feel something of the strengthening influence which comes from their immortal pages. He pierces beneath the forms to the principles. Through the language he imbibes the spirit. His mind enlarges; the chains of ignorance fall from around him; gradually he attains to a comprehensive knowledge of the great themes which he studies. He learns accurately t estimate the merits and defects of the systems of go ernment, law, and polity with which his mind is con versant. All the while his eye is trained to appreciate the graceful forms of Plato, and his ear to drink in the subtiler melody which comes from the pages of that " old man eloquent." His taste is quickened and purified, till he attains the highest style of the scholar, a susceptibility for all truth and beauty, a power of kindly appreciation for all science and literature.

In the preparatory course, too, the elements of the mathematics should be studied. The youth between the ages of fourteen and seventeen or eighteen is competent to master portions of algebra and geometry. Sufficient time for this purpose ought to be spared from the classics. The latter should be, indeed, the prominent and leading study in the preparatory school, as they are fitted beyond almost any other branch of knowledge to the lively susceptibilities of youth. Still, a good beginning may be made in the other great department of collegiate learning. The mental powers which are addres__d by mathematics begin to be developed in the later stage of the preparatory school. This study, likewise, will furnish an agreeable relaxation from the classical routine.

The young scholar, having thus laid the foundation in the classical school, by mastering the elements of abstract science, and by becoming familiar with the forms and principles of the two great languages of antiquity, will be prepared for the wider fields which wait him. Exact knowledge in the earlier course has tted him to climb loftier heights, has given him a keen lish for the profounder truths and more beautiful orms to which his attention will be called. If the classical school has done its work well, if the three years have been wisely occupied, the education is in one sense complete. Just habits are formed; the great aims of a student's life are appreciated; real, and perhaps the greatest, difficulties are surmounted, and that course is begun which will lead to the loftiest attainment. In short, the preparatory school occupies in some respect the most important place in our system. It holds the keys of knowledge. It has in its hands almost unlimited means of good. It may easily shape the destiny, both as scholars and moral beings, of most who are committed to its keeping. It should be fostered with the most benevolent care. It should be elevated to its high and true rank. The few who are now toiling for its improvement should be cheered with all good omens, and with all substantial aid. It is said that the endowed classical schools of England exert a greater influence upon the higher education, than the universities themselves.

One of the most obvious and important results of classical study is the habit of discriminating thought which it insures. It involves from beginning to end a nice analysis, a delicate perception, a constant collocation of words, a sharp definition of synonymous terms, a patient process of comparison till the words which hit the case are determined, a weighing of evidence, a balancing of shades of thought almost imperceptible. In these processes, the mind acquires the power of recognizing the slightest varieties in thought and speech, something like a quick and unerring instinct; the judgment becomes, like the scale, capable of weighing the smallest particles, of detecting the slightest variations. Language is no longer an uncertain instrument. Many apparent synonymes are shown not to be such in reality. Forms of speech long acquiesced in as of a general or indefinite character, are divested of the haze which has settled around them. The ancient writers stand forth vindicated as masters of the subtilest elements of thought, as possessing weapons of the most perfect temper and of the keenest edge — a system of symbols for communicating the finest mental conception·· such as the world has never seen. This power of discrimination has respect, be it remembered, both to words and thoughts. One trained under this discipline has acquired, at the same time, the elements of the most effective style, and the ability to form the most careful moral judgments. He can detect the plausible sophism, disentangle the web of error, and exhibit truth in its just proportions. He will not be so likely as other men to adopt an erroneous theory, to defend a system whose plausibility consists in the ambiguity of its terms, or to make war, in the temper of a bigot, upon his brethren, who differ from him only or mainly in the language which they employ.

Again, the study of the classics ensures a copious vocabulary. The careful student of Cicero and Plato has enriched himself with many spoils. He has laid in a large stock of invaluable materials, gathered from the choicest fields of literature. In all the exigencies of life, in the thousand calls of duty, at moments when no preparation can be made, he can draw upon resources which are admirably classified and whose value has often been tested. The copious stores of the English tongue have been necessarily digested, compared, arranged, as the emergencies required. Successive terms, one phrase after another, have been carefully weighed, and while one has been chosen, the entire series have been sedulously deposited in the records of the memory, ready to trip as "nimble servitors" at the bidding of him who needs them. That the acquisition of a copious stock of select language is one of the effects of classical . udy might be proved from the experience of distinguished men in all the learned professions. We have in our eye an eminent American senator, now deceased, who could clothe his beautiful and effective thoughts in the most varied as well as pertinent forms, who was listened to with delight·by all his auditors, and who was an earnest classical scholar when he was an octogenarian.

We may advert, in the third place, to the effects of the study on the taste, imagination, and general culture. The sculptor, who is aspiring to the highest excellence, repairs to Rome to study the Belvidere Apollo and the wondrous group of the Laocoon, or to Florence to gaze upon the Venus or the Dancing Faun. The young painter idealizes his conceptions before the great masters of his art at Dresden, Venice, and Rome. The landscape painter plunges into the recesses of the Alps, or lingers under the " purple " light and amid the eternal spring of Southern Italy, that he may copy his model in her most awful or fairest attitudes. The forms of mediaeval architecture, which shoot up so gracefully and in such inimitable proportions in the Netherlands, are patiently studied by him who would produce works worthy to live. So he, who would be drawn to the beauty of written symbols, who would gaze at the " winged words " of the masters of language, who would worthily educate his own instinctive love for beautiful sounds and forms, who would place himself under the full influences of compositions which combine the freshness and simplicity of nature with the last polish of an art that conceals itself, will repair to the pages of the classics. He will carefully study their finished sen‑ tences. He will mark the perfect truth of expressions which can never grow old. He will dwell upon some word or phrase exquisitely chosen which is a picture in itself. To these cherished passages, he will revert so fondly, that they will be forever singing in his ears, or be vitalized as it were, and incorporated into his own being. We need not refer any true scholar to the passages which can be excelled by no specimens of sculptured or pictured beauty. The Odes of Horace, the Georgics of Virgil, the Poems of Homer, the Dialogues of Plato, will at once recur to the mind. They furnish models which combine all the excellences of which the subject is capable — perfect truth to nature, sweet simplicity, most felicitous selection of epithets, a collocation of words which is music itself, the repose of conscious power. It may be said, indeed, that this is in part a deception. The antiquity of the poems casts a deceitful halo around them. The rich clustering associations of two thousand years are with them. So much the better, we reply. If to their unapproached intrinsic excellences, we add the mellowing and exalting influences of time, then they will be only the more worthy of study.

The distinct benefits which the classics confer on the taste and imagination are such as these : The mind learns to delight in order, proportion, fitness, congruity. It instinctively shuns extravagance, finical terms, unseemly plays of words, all straining after effect, all ostentatious parade, all dainty expressions, all cant phrases, all tautology and wearisome diffuseness. It would be an unpardonable offence against his old teachers, if the scholar should deck out his compositions with tawdry ornament, or deform them with unseemly adjuncts. He feels as the student of Raphael or Michael Angelo does, that they will frown on aught which interferes with the severe simplicity or the heavenly beauty which speaks in every lineament of their works. These excellences are strikingly contrasted with the defects of many of those writers who do not make the classics their model. They may possess great force of thought and language, and in certain directions great power of execution. But in an unexpected moment, a sad prejudice will be revealed, an extravagant opinion will be broached ; the mind will be developed in a one-sided and disjointed manner. The charm and useful-ness of symmetrical culture never meets our eyes. They are able but not finished thinkers and writers. We never repose upon them with entire affection and confidence. We always suspect some lurking weakness, or dread some unlicensed outbreak. We do not look to this class of men for finished writers, for men of the purest taste or comprehensive views, or perfectly sound opinions.

There is another class of these influences, to which we have already alluded, and which must be felt rather than described. We refer to those reminiscences which forever linger in the memory, which people the fancy, which excite the imagination, which attract the affec-tions, like strains of the sweetest music. There are passages in Cicero's works which seem like the dear faces of departed friends yet remembered. They are full of an elevating, genial influence. They crowd the mind with solemn and affecting impressions. They suggest thoughts which, for the time being, expel every low desire and frivolous fancy. They have not indeed a religious efficacy, yet they are powerfully auxiliary to all virtuous tendencies. The music of their words does not sound harshly along with the holier strains that come from the hill of. Zion. Passages in nearly all the greatest writers of Greece and Rome embody the beautiful yet fragmentary notes which natural theology utters through all her domains. It is this melancholy association in part, in company with words of the most exquisite fitness and grace, which gives to the passages in question their deathless power. Some of them are the words of men who saw the ancient glories of their country fading away, never to return. Hosts of barbarians, or the sands of the deserts, were mutilating or burying works which their authors fondly thought they were fashioning for eternity. But, whatever may be the causes of this peculiar influence, it certainly exists, and is like a perennial spring in the hearts of all genuine scholars, and it is an influence which no literature but the classical supplies, except in a very limited measure. We look in vain for it to the student of Johnson or Burke or Addison. We find it in a degree in the pages of great poets like Milton and Wordsworth, for they were imbued with the spirit of classic song.

We may refer to a recent but eminent benefit which results from classical study. It introduces us to a vast body of varied and profound criticism. It unlocks treasures of inestimable value. Some of the greatest minds of the present day have traversed the fields of classical literature, and have illuminated with the light of a happy erudition, the most secret nooks, and the remotest corners. Great classical scholars, like Niebuhr,

Müller, Savigny, Hermann, have brought stores of
learning to bear upon the illustration of the classics,
no more admirable in amount than in selection, perti-
nence, and sterling value. Multitudes of very able men
have labored, not in verbal criticism merely, not in the
lighter matters of metre and prosody, but on the great
questions of law and government and revenue, and on
the still greater questions of moral philosophy and
theology. The profound problems relating to man's
eternal destiny as stated by the Greek and Roman
moralists, the degenerating process of heathenism as it
wandered further and further from a primeval revelation,
the true significance of pagan mythology, etc., have
been handled with a depth and fulness of learning,
with a clearness of method, and with a satisfactoriness
of results, which should seem to leave little for the
future inquirer. The laws of the two classical languages, the principles of syntax, the relations of these
languages to others, opening the rich fields of comparative philology, have been investigated with eminent
success. These investigations impart to the subject a
truly scientific worth, and command the attention of
all who feel any interest in the origin and fortunes of
our race. Now this vast body of classical criticism,
and historical literature, for which we are indebted to
hundreds of able scholars in Germany and elsewhere,
can be adequately appreciated only by the classical
scholar. In illustration, we may refer to works on the
philosophy of Plato and Aristotle ; to those comparing
at large the origin, structure and relations of the Latin
and Greek languages ; to the profound, acute, and, in

one sense, creative labors of Niebuhr, and of the very
able scholars who have followed in his steps, in investigating the ante-Latin languages of Italy, and the
general antiquities of that country; to profound treatises
on Roman law; to acute researches in ancient and
modern history; and to studies of a more general
nature, sweeping over the vast regions from India to
the Atlantic, and deducing by a rigorous inquiry the
mutual laws of the most important languages of past
and present times, and showing the identity, in origin
and locality, of the races that spoke them. In short,
a vast field has been traversed, and is now thoroughly
exploring, by hundreds of eminent scholars in Germany,
France, England, and other countries. The rich fruits
of these explorations can be enjoyed only by those that
have mastered the two classical languages. These, in
some respects, constitute the central points — embrace
the germinating principles of the inquiry. They possess
a literature perfect in form and adequate in amount.
Being understood by large numbers of scholars, they
can be appealed to as common umpires in a dispute.
Through them, as a mirror, we can see the culture and
development to which all the sister dialects might have
attained, or did actually reach.

Classical studies, too, are eminently humane. Well
were they styled the "humanities," from their enlarging,
unselfish influences. They have no special affinities
with what are called " the material interests." They
lead to the cultivation of tastes, which throw a charm
over the dealings of trade, lighten the heart of the
banker, and lead the mechanic and the land-owner to

cherish enlightened views and perform philanthropic deeds. " It is delightful," says Mr. Talfourd, " to see the influences of classical learning not fading upwards, but penetrating downwards, and masses of people rejoicing to recognize even from afar the skirts of its glory."

IX.

It may, perhaps, be conceded that the language of Rome is not inferior in educational value to that of Greece. An inflected language with a highly elaborate syntax, Latin may challenge comparison with any, as a means of mental discipline. On historical grounds, no tongue can possess stronger interests for civilized humanity than the speech of that victorious city, which, beginning with almost daily struggles for life with the petty tribes of its own narrow peninsula, succeeded in breaking to pieces the power of one nation after another, and finally in its imperial decline gave laws to the world. Language is always more truly national than literature: they act and re-act on each other; but the broad distinction remains, that one is the spontaneous product of the nameless many, the other the artificial creation of the illustrious few; and though the remnants of early Latin are scanty and imperfect, its formal part — that which makes it what it is — was in being long before the days when, as Horace expresses it, the Roman sat down to rest after the Punic wars, and speculated what might be made out of Sophocles and Thespis and Aeschylus. But it is too late to expect

This Chapter is from an Inaugural Lecture on the "Academical Study of Latin," delivered at Oxford, December 2, 1854, by John Conington, M.A., Professor of the Latin Language and Literature, and Fellow of University College.

that any single language, except it be the vernacular, will continue to be studied for educational purposes apart from its literature, at a time when comparative philology is exhibiting to us the structure of articulate human speech in all its world-wide extent, and a more profound psychological analysis is searching for the principles of universal grammar in the unfathomed depths of the individual mind. What, then, are the grounds for recommending the minute study of Roman literature to one who has been taught truly to estimate the literature of Greece ?

The answer, I believe, lies on the surface : it is to be found in the historical position actually occupied by Roman literature, in relation both to that which went before and to that which has followed it.

We are entitled to claim, as belonging to Rome, not only what it did for itself, but what it has wrought in the nations which succeeded it. What Greece was to Rome, Rome has been to modern times — the great educator, the humanizer of its barbarous conqueror, the mother of intellect, art, and civilization. That part of our culture which we have not worked out for ourselves, or received from contemporary nations, we owe almost wholly to Rome, and to Greece only through Rome, just as our language, saturated throughout with Latin, has assimilated but few particles of Greek. If the Romans viewed the great works of Greece through the medium of Alexandrian criticism, our fathers viewed them through the medium of Roman imitation. *Paradise Lost* may ascribe its form, and much of its detail, to the conception of Homer framed by the educated

men of later Greece, accepted by Virgil and the epic
writers of Augustan Rome, and finally sanctioned by
the heroic muse of modern Italy. The foreign element
of the Shakspearian drama is traceable, ultimately, not
to Aeschylus and Aristophanes, but to Plautus and
Seneca. The tragedy of the Restoration period is
formed on the model of the French, which itself copies
the declamatory dialogues of the Roman sophist. In
the eighteenth century, the influence of Rome is yet
more direct and exclusive : in fact, we may say that
an acquaintance with the principal Latin writers is the
only way to a literary appreciation of that phase — the
most brilliant, as some may still esteem it — of English
authorship. The position of the Augustan era is reversed : it had openly rivalled Greece, and it is now
itself openly rivalled by England. There is the same
consummate dexterity which is characteristic of all high
imitation, the same universal ambition to be eminent,
not only in one department of imaginative composition,
but in several. The great Augustan artist would be
Theocritus, Hesiod, and Homer in one : the poet of the
reigns of Anne and George I. aspires to unite the
features of Ovid, Horace, and Virgil. The two forms
of composition which have been mentioned as the
peculiar property of Rome are precisely those which
are most congenial to this Roman period of the English
mind. Pope and Swift recall Cicero and Atticus : nearly
every wit, whatever his intellectual temperament,
writes a satire or an epistle ; and two of the greatest
not only follow Horace and Juvenal, but expressly and
directly copy them. This may now be, to many of us,

merely a thing of a bygone time: the deliberate imitation of Latin models was impossible after men became alive to the power and beauty of earlier and later literature.

It is on these grounds that I would venture to recommend the study of Latin literature, as such, to any one inclined to question its value, as I believe that to neglect it would be to neglect a whole epoch in the history of letters, most important intrinsically, and most unequivocal in its influence on ourselves. As the first to feel and obey the impulse given by Greece, Rome might well excite our attention; as the communicator of that impulse to modern Europe, it sublimates attention into sympathy and earnest regard. That which has actually had so much to do with the formation and discipline of a culture which the lapse of many generations of men has proved to have been no weakling, but a vigorous birth, can never cease to be studied wherever that culture is made an object of paramount interest. To allow it to pass into the shade because we have come to appreciate its relation to Greek literature more truly than heretofore, is as idle a thought as it confessedly would be to speculate on the larger results, as we may deem them, which would have accrued to humanity if Greece had been permitted to influence later ages without any interposing medium. Indeed, the historical position of Roman literature enables it to vindicate itself. We are not left to our own choice whether or no we should study that which, being as we are, we cannot afford to forget. The scholar may feel that Latin, as compared with Greek, is but

" as moonlight unto sunlight "; but if the time should
come when those who wish to preserve a classical
education for the generality of instructed Englishmen
find it necessary to abandon one of the classical languages in order to save the other, it is not difficult to
foresee that practical convenience will overturn other
considerations, and plead for the language which for so
many centuries has been held in England to be the
symbol of cultivation, against one of whose existence
there is scarcely anything in our daily speech to remind
us, and whose very alphabet has to be made a matter
of learning. Happily, to us in this place the alternative
does not present itself: we have not to choose between
a distant and a proximate benefactor — between originality and utility. Homer and Virgil, Pindar and
Horace, Thucydides and Tacitus, Demosthenes and
Cicero, may be studied side by side: we may acknowledge the commanding pre-eminence of the master, at
the same time that we admire the skill and discrimination which the pupil has shown, not only in following,
but in deviating from, his model. The same method
of study will enable us to acquire both: the specific
differences of the knowledge to be realized will occasionally involve a difference in the manner of knowing;
but the powers of mind called forth are the same, and
the discipline administered to them partakes of the
same character, though it may be not always in the
same degree. Of this part of the subject I have now
to speak.

The object which the study of literature proposes
may be described as the entering into the mind of men

eminent in thought and in power of expression. It may seem hardly worth while to note that it is requisite not only that the student should gain certain conceptions of power, beauty, and the like, but that they should be such as the writer intended to convey. In the case of other things of a similar nature, the distinction is one which scarcely occurs to us. When we look at a painting, we seldom set ourselves deliberately to discover the intention of the artist; we know that though we may fail to understand all that was meant, we are not liable to substitute a wrong meaning for the right, much less to perceive graces which really result from accident or exist only in our own lively fancy. Words are acknowledged to be a more palpable and less transparent medium than forms or colors: still, in the average course of a vernacular literature, the instances are comparatively rare where a man has to ask himself whether he comprehends what he is reading; and even then the knot is generally solved, not by investigation and study, but by reflection and an appeal to common sense. Truth, as such, seldom or never has to be made a distinct object of pursuit: it seems to come unasked, and so rarely obtains even a passing glance of recognition. But when we approach the literature of another country, our view is at once changed, if not reversed. Then the difficulty of the medium is seen to be such that the thoughts which lie beyond are apt to appear easy in comparison. If the language is a modern one, the labor will be more or less mechanical. The method of discovering truth consists chiefly in looking out words in the dictionary;

that done, a little experience of idiom and style supplies the rest. The trouble may be considerable for the time, but it is short, and the student soon comes to read a foreign work as he would read one written in English, and finds the process of interpretation go on intuitively. It is precisely here that the real difficulty of studying an ancient language begins. To the schoolboy, reading Latin and Greek is virtually the same as reading French or German; to the scholar, there is all the difference in the world. The books of reference which he uses, the lexicons and the grammars, are far more elaborate and more helpful than anything which he could obtain for studying a modern language ; but they remind him that the need of assistance is far greater. They furnish him not solely or principally with patent and unquestioned facts, such as a few days' travel might verify, and the slightest authority may consequently guarantee : the certainties in which they deal are frequently such as it requires the toil of months or years to discover, and perhaps the reputation of a life to accredit. He finds that others have thought and investigated, not that he may be spared the trouble of thought or investigation, but that he may think and investigate for himself. The sense of many of the words before him is to be made out, not on direct evidence, but by a long induction of instances : the full appreciation of an idiom or construction has often to be gained by the inward exertion of sympathetic thought, as well as by wide reading : nay, the very text of the author is often itself a matter of doubt, so that the critic has, as it were, to tell both the dream and the interpretation. History has to be ransacked in the hope of finding the key to an indirect allusion in a single line ; the windings of a writer's mind have to be tracked not only in his own works, but in those of the contemporaries with whom he lived familiarly, or the predecessors whom he regarded with filial reverence : the arrow, like that in the fable, has to be aimed at a mark which the archer's eye is allowed to see only as reflected in some other substance. In a word, he is constantly brought to feel that the language with which he has to do is a *dead* language, buried under the weight of interposed centuries, and only to be reached by one who has skill and resolution to penetrate through their manifold incrustations.

There are, I know, persons to whom the enumeration of the obstacles to the understanding of the classics suggests regretful, if not contemptuous feelings. They lament the waste of labor spent, not in the discovery of the unknown, but in the recovery of the lost, and make light of divinations of truth which the unrolling of a single new manuscript may supersede or disprove. The complaint is the same which is put so epigrammatically by the author of *Hudibras*, where he says of Time and his daughter Truth,

> 'Twas he that put her in the pit
> Before he pulled her out of it.

I need hardly say, that if valid at all, it is valid, as Butler doubtless intended it, against all historical research. There, as here, we have the spectacle of human thought toiling painfully to repair the losses caused by human thoughtlessness, as well as by the un-- advoidable chances of time: there, as here, the utmost that can be done may disappear before the contradiction or the fuller affirmation of an accidental discovery. But is the case so different as regards other parts of knowledge ? Is not the attainment of all intellectual truth a labor which might have conceivably been spared to us ; nay, which doubtless would have been spared, had the mere possession and enjoyment of truth been the end which we were meant to compass ? Even the very word " enjoyment," so used, implies a misconception. The intellect enjoys truth, not by simply contemplating it, but by feeding on it, by assimilating it, and thus making it instrumental to the perception of further truth, which in its turn ministers to other and higher realizations. The toil of getting and the joy of using are not, as in other things, separate, but identical; if distinguishable in common speech, it is only as we may choose to distinguish parts of a process which is really uniform and indivisible. In this sense, no one need hesitate to join in Lessing's celebrated profession, that if called upon to choose between truth and the search after truth, he should prefer the latter. It is not hard to see that, the constitution of our minds remaining as it is, the immediate communication of all knowledge would not be a blessing, but an incalculable curse. "There is," indeed, "nothing better for a man than that he should make his soul enjoy good in his labor"; that he should accept the knowledge and discipline which each day brings, instead of deferring his satisfaction till the end of a pursuit which, rightly understood,

18

never can be ended on earth, and which, if followed only in the hope of some ulterior reward, even though that reward be truth itself, will but yield "vanity and vexation of spirit." Thus the question is, not whether we *must* seek for truth, but whether we *may;* not whether the child can be excused his task, but whether he is to be allowed the gratification of guessing the riddle. Whoever may complain of the difficulties which beset the pursuit of classical scholarship, assuredly it will not be the scholar himself. He knows it is precisely by means of these difficulties that he is made perfect in his work. If he is led to repine at times that knowledge should be hidden, it is not as wishing to evade the pains of searching, but because he is already longing to bestow his labor on some other part of the field. It is nothing to him that his time has often to be spent on minute and seemingly trivial points, for he feels that the smaller is to be estimated by the standard of the greater, and that in accepting his calling he has accepted a duty, more or less defined, to everything that appertains to it. The task of recovering a lost word or allusion is not resented as a gratuitous hardship, but embraced as a welcome boon, which compels the student, as it were, to enter the author's laboratory, not as a spectator, but as a follow-worker, and rewards the restoration with something of the same delight which must have attended the original invention. It is his labor that he has to go down among those who have long been dead ; but there is conscious pleasure in every step of the way, and it is his glory that he can break their sleep and revive them, that he can make them drink the blood of life and speak living words, that he can endow them, if not with the gift of prophecy, at least with the human power of memory.

I have anticipated much of what I had to say about the manner of studying Latin literature; but I feel that if my conception of it be a true one, its worth is to be appreciated, not by generalities, but by a more detailed account. There is something ambitious in the term " method," as applied to so simple and obvious a process; and yet, when we think of its capabilities as an intellectual discipline, we shall hardly be able to find a more appropriate name for it. I cannot hope to explain it so that the statement shall not appear the merest truism; indeed, I hardly wish to do so. The way to study Latin literature is to study the authors who give it its characters: the way to study those authors is to study them individually in their individual works, and to study each work, as far as may be, in its minutest details. For other purposes, we may be satisfied with a general view of an author's mind, or with a cursory perusal of some one or more of his writings; but the peculiar training which is sought from the study of literature is only to be obtained, in anything like its true fulness, by attending, not merely to each paragraph or each sentence, but to each word, not merely to the general force of an expression, but to the various constituents which make up the effect produced by it on a thoroughly intelligent reader. Nothing but practical experience can give any notion of the number and variety of the subjects of knowledge and thought presented by the careful study even of a small portion of a work, without travelling beyond those considerations which properly belong to the particular passage, as having been present, consciously or unconsciously, to the mind of the author. Perhaps it will not be thought tedious or inappropriate if I venture, for the sake of clearness, as well as of variety, to analyse, in this spirit, a very short passage, which must be familiar to us all — the first seven lines of the first Book of the *Aeneid* of Virgil. I am not sorry to choose one upon which I have myself scarcely anything to offer beyond what may be found in the ordinary commentators, such as Wagner or Forbiger, because my object is to show the improvement which may be derived from this study at any time, as an every-day exercise, not the discoveries to which it may occasionally conduct us, interesting and encouraging as these undoubtedly are.

The first inquiry respects the four lines which in many copies are prefixed to the *Aeneid*. We examine the external evidence, and are struck by one fact, among others, that the testimony which would exclude them tells still more forcibly for excluding the passage about Helen in the second Book of the *Aeneid;* nor can we well escape without gaining some rough notion about the authorities for the text of Virgil. We examine them internally, noting not only their own peculiarities of expression, but their relevancy to the passage which they are intended to introduce. We discuss the probability whether Virgil in particular, or any poet of the Augustan age, would begin by a reference to himself, or rush at once upon his subject and his hero. We estimate the collateral testimony of those contemporary or subsequent writers who mention the words *Arma virum*, as if they were the key-note to the whole *Aeneid*. After thus pausing on the threshold, we proceed to the work itself. We ask whether the word *Arma*, bursting thus suddenly on the ear, may not be meant to imply the contrast between this and Virgil's other poems, which the interpolated lines so clumsily endeavored to express. We compare Virgil's opening with Homer's, and with the apparently parallel passage in one of the Cyclic writers, noting that he begins in the first person, like the poet ridiculed by Horace, and defers his invocation of the muse till afterwards. We observe that Virgil himself uses the words *Arma virum* together elsewhere in the *Aeneid*, as if he intended them to be linked by a real connection. We remark on the sense of *primus*, not as excluding an earlier journey, but as pointing to the beginning of Roman history, and thus reminding us of the purpose of the Augustan epic. The word *Italiam* opens another question, having actually given rise to a treatise by a German scholar, which is highly spoken of, on the anomalies of quantity introduced by the Roman epic writers. *Fato* leads us to inquire into Virgil's conception of destiny, and of its relation to the power of the gods, in short, into his theological belief. We then come to a question of reading between *Lavina* and *Lavinia*, when we have to consider the imitation of the passage by Propertius, and to observe the circumstances under which Virgil elsewhere employs a synizesis. In the third line, we note the rhetorical pleonasm of *ille*, established by other passages of Virgil, remarking on the use of pronouns, both in Greek and Latin, to express other than pronominal relations, and on the grammatical considerations involved therein. The fourth line presents a difficulty of interpretation in the words *Vi superum*, the common rendering of which has recently been disputed as implying that Juno acted in concert with the gods, whereas the whole tenor of the *Aenied* represents her as Aeneas's sole enemy. Thus we have to examine Virgil's theology again, as well as to decide on the possible meaning of the words, considered grammatically. *Memorem iram* recals us to Homer, and reminds us also of the μνάμων μῆνις of Aeschylus. In the next line, the construction of *dum* with the imperfect conjunctive opens a subtil grammatical question, the answer to which is to be sought in a consideration of the nature and force of the conjunctive mood. The two remaining lines introduce us to questions of mythology and antiquities: what the *Penates* were, how they differed from the *Di Magni*, why the *Albani patres* are so called, and, generally, what was Virgil's view of the beginnings of Rome, — all to be settled by a careful reference to other passages of the *Aeneid*, which in their turn frequently start fresh questions, even when discussed only so far as is necessary for purposes of illustration. Lastly, we are led to regard the exordium as a whole, admirably adapted as it is throughout to express the poet's full sense of the greatness of his subject — a broad and striking contrast to the unconsciousness of Homer, who presents himself as the teller of a wonderful story, not as the author of a grand national poem.

Those who are accustomed to a careful study of the

classics, will see that I have by no means exhausted all
that could fairly be said on these lines, in other words,
all that is required for a complete appreciation of them,
at the same time that I have been careful not to make
them mere pegs on which to hang irrelevant questions
in philology or aesthetics. Yet, surely the amount of
education which such a study presupposes or imparts
is very considerable. In considering his author's general character in itself, or in contrast with that of
another, the student is led to take broad views of rhetorical or poetical art: in analyzing particular expressions, and disclosing the images which they involve,
he is made to trace that art in its details. He has to
skirt the undefined bounds which separate rhetoric
from grammar, and ascertain the conditions under
which words grammatically appropriated to one conception can be put for those denoting another. He is
frequently called to investigate grammar itself, by the
occurrence of constructions which have to be explained
by some general law, or left unexplained under the
shelter of some unquestionable idiom. At other times
he will have recourse to comparative philology, to illustrate a word or usage, of the true nature of which the
writer himself, learned as he may have been in the
antiquities of his country's language, had but a dim
confused consciousness. The casual allusions scattered
through the work will familiarize him with much historical knowledge ; the subject of the work, even though
it may have no direct bearing on history, with much
also. This enumeration is a very imperfect one, even
as compared with my own conception and experience ;

yet it will be seen that it includes many of the elements
which are usually held to constitute a general cultivation, thus insuring a discipline of the various parts of
the mind, more comprehensive, probably, than can be
afforded by any other single subject of knowledge.
But this is not all. These several lines of thought and
research are not followed for themselves, but as means
to something further: they make up the method by
which the truth of the writer's meaning is to be attained.
However great their heterogeneity in relation to each
other, in this point they all converge. It is difficult to
secure anything like completeness in the method, as no
man can hope to realize all the aspects in which a word
or conception has appeared to the mind of another,
especially when separated from him by a gulf of centuries ; it is seldom that we can expect to make the
best even of our incompleteness, as in any single track
of investigation we are liable to meet with failure, or
at any rate, with only partial success. Such defects,
however, do not destroy the value of the results which
can be obtained ; and it only requires a careful use of
the various means in our power to convince us that the
method of interpretation is one that really deserves the
name, leading not to specious plausibilities, but to substantial truths. I know not how it may be in the case
of other sciences, but I can testify to the genuine
intellectual satisfaction which the mind receives when
some discovery, in itself, perhaps, of quite minor importance, a latent metaphor, a concealed imitation, the
substitution of one insignificant word or inflection of a
word for another, or even the mere position of a word,

hitherto overlooked, and now noticed accidentally, has flashed light on an entire passage, and a vague sense of disproportion has given place to a clear perception of harmonious symmetry. Or again, where the lighting up has been not sudden, but gradual, it is not the less reassuring to recall the first aspect of a sentence, seemingly complete in itself, and sufficient to the eye of the ordinary reader, and compare it with the full appreciation which is gained at last, when every point has been accurately scrutinized, and the student once more comes to survey it as a whole. Thus the exegetical study of the classics, as it appears to me, fulfils the two great conditions of an educational instrument; it gives at once a general and a special discipline; it encourages exuberant variety of interest along with severe precision of aim. I do not say that it has always had this effect on the mind of the student; but I believe that where it has failed to do so, the fault has not been in the method, and that if even really great scholars have sometimes been narrow and one-sided, they have been so far less complete, not only as men, but as scholars. I believe also that, like all methods, it has a salutary tendency to equalize human capacities, so that though the greatest reward will always fall to his lot who, having the greatest natural powers, economises them most prudently and disposes them to the best advantage, there will yet be an abundant harvest which inferior minds are certain to reap, by the mere fact of their honest compliance with prescribed rules; while those who go out in their own strength, disdaining all labor that appears uncongenial, find for the most part barrenness and comparative scarcity.

Such a mode of reading, I need hardly say, cannot but be a work of time ; even a professed teacher can scarcely expect to attain so close a familiarity with more than a very few authors ; for a learner, who does not intend to pursue the study, a thorough mastery of one or two books, or parts of books, is perhaps the utmost that can be proposed. But I am sure that a single work, studied in this manner, may be of indefinite use to the mind ; and though of course he who has read much will have an advantage, in explaining a text, over him who has read little, yet, on the other hand, under the treatment of a diligent student, an author becomes, to a great extent, his own interpreter, and the various books of reference which come into requisition will indicate collateral sources of information, which may obviate, if they cannot supply, the want of strictly independent research. It need not, it ought not, to exclude the more rapid and cursory reading of the principal classics. What I have said of the peculiar value of Roman literature as a regularly developed whole, will show that I would have the student's acquaintance with it general, as well as particular ; extended, as well as intimate ; but no diffusive reading, however it may expand the views, can be accepted as a substitute for that scrupulous training in the minutiae of thought and feeling, of grammar and rhetoric, of historical allusion and textual criticism, all rigorously directed to one end, which it is my present object to set forth.

X. .

PROBABLY it will be conceded on all hands, that the chief object of primary education is not knowledge, but discipline, and facilities for acquiring knowledge. The absolute knowledge of things which the boy learns out of his school books is next to nothing, — scarcely more in a course of years than the man of full-grown and well-trained faculties might acquire in as many months. The object, then, is rather to create habits of application; to call into action that greatest principle of all human greatness, attention; to give a command of the faculties, to such degree of investigation as their tender expansion will permit; to enlarge and strengthen them by judicious exercise; and for this purpose language is selected, as being by God's own appointment more easily learned in youth than in maturer years, and a foreign language, because it is of necessity learned in a more exact manner, and with greater intension of the mind than our vernacular tongue. But surely accuracy in this learning is the whole evidence that the end for which it was learned at all has been attained. The attention has been roused, the faculties have been stretched; and therefore the knowledge of those things

This Extract is from an Address delivered before the Phi Beta Kappa Society of Harvard University, August 28, 1834, on Classical Learning and Eloquence. By William Howard Gardiner, Counsellor at Law.

towards which the mind was directed is accurate. The more accurate the stronger is this evidence.

And since the object is not so much knowledge as the means of knowledge, the command of powers and use of tools, the Greek and Latin languages are selected, by common consent, not only for the immortal treasures they contain, but because they incorporate themselves into all the living languages of civilized man ; so that he who has once mastered these ancient vehicles of thought, descends, as from an eminence, how familiarly, compared with the mere vernacular scholar, into all or any of the dialects of modern Europe, and, which is of more importance, better understands his own. For we cannot read a single page nor utter a solitary sentence in our native language (the very words I am compelled to use, the *single page*, the *solitary sentence*, the *native language*, speak to the fact) without recurring to Rome or Greece, or both, for most of the nice shades of thought which mingle and coalesce in the full meaning of every phrase that is uttered. Thence is it that " even as a hawk fleeth not high with one wing, even so a man reacheth not unto excellency with one tongue." The ancient instructor of royalty whom I quote would have had for its fellow a learned tongue at least, doubtless little better than heathen Greek. But are not the ends for which these languages are selected in preference to all others answered precisely in proportion to the accuracy with which they are learned ? And shall we, above all things, stop short of that point of accuracy which alone gives the power to perceive with clearness the beauties of the thought and the delicacies of expression they contain ? Shall we learn a little of language, and stop short of its literature ?

So far from doubting the advantage of the critical accuracy of Europe, and especially of England, in this branch of education, the more rational doubt is that of some of the sweeping reformers, whether there be any benefit, or at least a benefit proportioned to the time and labor consumed, in learning these languages so superficially and inaccurately as we for the most part do. For of what avail is it to talk of the simple majesty of Homer, or the deep pathos of Sophocles, to him who scarce reads with any tolerable fluency the mere character in which their works are written, and knows no more of the genius of their language than he does of the genius of the Cherokee ? Yet of how many who have received the advantages of what is termed a liberal education is this literally true ?

Accurate knowledge of the ancient languages useless ! A waste of life to spend its best years on syllables and sounds — mere names of things, and those dead and forgotten ! Rather let us say, that it is a waste of life to stop short of accuracy ; that language is thought, and the memory of words the memory of things. For God and nature have so mysteriously mingled body and soul, thought and expression, that man cannot set them asunder. They are one and indivisible. The principle of intellectual life hangs upon their union. We cannot think but in words. We cannot reason but in propositions. Or if the excited intellect should sometimes leap to an intuitive result and flash upon truth, it is

19

yet a useless result, an unutterable, incommunicable,
voiceless truth, a waste flower in the wilderness, a gem
buried in the ocean, until it has been embodied in language, and made visible by signs or audible by sounds.
And however it may be rarely true that the man of
accurate thought is incapable, because he has not studied language, of accurate expression, it is universally
true that he who has greatly studied accuracy of expression, words, their arrangement, force, and harmony
in any language, dead or living, has also greatly attained towards accuracy of thought, as well as propriety
and energy of speech. " For divers philosophers hold,"
says Shakspeare, clothing philosophy in the mantle of
the muse, " that the lip is parcel of the mind."

A waste of life! Why, what is man, his pursuits,
his works, his monuments, that these niceties of language, the weight of words, and the value of sounds
should be deemed unworthy of his immortal nature?
He is fled like a shadow. The wealth which he toiled
for is squandered by other hands. The lands which
he cultivated are waste. That hearthstone on which he
garnered up the affections of his own home is sunk into
the elements. The very marble which his children
raised over his ashes for a memorial unto eternity is
scattered to the winds of heaven. His sons, his kindred, his name, his race, his nation, all their mighty
works, their magnificent monuments, their imperial
cities, are vanished like a mist, and swept out of the
memory of man. Yet the very word that he spoke —
that little winged word — a breath, a vapor, gone as it
was uttered, clothing a new and noble thought, em-

bodying one spark of heaven's own fire, formed into
letters, traced in hairy lines upon a leaf, enrolled, copied, printed, multiplied and multiplied, spreads over
the whole earth, is heard among all tongues and nations, descends through all posterity, and lives forever,
immortal as his own soul. Homer, and ye sacred proph-
ets, attest this truth !

There is one view of this subject so peculiar for us,
so national, so practical, that it conveys to my mind an
irresistible feeling, that in this country, more than all
others, the learning of the ancient languages should be
deeply cultivated. It is for its effect upon eloquence.
It has not been my purpose to go into a consideration of the general scheme of education which would
best conduce to this end. My whole object is to impress upon all who hear me, so far as my feeble
ability may permit, the vast practical importance of
bringing up our classical learning here in New England
to the mark of true scholarship ; and especially for its
effect upon the writing and speaking of the country.
For I hold it to be the dictate of reason, confirmed by
all experience, that the early education best adapted to
produce accomplished writers and accomplished speak-
ers, is that, which, while it sharpens and invigorates
the faculties, while it settles habits of attention and
investigation, gives the most accurate knowledge of the
construction, power, and harmony of language, with
the greatest command of it in choice and arrangement
of words, fills the memory most copiously with noble
sentiments, agreeable images, and striking turns of expression, and most kindles in the youthful soul that

enthusiasm for liberal pursuits, and generous ardor in
the cause of regulated liberty, which so distinguished
those admirable ancients. What has yet been discovered or invented by men which 'so well answers all
these ends at once, as accurate study of the ancient languages, and familiar acquaintance with their glorious
literature ?

Is this all theory? Do you want practical proofs?
Shall I point to examples then ?

> " Hence to the famous orators repair,
> Those ancients whose resistless eloquence
> Wielded at will the fierce democracies " ;

and those modern, too, whose names are names of eloquence itself. Time would fail me were I barely to
run through the illustrious catalogue, and point out
the distinguishing fact in the life and education of each,
which bears upon the illustration of this truth.

Look for yourselves at those departed orators of England, who stood pre-eminent, *longo intervallo*, in the
ranks of eloquence, parliamentary or forensic, and
you will find not one out of the host who was not
deeply imbued with classical literature ; scarce one who
was not so accurately instructed in the ancient languages as to be a scholar among scholars; not one who did
not extensively study language and eloquence. I select Charles Fox and William Pitt, because, while they
illustrate equally with others the main point of this
remark, they are at the same time peculiar and striking examples of the effect of a general system of education directed to the purpose of creating orators and

statesmen. For, in the persons of Lord Holland and Lord Chatham, the world beheld the singular spectacle of two rival political leaders educating their children expressly to be what both became — the first parliamentary orators of their age, and premiers of England.

And, to accomplish this purpose, both these distinguished parents, themselves practical orators, — Lord Chatham certainly one of the greatest that ever lived, — concurrently judged that the strength of youth should be expended in acquiring accurate knowledge of the ancient languages and extensive learning in Greek and Roman literature.

Fox was one of the best Grecians in England ; accurate enough after he had reached the full height of his parliamentary fame, at an age when most men have forgotten this half-learned knowledge of their youth, to cope with Wakefield, that famous and professed philologist, in criticism on the merest niceties of Greek prosody and dialect. From the correspondence between them it appears that Fox was amusing his leisure in the country with reading the Greek tragedians without commentary or translation, while he was constantly citing *memoriter*, because he had not his Homer with him, verses from all parts of the Iliad and Odyssey to illustrate his critical remarks. The learned tutor of Pitt has recorded that, when his pupil first came to him at the age of fourteen, his proficiency in the learned languages was probably greater than ever had been acquired by any other person in such early youth. " In Latin authors he seldom met with any difficulty ; and it was no uncommon thing for him to read into English

19 *

six or seven pages of Thucydides which he had not previously seen, without more than two or three mistakes,
and sometimes without one. "And after that," says Dr.
Prettyman, " he became deeply versed in the niceties
of construction and peculiarities of idiom, both in the
Latin and Greek languages." He adds: " There was
scarcely a Latin or a Greek classic of any eminence,
the whole of whose works Mr. Pitt and I did not read
together."

Look at those who have been most distinguished
among the orators of our own country, and you will be
struck with the same fact; not to the same extent
indeed (though James Otis was so exact a scholar as to
have written treatises on Greek and Latin prosody), still
in general not to the same extent, because our means
of early education have been inferior; but you will
find all who have attained great eminence with the
single exception of that phenomenon of orators, Patrick
Henry, good classical scholars for their age and country.
You will find all of them, at some periods, students in
these niceties of language; some, late in life, laboring
in classical literature to repair the imperfect education
of their youth. And since Patrick Henry stands a solitary exception to the whole current of examples, one
singular fact should be noted, which is among the best
authenticated of the imperfect traditions of his early
history. It is this: when at last he began to read,
somewhat late for the commencement of an education,
and then reading in the spirit of idleness and for mere
amusement, as it seemed, one of the books which happened to fall into his hands, and upon which he imme-

diately fastened with delight, was a translation, for he could not read the original, of the oratorical Livy. This history became his standing favorite. He was in the habit of reading it over and over, again and again. And thus, as his classical biographer with reason conjectures, he derived, at second hand, from Rome his first notions of that peculiar oratory for which he was afterwards distinguished, and much of that Roman magnanimity, enthusiastic love of country, and ardor of liberty which gave soul to his eloquence.

But why this to us? Have we yet an education to perfect? Are we so ignorant or insensible of the value of classical literature, or of its necessary precursor, accurate instruction in the learned languages? Or are we an association of tutors and pedagogues to be held responsible for the default of the age?

Little indeed would it become one of the least informed among you in that learning of which I have ventured to speak, not certainly from any present familiarity, or even past accuracy in the studies, but rather from an old and hereditary regard for them, coupled with a deep conviction of their substantial value and neglected merit, to address these remarks to you, otherwise than as claiming your interest in a great public cause. If there be anything in the argument to which you have thus patiently listened; if it be true that science and those departments of learning, the utility of which is most directly and superficially apparent, will be cultivated of course among us, falling in as they do with the immediate and pressing demand of the time and of the people in all times, but that letters

and the fine arts need to be fostered and cherished
in this republican soil with peculiar and extraordinary
care, lest they should fall into utter neglect and oblivion; if it be true that these liberal pursuits do indeed
elevate, dignify, and adorn the character of men and
nations; if it be true that our government is built
upon public opinion, and that opinion is controlled by
the tongue and the press; that effective writing and
effective speaking are, or should be, leading objects of
republican pursuit and youthful instruction; and that
classical learning and literature are the best foundations
of an education conducted with these views and for
these ends; if there be anything in this argument, if it
be not all error, all fallacy, I appeal to you, gentlemen,
whether there is not need of great and substantial reform. There is no end to the invention of new and
visionary schemes for the infusion of learning without
labor, of knowledge without discipline, into the young
and growing mind. There is no end to the diversity
and multiplicity of objects proposed for youthful pursuit, in the vain attempt to make absolute infants over-
take the modern steamy flight of full-grown intellect.
But if these schemes are, in truth, visionary and base-
less, our course is partly to retrace our steps; to begin
again with the slow toil of laying broad and deep foundations, stone by stone, for the Athenian structure we
would raise, firm in its fair proportions, graceful in its
strength. Make our youths accurate in the first rudi-
ments of classical learning. Lead them far into the
niceties of those languages which are chosen to enrich
their souls. Overcome for them, at least, that strange-

ness and confusion which obscure a half-learned tongue. Give them to see the beauty and magnificence which lie beyond these clouds. Wake them to some sense of the harmony and grandeur of the Grecian muse. Let the eloquence of Rome and of Athens speak to them in a voice which they will feel as well as hear. Induce them to drink largely at those classic fountains of which our fathers deeply drank, while we do but taste the scanty rills which ooze over the common path. Thus, chiefly, may we hope to raise up in the body of this great republic, men who by their knowledge, and their power to use that knowledge, shall guide the public weal; men fitted to adorn the councils they direct; to scatter light among the people with whom they mix; to purify and exalt the national taste, as well as to expand its intellect; to build up for us a literature which shall immortalize the people which brings it into being; and to conduct the prosperous queen of modern republics to the head of the refined and intellectual nations of the earth.

XI.

THE question as to the utility of instruction in the Classics is by no means a new one; but it has been agitated of late by the adverse party with more than ordinary earnestness and pertinacity. "Why," it is asked, "should so much time and care be expended in learning to call the same things by two or three names instead of one? and, even admitting such attainment to be desirable, why insist that these names (if they must be learned over and above the vernacular terms) shall belong to two languages which have not been spoken, as we wish them to be acquired, for nearly two thousand years? Do we add much to our stock of useful ideas by learning that that which the word *apple* tells us in our mother tongue is a fruit of certain properties, was called *pomum* by one people and μῆλον by another, both of whom, with all their institutions, have long since passed away from the earth? Is there any knowledge in these classics so very much worth having, or so unattainable in our own tongue, that we must devote the best hours of the most precious years of our boyhood to acquire the power of gathering it with difficulty

This Chapter embraces the greater part of the last of "three Lectures on the proper Objects and Methods of Education, in reference to the different Orders of Society; and on the relative Utility of Classical Instruction, delivered in the University of Edinburgh, November, 1835." By James Pillans, M.A., F.R.S.E., Professor of Humanity in that University.

in the original language, rather than with ease in our own ? " These are questions which every one has a right to put, and a right to have answered. It is in vain that we try to avoid a direct reply, by affecting an air of mystery — by quoting the fable of the fox and the sour grapes — or by talking of some indescribable charm, some *nescio quid* of excellence and perfection in the language and literature of antiquity, which the initiated alone can apprehend and appreciate; and by refusing on these grounds to reason at all with the opponents of classical education, just as one would decline to discuss colors with a blind man. If we mean to defend either the principle or the practice that has hitherto prevailed, we must descend into the arena and grapple with our antagonists; some firmer ground of defence must be taken than custom or usage can furnish.

Proceeding, then, upon this view of the matter, and abjuring all right of appeal to anything but argument and fair reasoning, I am ready, for my own part, to admit, in the fullest extent, that whensoever the teaching of Greek and Latin is directed to no other object, and goes, in point of fact, no further than to give the power of substituting one word or set of words in the place of another; when it is limited to the simple act of transferring the sense of an ancient author into something equivalent in English, or even to the more difficult task, and requiring higher powers, of converting portions of our own language into something resembling the composition of an ancient, — in all such cases I admit that the true aim of education has been lost sight of; that the memory has been cultivated far too exclusively, and that faculty itself not in the best direction, nor in the most wholesome exercise; and that, instead of attempting to justify such practice, we cannot too soon alter or amend it. I will admit, also, that for the two or three centuries during which classical acquirement has been made a prime object in the education of the middle and higher ranks over Europe, it has been very generally taught in such a way as to give a colorable pretext to the statements of the objectors.

But while I make these concessions, while I freely admit that a mere multiplication and heaping up in the memory of words and phrases is little better than unprofitable waste of time and labor, I am prepared at the same time to contend that no instrument for training the youth of what may be called the educated classes has yet been invented, which is so well adapted for that purpose, as a course of classical instruction conducted on enlightened and philosophical principles. I have not stated the proposition as one of universal application. If a youth is destined to be a ship's carpenter, an optician, a practical engineer, or to pass his days in the details of some mechanical employment, without any higher aim than excellence in his particular department, however scientific that may be; in all such cases a course of classical education might fairly be considered as misplaced. But with a view to that general cultivation of the mental powers and capacities which is to give a man the use of his faculties in their most serviceable state, to bring him up to the level of other men's thoughts, and make him an acute, observ-

20

ant, and intelligent member of the community he belongs to, I am not aware that any method has yet been
devised which either has produced, or in the dispas-
sionate judgment of philosophy, is so likely to produce,
a succession of citizens at once useful and ornamental
to the commonwealth, as a course of intellectual discipline which takes classical instruction for the groundwork.

In proof of this position, it will be necessary to enter
a little more into detail, and attend to the successive
steps and processes which such a course of instruction
consists of.

In the first place, then, of all the faculties of the
mind, memory is that which admits of being earliest
exercised, and trained to habits of susceptibility and
retentiveness. Now, the initiatory processes of classical
discipline are of a kind particularly well fitted to call
forth and to strengthen that faculty; for, next to the
immediate perceptions of the external senses, language
is doubtless the subject in which a young mind feels
itself most at home.

I have said, next to the perceptions of the senses;
for, far be it from the advocate of the classics to consider the study of the languages as opposed to, or exclusive of, a knowledge of external nature. This is the
error into which many of our adversaries fall, when
they insist on our abandoning ancient literature, and
devoting all the attention of our youth to the powers,
properties, and appearances of the material world. But
why not have both? A desire to become acquainted
with the objects and phenomena of nature, and a very

considerable actual amount of such knowledge, it is
quite possible, by a judicious system of infant tuition,
to impart in a still earlier stage of education than that
we are now referring to; at a time when the senses,
and particularly those of seeing and hearing, being fresh
and young, and full of curiosity, should be directed to
their appropriate objects, and inured to habits of accurate and discriminating observation. This is all that
is desirable, all indeed that is practicable, at a very
early age. The demonstrations and deductions of physical science, and the minute classifications of natural
history, must come at a much later period. The attempt to anticipate them before the natural development of the faculties at the approach of manhood might
produce a few prodigies of precocity; but, if applied
generally, would stunt the mind's growth, which cannot
be healthy, unless, like that of the body, it be gradual.
In the meanwhile, so nearly instinctive is the faculty
of speech in man, that the study of language affords
the finest instrument for evolving the powers of the
youthful intellect, and particularly that which it is then
most important to cultivate — the memory. There is
ample room, at the same time, in the initiatory steps,
for cherishing the first feeble efforts of the reasoning
faculty and of the judgment, and above all, for bringing out and exercising that reflex power of attending
to what is passing in the mind itself, which is the dis-
tinctive characteristic of intellectual existence.

It is in this preliminary stage, I admit, that the helping hand of philosophy is eminently required, to remove
difficulties, to smooth asperities, and to seize and take

advantage in teaching, of those analogies and generalizations in language, which, when dexterously presented to a boy's mind, are apprehended with the rapidity of lightning. There is no doubt that much of the obloquy that has been cast on the study of the ancient languages, and most of the failures that occur in the teaching of them, arise from the want of philosophical views in the construction of the grammars generally employed. Instead of following nature by presenting in strong relief to the young mind the great outlines to the language; instead of illustrating these by comparing or contrasting them with the corresponding parts of the vernacular tongue, and thus fixing indelibly the leading rules by appeals to the testimony of consciousness, it is but too common to confound and appall the pupil at the very outset with an undigested mass of rules without reasons, where the facts of the language, whether they be of the broad and general kind which belong to universal grammar, or whether they be mere peculiarities and idioms which are reducible to no principle, are all, rule and exception, huddled together, taught at one and the same time, and confounded in the boy's memory as if they were of the same description and of equal importance. If grammars for the use of schools were what they ought to be, they would serve as text-books to guide the teacher in eliciting and exercising the finest capacities of youth, and in giving a right direction to what I scarcely hesitate to call the noble *instinct* of speech.

The leading facts and general rules in the structure of any language result from the laws of human thought, and when put into words, are the expression of principles and mental operations common to all mankind, which develop themselves spontaneously, and which begin to be unconsciously acted upon at a very early age. When simply expressed and judiciously explained, they find an echo in every breast, and scarcely ever fail to interest the attention and command the assent of the young. If too little advantage is taken of this appeal to the principles of our nature in the actual business of teaching, the fault lies in our grammars, and furnishes an argument, not against the study itself, but for improving the method of pursuing it.

But without dwelling longer on the initiatory steps, let us suppose the boy advanced beyond the threshold, and engaged, after due preparation, and under the guidance of an able and judicious teacher, in perusing the works of the ancient writers. If, indeed, the system pursued in this stage be one of hard, dry construing, involving all the intricacies of parsing, syntax, and prosody, and concluding with a literal version of the passage, and nothing more, the process, it must be confessed, tends rather to sharpen than to expand the youthful faculties, and, if carried no further, will fall lamentably short of the great ends of education.

I would not, however, be understood to undervalue such analysis of sentences and minute examination and decomposition of words, or to represent it as a part of classical training that can or ought to be dispensed with. On the contrary, it is not less useful and necessary to the young scholar towards becoming familiar with the structure and idiom of a language, than dis-

20 *

section is to the young anatomist; and, when skilfully conducted, is one of the finest exercises of the youthful understanding, admirably adapted for rendering more acute its powers of memory and analysis, for throwing it back on its own resources, and for teaching it to sift, to discriminate, and to decide. Its efficacy in these respects may indeed be justly regarded as one of the most important benefits of a well-ordered education, and one which I know not where else to look for the means of conferring so certainly and so completely. Those of my hearers who are at all conversant with the great prose writers of antiquity, and particularly with Cicero and Livy, will understand what I refer to when I speak of the long and intricate sentences with which those authors abound. Now, let any one select such a sentence, and observe the great variety of parts or clauses of which it consists; the manner in which they are dovetailed into, and made dependent upon, one another; the distance words are placed at, which their use in the sentence and their concord or government prove to be connected; the involution of the sense, one assertion circumscribing and being qualified by another, and that again by a third, and the whole wrapt up and infolded, clause within clause, in mutual dependency, like wheel within wheel in a piece of complicated machinery; and then let him say whether the analytical process by which these relations and reciprocal bearings of the long period are detected and explained, and the form and pressure of the main affirmation with its whole retinue of subordinate parts are exposed in lucid order, be not an exercise of mind which is not merely useful for the particular passage under discussion, or the particular language the pupil is engaged in acquiring, but one which can scarcely fail to excite and quicken his faculties, in a way most conducive to the general improvement of his intellectual character. I have no wish to utter a word in disparagement of accurate observation and attentive study of external nature, and of the powers and productions that are known to us by the senses — an employment of the faculties not to be neglected in any stage of education, and which can scarcely, as I observed before, be commenced too soon; but it does appear to me that no gathering, naming, and ticketing of plants and minerals, no system of pullies and combination of mechanical forces, no watching of retorts and crucibles, can supply the place of the keen and searching exercise of mind which I have just described, or ought to supersede and supplant it.

Great, however, as I conceive the benefits to be of a minute anatomy of sentences, followed up by a version so literal as to vouch for a perfect comprehension on the part of the pupil of all the minutiae of grammar and syntax, I regard this preliminary process, after all, as but a subordinate branch of classical instruction, — indispensable, no doubt, as a basis on which to rear what is to follow, on account both of the actual knowledge it conveys and the habits of mind it induces; but no more to be considered as the whole, than a building is thought to be complete when the foundations are laid and the scaffolding erected. It is common enough, I admit, to stop short with this process, and to think that everything is done when the pupil has acquired dexterity in this grammatical analysis. But it is to degrade and desecrate the writings of the ancients, thus to make their noblest passages no more than a vehicle for exercising on flexion, conjugation, syntax, and idiom. And to the frequency of such practice we may fairly ascribe the clamor which has been raised, and so far not without reason, against classical education. But we must not argue from the abuse of a thing against the use of it; we are not in search of what is wrong in practice, but of what is right in principle.

Let us, then, in the next place, survey the wide field that opens before us, as soon as the preliminary work we have spoken of is completed.

The pupil is now to be considered as engaged in the perusal of those works of ancient genius to whose very excellence we owe it, that they did not perish in the flood of barbarism that swept inferior productions into oblivion — works therefore, which, having been the admiration of every age since they were written, are invested with a glory and an authority which time only can bestow upon excellence. And of these works, containing the most matured thoughts of the noblest minds, clothed in a language of peculiar pomp, expressiveness, and melody, it is the teacher's fault if the pupil shall not read the fittest and choicest portions.

How are the " thoughts that breathe," " the words that burn," to be unveiled to the apprehension of the youthful scholar, and so brought home to his understanding, his fancy, and his feelings, as to produce those sensations of wonder and delight which they never fail to excite in the mind of the adept.

The same care, I answer, that presided over the selection, must be exercised also in the illustration, of the passages read. In the *first* place, obscurities must be cleared up which may arise from allusions to the peculiar manners, customs, and laws, and to the institutions, civil, military, and religious, of antiquity. Under this head it is evident that frequent opportunities are afforded, not only of throwing light on the most interesting topics of Roman and Grecian antiquities and history, but of comparing or contrasting them with the corresponding parts of our own constitutional system, of awakening curiosity to become better acquainted with both, and of introducing the pupil to ever-varying, and to him no less attractive than improving, views of human character and human affairs. *Secondly*, scarcely a page of the classics can be read without some river, mountain, city, or remarkable site being mentioned or alluded to, — thus presenting occasions, from time to time, of dwelling on the condition, physical and political, of the ancient world, — of comparing it in both respects with the present, and of thus inspiring a taste for geography and topography, by investing the study of them with a deeper interest. In the *third* place, after all kinds of illustration, direct and collateral, have been thus brought to bear on the individual passage, and its sense has been fully made out, it remains to trace its connection with what goes before and follows, to fit it into its place as an integral part of the whole, and in this way to accustom the youthful mind to connect the several links in a chain of ideas. Accordingly, whether it be history he is engaged in perusing, he is

led to mark the series of events as they evolve themselves in the narrative, the skill of the historian in dis-
posing and grouping them, and the bearing they all
have on the main points of the story; or, whether an
oration of Cicero or of Demosthenes be in hand, he is
led to follow the train of the reasoning, and mark
the dexterity with which the pleader marshals his arguments, giving prominence and full display to the
weighty, and using them to mask the weaker points
and to cripple and break down the array of his adver-
sary; or whether it be a poem that forms the subject
of prelection, he is led to admire the beauty of the
descriptions and allusions, and the richness of the imagery; and amidst the ornaments and graces with
which the poet's fancy embellishes his work, to trace
his unity of purpose, and the consecutive train of his
ideas.   And in all these different kinds of composition,
and particularly in the last, we shall fail to extract all
the good they are capable of yielding, if we do not, in
the *fourth* place, embrace every opportunity of placing
alongside of the most striking passages read, parallel
ones, either from the same author or from other classics,
or from the distinguished writers of our own country.
This is an engaging, no less than an improving, exercise
for young minds; they require only to be put on the
track, and they will hunt out many resemblances of
thought and expression; and in the very pursuit they
become acquainted with, and acquire a relish for, the
standard poets of their own language.   To be thus invited to observe whence and how modern poets have
borrowed from or imitated the ancients, and how, with-

out borrowing or imitation, different writers handle the same subject, is one of the best modes of inoculating with the love of literature, and forming the taste.

And all the various information and mental exercise under the different heads I have described, it is important to observe, are thus presented and conveyed, not in formal lectures and continued discourses addressed to minds indifferently prepared and therefore but little disposed to profit by them, but in short, familiar, and almost conversational notices, listened to with avidity, because they spring out of a passage on which attention has been recently bestowed, and which serves as the text to impress and recall the information communicated. The instruction, too, is exactly of the kind and to the amount which excites curiosity without satisfying it, which promotes rather than stifles further inquiry. It opens up glimpses and vistas of knowledge as diversified as the minds to which they are presented, and thus exposes all to receive an impetus in the direction in which the tendencies of each are most apt to carry him, giving to the pupils an additional interest in whatever they either read or see passing around them, nay, occupying and coloring even their solitary thoughts.

Such is the nature and tendency of the *oral* instruction that flows naturally from a judicious method of teaching the classics. But we are yet far from having exhausted the benefits to be derived from such a course of discipline. For, let us consider what endless variety of themes for *written* exercises, adapted to every diversity of talent and capacity, must be furnished by the discussions and illustrations mentioned above. Of this kind are translations, English and Latin, in prose and in verse, which themselves furnish a theme for valuable information in the remarks made and judgments passed on them by the teacher ; abstracts of historical narrative or of oratorical argument ; dissertations on points treated by the author in hand ; criticism on the passages read, and summaries of grammatical and philological discussions. The resources of the instructor are thus multiplied a hundredfold. Sparks are constantly struck off from the sacred fire that is ever burning on the altar of ancient genius, which, flying in all directions, light on the susceptible minds of the young, kindle in their hearts the love of freedom and of virtue, and inform their whole thoughts with nobleness.

If, in addition to all these different means of illustrating the classics, we make occasional excursions into the field of general criticism, and endeavor to ascertain the principles upon which we feel admiration for the masterpieces of antiquity; if, deducing from those principles the rules of judging, and refusing to be guided by blind partiality, we venture, not petulantly, but with the reverence due to names so sacred, to " hint a fault and hesitate dislike ; " if, to quicken our perception and our relish of what is exquisite in writing, we institute a comparison between the kindred productions of ancient and modern genius, detecting the imitations which often do equal honor to both, and adjusting their respective claims to our homage and admiration, we shall be laying the foundation of that refinement and delicacy of taste which gives the last finish to the character of an accomplished gentleman.

After even so brief and hasty a sketch of what may be done for the training of youth by a course of classical discipline, I think myself entitled to ask its impugners what is the process they propose to substitute for this, it being taken for granted that the end in view is not so much to rear a youth for a particular trade, craft, or profession, as to bestow on his mind that general culture, and give him that free and dexterous use of his faculties which will enable him to excel in any.

What means, let me ask, shall we have recourse to, different from those above described, to accomplish the youthful mind for the purposes of life, and give it the culture required for a liberal profession? By what other treatment or manipulation shall we prepare so rich a mould, trench it so deeply, pulverize it so thoroughly, plough it and cross-plough it so frequently, give it so effectual a summer fallow, and sow so much precious seed, and promising so abundant a crop of all that is required for the use and embellishment of life? It is so much easier to destroy than to build up, and it is, besides, so impossible, I conceive, to meet this question with a direct answer, that the enemies of the classics will probably shift their ground, and evasively reply : "All this is well enough, if it were done ; but nobody will pretend that such practice is general; the picture drawn is purely ideal." But even if the practice were more rare than it is, we cannot, as I have said before, admit the argument against the use of a thing from the abuse of it; it is enough for us to show the

tendencies and capabilities of the study, and to challenge our adversaries either to disprove their existence,
or to show us a course of early discipline which possesses them to a greater extent, and with less chance
of imperfection and abuse in the teaching. A single
instance of success, and there are many, is as good for
our purpose as a thousand. The argument from present practice proves nothing against the principle.

. But again it may be argued : Why might not all this
be done, and done more compendiously and expedi-
tiously, by taking the works of our own English authors
for the substratum of this intellectual and moral training ? My answer is, that with such means, it could
not, I think, be done at all. In order to maintain this
argument, it is not necessary that one should be an
exclusive admirer of ancient literature, and blind to
the merits of our own English writers. I claim for the
ancients no faultless excellence, no immeasurable superiority. The raptures which some people seem to feel
in perusing Homer and Virgil, Livy and Tacitus, while
they turn over the pages of Shakspeare and Milton,
Hume and Robertson, with coldness and indifference, I
hold to be either pure affectation or gross self-delusion ;
being fully satisfied that we are in no want of models
in our own English tongue, which, for depth of thought
and soundness of reasoning, for truth of narrative, and
what has been called the philosophy of history, nay,
even for poetical beauty, tenderness, and sublimity, may
fairly challenge a comparison with the most renowned
productions of antiquity.

The languages, however, in which these qualities are

embodied, are essentially and widely different, not so much in the words or combinations of letters that respectively compose them, but in genius, in structure, and in idiom. The ancient are languages of flexion and conjugation, expressing the relations of things to one another, and the variations of the verb in time, person, number, mood, and voice, by changes in the termination of the words, all, or nearly all of which we express by separate small particles and monosyllables, which, to prevent ambiguity and confusion, have their places fixed, and must stand in juxtaposition to the words they are intended to affect. Hence two results ; one, that our English sentences admit of very slight and rare deviations from a precise definite arrangement of words ; and the other, that modern, and more especially English composition, is necessarily overrun with monosyllables, most of which, in our language at least, terminate in consonants. The ancient languages, on the contrary, from the circumstance of their incorporating the expression of various relations among objects and ideas into the words themselves, derive two advantages ; first, by avoiding a crowd of such little words as encumber our diction, they acquire a pomp, sonorousness, and condensation of meaning, " a long-resounding march and energy divine," which we cannot look for in our modern dialects ; and secondly, they admit a variety in the collocation of words, and a freedom of transposition, which materially contribute, in the hands of an accomplished writer, both to mould his periods into the most perfect music and melody to the ear, and what is of more consequence still, to present

them in the most striking forms to the understanding
and imagination of his reader.

It is, indeed, a great and just boast of these languages (which have been called, from the circumstance,
transpositive), that this liberty of arrangement enables
the speaker or writer to dispose his thoughts to the best
advantage, and to place in most prominent relief those
which he wishes to be peculiarly impressive ; and that
thus they are pre-eminently fitted for the purposes of
eloquence and poetry. It is owing to the same peculiarities in the structure of the ancient languages, that
the writers in them were enabled to construct those
long and curiously involved sentences, which any attempt to translate literally serves only to perplex and
obscure, but which presented to the ancient reader, as
they do to the modern imbued with his taste and perceptions, a beautiful, and, in spite of its complexity,
a sweetly harmonizing system of thoughts. I have
already alluded to the exertion of mind required to
perceive all the bearings of such a sentence, as to an
exercise well fitted for sharpening the faculties ; and
this view of the ancient tongues — considered as instruments of thought widely differing from, and in most
respects superior to, our own — is one which recom-
mends them to be used also as instruments of education.

Again, our mother tongue is so-entwined and identified with our early and ordinary habits of thinking and
speaking, it forms so much a part of ourselves from the
nursery upwards, that it is extremely difficult to place
it, so to speak, at a sufficient distance from the mind's

eye to discern its nature, or to judge of its proportions. It is, besides, so uncompounded in its structure, — so patchwork-like in its composition, so broken down into particles, so scanty in its inflections, and so simple in its fundamental rules of construction, that it is next to impossible to have a true grammatical notion of it, or to form indeed any correct ideas of grammar and philology at all, without being able to compare and contrast it with another language, and that other of a character essentially different.

But how much is the title of the ancient languages to the distinction we claim for them strengthened and enforced by the consideration, that to them our own and most of the other dialects of modern Europe, changed as they are in form and structure, owe a very large portion of their vocabulary. The more immediate descendants of the Latin — the Italian, Spanish, Portuguese, and French — are little else than corruptions of the parent stock, altered in shape, and frittered down in the parts, but the same in substance; and the complicated tissue of our own tongue is so wrought up and interwoven with the Latin chiefly, and also with the Greek, that it is impossible to unravel its texture or understand its nature and uses, without a competent knowledge of both. It may be regarded as a most agreeable and improving exercise to young minds, and one which will engage much of our attention here, to trace English words through the various forms and significations which they have assumed in the intermediate stages of French and Italian, up to their roots in the Latin or Greek tongues.

Indeed, when one considers these venerable forms of speech in connection with the history of Europe from the times in which they were spoken to the present day, one is tempted to compare them to splendid edifices reared by the genius of antiquity, fairly proportioned, and presenting an elevation of squared and polished blocks of the finest marble; but which, at a period when time had begun to impair without destroying their beauty, an earthquake and tempest, suddenly coming on, shook from their foundations and shivered into fragments. Out of these fragments, with whatever other materials came in our way, we moderns, when the storm had subsided, built ourselves habitations, convenient enough in point of accommodation, and destined to lodge many a gifted tenant, but nevertheless devoid of the grace and decoration and exquisite symmetry of the original structure. And if a few specimens of this architecture have escaped the wreck of ages, and survive in all their primitive chasteness and elegant simplicity, shall we not teach our youth to visit them, to admire their fair proportions, to study their cunning workmanship, and to imitate whatever is imitable of their perfection? In the volumes you have read or are preparing to read in this place, there are remains of antiquity, nobler, more graceful, and more entire, than the ruins of Paestum and the Acropolis; and while our very antagonists pretend to join in the admiration which these architectural ruins inspire, and to envy those who have had the good fortune to behold them on their site, shall we, by a cruel and infanticidal act, block up the avenue to still holier monuments—

those sacred repositories of mind wherein its brightest manifestations are consecrated, and which, instead of being, like the other, distant and almost inaccessible, are with us and about us, and ever ready when invited, *pernoctare nobiscum, peregrinari, rusticari?*

The very difficulties encountered in the way to these treasures—though they ought not to be multiplied, and there is much room and a strong call for diminishing their number—are not without their advantages to the student. There is no royal road to great attainments, nor is it desirable there should be; the labor of acquiring is itself half the reward, both in pleasure and in profit. What is easily learned makes little impression, and is soon forgotten. Hence an advantage in classical education, which may be regarded as an important one; that the variety of aspects in which, as I explained at the outset, the portions read are viewed—grammatical, syntactical, antiquarian, historical, mythological, geographical—are all, besides their own peculiar uses, just so many means of riveting the sense, when at last brought out in all its fulness, permanently in the memory. And this, indeed, is one of the sources of the secret charm and depth and dignity, which to well-trained minds seem to invest and hover around the choice passages of the classics. It would be impossible to dwell at such length and with such improving effect on equal portions of our mother tongue. The Paradise Lost is perhaps of all compositions in our language, that which would best admit of being made the groundwork of curious prelection and interesting discussion; and I should be glad to find that divine poem adopted as a text-book in school or college, and taking its place, as it might most worthily do, alongside of the productions of Homer and Virgil. But the circumstance which marks out Milton's poetry for this distinction, is the reverence and devotion he everywhere shows for those ancient models, in whose steps he was proud to tread. Hence the necessity of recurring perpetually to the classics if we would enter into the mind of the author, or comprehend one half of his beauties. Strip Milton of his translations and imitations of the classics, and still more of those direct and distant allusions to particular thoughts or expressions of theirs, and he will be found, to use a phrase of his own, " shorn of his beams."

Finally, much as I dislike mysticism and factitious extacies, I am not disposed to overlook or discount the delightful associations connected with compositions, which, though they carry us back to a remote antiquity, and an order of things very different from the present, are true to the great principles of our common nature ; nor am I inclined to quarrel with prepossessions and preferences for works which are stamped with the approbation of all the intervening ages. Is nothing to be allowed to the witchery of a great name ? no weight or value to be attached to the evidence of a cloud of witnesses who have testified to the worth of the classics by the use they have made of them in works of their own, imbued with the spirit of the ancients, and breathing, as it were, through their lips ? Must we adopt the utilitarian logic so far as to become henceforth insensible to all the references and felicitous expressions which our own classics are constantly making to, or borrowing from, those of antiquity — expressions and references so inseparably wrought into the web and tissue of our finest literature, that they give to the whole of it a relative character? Must we renounce all attempts to execute, and all power even to comprehend, those delicate touches and happy allusions to matters classical, which distinguish the speeches of our most eminent orators? Must we doom ourselves nevermore to hear, or if we hear, to have no relish or understanding of, those appropriate quotations which come like a gleam of light on the landscape, or " rise like a steam of rich distilled perfumes," diffusing around an atmosphere of odors redolent of joy and youth, and filling the mind with noble fancies and cherished recollections? Must such ornaments be discarded in all time to come from our senate? and where they are already recorded in the published specimens of parliamentary eloquence, as having fallen from the lips of a Burke, a Pitt, a Fox, a Wyndham, and a Canning, must they become to the next generation a sealed letter? Taste, feeling, public character, all the fondest remembrances of ancient and modern times, oppose themselves to so lame and impotent a conclusion. Introduce such a change in the training of our ingenuous youth, and we shall soon justify the bitterest taunts of our enemies, by degenerating, in the worst sense of the term, into a nation of shopkeepers.

But while we adhere steadfastly to the principle that a classical education is the best training for the youthful mind, and the finest equipment for exploring the fields of science and for playing our part in life, we must not shut our eyes to the fact or our minds to the conviction, that much is yet wanting to improve and perfect the discipline.

Let us drive the enemy from his last and strongest hold, by applying ourselves, with all earnestness, to rectify what is amiss in our methods of classical instruction, to disencumber the earlier stages of all that is mere rubbish and lumber, to simplify our grammars, and to infuse more philosophy into our treatment of the youthful mind, adopting whatever is proved to be most effectual for exciting it to healthy action, for increasing its knowledge, and for invigorating its powers, but rejecting all nostrums that only fill the head with a jumble of words, and dispense with the exercise of every faculty but memory. Let us multiply our holds upon the pupil's attention, and double the interest of his lessons by associating the science and literature of our own country with those of Greece and Rome ; thus entwining, as it were, the most graceful shoots of modern genius around the majestic pillar of ancient learning. It is then we may indulge the hope — that while we strengthen and multiply the stays and buttresses that give stability to the temple of our commonwealth — no sacrilegious hand will be raised successfully against the graceful shaft and Corinthian capital which at once support and adorn it.

XII.

But not upon the state alone has the power of our colleges been exerted and felt. The classical education, which has constituted their foremost work thus far, has refined and elevated society, and has furnished that broad foundation of general culture upon which all special knowledge may most securely rest. It may, perhaps, be true, as has been said: "That when fifty years have passed, not one fourth of any college class will be found to have been of real, visible use in the world, except the humble use of keeping the great machine going"— though no man here will believe it. But these discouraging critics should remember that it is from this class in society, raised as they are into the atmosphere of letters, if not all invigorated by it, that the great lights of learning always spring. We turn our eyes to the beauty and grandeur of the heavens, to be reminded that in all that shining throng there are but few which we can call by name, and that under the divine decree, " one star differeth from another star in glory." But we do not ask that darkness may again o'erspread the heavens, and that the constellations may be blotted out. One great scholar in an educated generation is all we have a right to expect; while we

This Chapter is an Extract from an Address on Classical Education, delivered at Amherst and Williams Colleges, in 1867, by Dr. George B. Loring, of Salem, Mass.

who walk, with unequal steps, the path which he has trod, may thank God that we are at least his brethren. And as we walk by his side, we must find ourselves in the companionship of the great men of the past whose spoken word is even now forgotten, as well as of the great company whose voices have hardly yet died away, if we would realize the full power and beauty of the order to which we belong. We are not all familiar with the wonderful humanity of Homer; we do not all dream in the mysterious thought of Plato; we cannot all walk the grove with Socrates; we have not all risen into the refined oratory and philosophy of Cicero; we are not all warmed by the genial verse of Virgil; but we all love those who are, and we feel that they bring down to us, from the language of the dead, refinement and beauty for the daily walk of life. What matters it if Homer's heroes are cruel, and Plato's philosophy is exploded, and Cicero's dream of immortality is to us a divine revelation and reality; our firmament would be dark without them, even to those who worship them as the Athenians did an "unknown God." I know the arts, and the church, and the state may be conducted without the immediate application of classical literature; but I cannot conceive of an educated community rising to the full measure of its capacity without it. The languages which compose it may be dead, their artic- ulation may long since have been forgotten; but though dead they yet speak, and will speak so long as man takes courage to his heart and strength to his soul from the thought that, among all perishable things, his spirit does not decay.

In order that I may come as near as possible to the plane of those who believe that all knowledge is useless, except as it applies to the practical affairs of life, and that the science of Technology has at last destroyed the value of letters, I desire to call before you some of the working scholars of our land, and the spheres in which they have labored.

The science of politics has many students among us; the business of public affairs has many devotees; and it is not claimed that it furnishes great opportunity for the scholar or the man of taste and letters to exercise his elevating influence. And yet, in this state, without considering at all the political sentiment which has controlled it, what a brilliant irradiation has our political history received from the scholarship of Edward Everett! He was in every sense a man of culture, familiar with the literature of ancient and modern times, the classic orator of Massachusetts for nearly two generations of men. When he differed from the popular voice, his presence was always felt as that of an accomplished and graceful antagonist. When the popular heart and his own beat in unison, and he uttered his last great speech in Faneuil Hall, his greatest speech for the glory and honor of his struggling country, how the eloquence of Demosthenes, pleading for the crown, rose up before us, and the great cause for which he labored received new life and grandeur! Do you doubt that the scholarship of Everett gilded all that scene? If you do, imagine how the assemblies of Massachusetts would rise and swell with exultation were the sound of his silver voice heard once more among them, and the public

22

affairs of this State were once more illumined by his presence.

The practical business of popular education has been brought to a system so nearly allied to the positive methods which Technology claims to teach, as to give to the model of a school-house a representative significance in the great Industrial Exposition of all nations. We all acknowledge the capacity of those who are engaged in this work, and we count the fruits of their labors as the most valuable of all the industrial products of our busy population. The course of education is intentionally adapted to the actual business of life. And yet, among all those who have labored in this field, no one has given it more renown, more elevation of character, more substantial vital force, than he who brought from the University his thorough scholarship, and demonstrated that a classical education and popular instruction may go hand in hand. President Felton was emphatically a scholar. Commencing his early mental discipline in one of the academies of this State, those rare old nurseries of our early classics, whose valuable service can never be forgotten, and which are still entitled to our pious care, he stepped at once, with all his zeal, into the society of the ancient men of letters. We are told that in the first fifteen months of his academic career, he " read Sallust four times, Cicero's Orations four times, Virgil six times, Dalzel's Graeca Minora five or six times, and the poetry of it until he could repeat nearly all of it from memory ; the Annals and History of Tacitus, Justin, Cornelius Nepos, the Anabasis of Xenophon, four books of Robinson's Selections

from the Iliad, the Greek Testament four times, besides
writing a translation of one of the Gospels, and a translation of the whole of Grotius de Veritate, which he
brought in manuscript to college ; he also wrote a
volume of about three hundred pages of Latin exercises,
and studied carefully all the mathematics and geography requisite to enter college.[1]   He was an accurate
Greek scholar, exploring every manifestation of Greek
mind and life."   The spirit of Aristophanes seemed
lodged in him; "he had the same sense of the ludicrous,
the same keen judgment of character, the same undying

---

[1] The following extract from the Inaugural Address of Mr. Felton as
Professor of Greek at Harvard University, delivered in August, 1834, will
show how fully he had imbibed the spirit of the Classics, and how richly
he had profited by them, even at so early a period in his studies. — [ED.

"The early language of the Greeks, like every other language, must
have been rude. But it was soon brought to a wonderful degree of full-
ness, strength, and beauty. Its words are made up of the most expressive
sounds. The breeze and the hurricane, the laving of the ocean over a
beach, and the tempest-tossed waves breaking against the shore, the
stream and the mountain torrent rushing to meet the tide of the sea, the
storm, and the coming out of the stars one after another, in a clear night,
when, in the language of Homer, 'the shepherd rejoices in his heart,' are
described by the early poets in terms of the most significant harmony.
All the works of man, too, whether in peace or in war, are depicted in
strong and lively colors. We see the warriors arm and go forth to the
battle; we hear the tramp of advancing multitudes, and the clash of the
onset. The council, the feast, and the sacrifice are made to pass before the
eye by such happy strokes of the poet's art, that we seem to be living in
the midst of them all. In short, this language of a freely organized and
developed people, formed under the genial influence of a serene and beautiful heaven, amidst the most picturesque and lovely scenery in nature, had
acquired a descriptive force and harmony, equally capable of expressing
every mood of the mind, every affection of the heart, every aspect of the
world. Its words are images, and its sentences finished pictures. It gives
the poet the means of clothing his conceptions in every form of beauty
and grandeur; of painting them with the most exquisite tints and hues;

earnestness of patriotism." His aesthetic power was
great, and he studied Greek poetry and art, until he
was fully imbued with the, spirit of that most aesthetic
of all people. With what enthusiasm did he discourse
of Athens, after he had trod the soil made sacred by
the poets, and philosophers, and orators with whom he
had, in spirit, spent his life! That marvellous and
almost voluptuous sense of beauty which produced in
Greece the only Venus and Apollo, and wrote the record
of great deeds and great men in marble, with the
sublimest grace, and realized all the divinity of form
and feature and soul of which man is capable, had
become a part of the daily thought of this great scholar,
who, we may be told, had so buried himself among the
dead, that he had no heart for the duties of the living.
But how was it with him? His own mental culture
filled him with a desire to cultivate others, and inspired
him with liberal views with regard to the fertilizing
power of every rill of knowledge. And when he took
his stand with the popular educators of our State, with
what new lustre did he clothe himself, and what radiance
did he impart to the work of education here!

It is not easy to soften the asperities of the law.
The hard and systematic practice of the courts belongs

of gathering around them the most appropriate images, wisely chosen and
tastefully grouped; and of heightening the effect of the whole by the
idealizing power of a chastened imagination. The curious mechanism of
its metre, combining softness and strength, its "linked sweetness long
drawn out," and its forcible brevity have never been surpassed. What
modern tongue has reproduced the stately march of Homer's majestic
hexameters? What translator has given us the compressed energy of
Pindar's Doric Odes?"

to that service which least of all others cultivates the broadest faculties and cherishes the loftiest sentiments. The greatness of this greatest of professions is attained only by the largest comprehension of what law is and what a state should be, supported by all the subtilty and self-possession of well-trained faculties. We ask, however, of our legal adviser only a thorough knowledge of the law, and expertness in its practice. And as we bring this great science down to the level of a mere useful machine, we lose sight of the opportunity it offers for the most accurate general culture. How are we surprised then, and how do the courts glow to our astonished vision, when a great cultivated mind lavishes upon them the wealth of its cultivation! The bar of Massachusetts has won for itself an imperishable renown, for its labors in that sphere where the greatest and the meanest of mankind seem to flourish alike. Its jurists are known wherever laws protect the people, and as a fountain of common law it is undoubtedly unequalled. But who of all men has given it its peculiar glory? Who is the lawyer whose rich intellectual cultivation has shed life and light around our bar, as the midsummer sun warms the capes that bound the polar sea? Need I tell the scholars of this commonwealth that it is Rufus Choate, the lawyer and the scholar, who in the courts never forgot the cloister, who enjoyed his "Horae Thucididianae" as common men do their newspaper and novel; who dropped his brief to translate Tacitus; who carried with him everywhere the letter and the spirit of the classics, of the dead languages and the living? It may be that his lore did not serve to interpret the law which he loved so fondly ; but it did ennoble his profession ; it did give the fraternity of lawyers a high place in the fraternity of scholars ; it did throw a light around our courts, which shall never be extinguished until

"All earthly shapes shall melt in gloom."

The study of the dead languages has done this, at least, for the law in Massachusetts.

It were easy to enumerate many similar examples of the effect produced by letters when carried into practical life. But these three distinguished illustrations are sufficient to show the deep sympathy which mankind in this age have for the intellectual efforts of the past, and the refining and invigorating influence of associations with experts in thought and modes of expression, even through an interpreter.

XIII.

THERE are two processes in the study of every important subject — the accurate mastery of its details, and the contemplation of it as a whole. We cannot, of course, pretend to exhaust the whole subject of classical antiquity. No scholar, nor all the generations of scholars, have exhausted, or probably ever will exhaust, the interest and meaning of the subject. But by reading considerable portions of the best authors, we can enter into their minds, and understand the subjects they treat of with far more truth and completeness of insight than when our vision is limited to a small part of their works. We raise ourselves, independently, to that higher level of study from which the relations to one another of the particular matters we have examined in detail become apparent. Every fact in ancient history, every feeling expressed in ancient poetry, every thought in ancient philosophy, acquires for us a new meaning when we perceive its relation to the whole character and civilization of antiquity. From the region of phenomena we rise into that of ideas, by which I do not mean bare abstractions, but truths of thought realizing themselves in experience. In other words, we enter

This Chapter is from a Lecture entitled "Theories of Classical Teaching," delivered in opening the Third Humanity Class, Friday, November 8, 1867. By W. Y. Sellar, Professor of Humanity in the University of Edinburgh.

on the philosophical study of ancient literature and history.

In determining what should be the work of the class, one naturally considers what are the objects which you probably have in view in attending it. I should fancy that these objects are twofold, one general, the other special. Many, I hope, indeed, all of you, come here animated by an interest in the subject, feeling the same kind of interest in the best Latin literature that you feel in the best English literature, conscious that the impressions you have received from Latin literature have fostered your intellectual growth, and desirous to deepen and enlarge those impressions. Virgil and Horace, Cicero and Tacitus, have helped to refine your taste, to enlarge the range of your ideas and sympathies, to open up to you a new world of human experience, and you feel loth to quit that world before you have brought it permanently under the domain of your intelligence. It is because of their inexhaustible human interest that the great writers of Greece and Rome maintain a life-long hold upon us ; a hold which is strengthened, not loosened, in proportion to the force with which the living questions of our own day affect us. To communicate, in so far as his longer familiarity with the subject enables him to do so, his own sense of this human interest, to act as a faithful interpreter to a modern generation of the thought and experience which the ancient writer imparted directly to his own generation, is the highest function which any teacher of the classical languages can perform.

But there is another kind of hold which the classical

languages have upon the world. The highly organized structure of these languages has recommended them as a formal instrument of intellectual training for minds still too immature to sympathize with the thought and experience contained in the ancient writers. Hence they have, in England at least, obtained to a degree which many of the strongest advocates of classical studies acknowledge to be excessive, a preponderance in the higher school education of the country. There are many signs that the days of this excessive preponderance are past or passing; and no liberal mind will regret the abolition of this or of any other monopoly. But at the same time, if there is one thing in the future about which we can augur more hopefully than another, it is that there will be a more general demand for, and a more intelligent appreciation both of popular and of liberal education, than there has been in this country in former times. And classical teaching, even though deprived of the monopoly which it has enjoyed in England, will share in the general impulse communicated to all liberal education. It is probable, indeed, that the elementary knowledge of the Greek language will not continue to be taught at school so generally as at present to all sorts of boys, whatever may be their capacity or their prospects in life; but for all who have the ability and can afford the time required for a high intellectual cultivation, for all true students of theology, philosophy, and political history, for all lovers of poetry and art, the study of the Greek language and literature must, I believe, maintain its unquestionable pre-eminence among literary studies. And though Latin literature does not lay any such claim to supremacy among the literatures of the world, yet its value as supplemental to the knowledge of Greek literature, and its independent value as expressing the mind and character of the race that has played the greatest part in human affairs, are likely to maintain for it too a leading position among university studies; while the practical uses of the language, as the best possible instrument of grammatical and philological training, and as essential to any proper understanding of our own language and of other modern languages, are likely to preserve its place among the essential branches of ordinary, though not of course as elementary, school-education.

But the two objects which I have mentioned, so far from being incompatible with one another, are really essential to supplement each other. The mere interest in the literature is apt to lose itself in vagueness and dilettanteism. The passive and receptive attitude of the mind in unfolding itself to the beauties of a great poet or the wisdom of a great thinker, though refining and elevating, may yet become enervating, if not combined with some active exertion of our own, some process of consecutive thinking, or some concentration of the faculties in mastering difficulties. In education the mind must act as well as receive, must learn to use as well as to acquire knowledge. On the other hand, the more masculine exercise of the understanding in gaining mastery over some subject remote from our ordinary associations, and of difficult access, — such as the language of the ancient Greeks and Romans, — while in the highest degree invigorating, has, if uncombined with the more feminine influence of human insight and sympathy, the tendency to leave the mind and character hard, dry, and unsympathetic; in short, to make pedants or doctrinaires instead of cultivated men. While accurate scholarship builds up and strengthens the active faculties of the understanding, the study and enjoyment of ancient literature awakens, expands, and educates the intellectual and moral sympathies.

The true theory of classical education lies, I think, like many other true theories, between two extremes; or rather, it combines into one two half-truths, acted upon or advocated by our extreme conservatives, and by the best of our extreme reformers in educational matters. The one extreme theory is, that education is purely a discipline of the understanding, that the form of the subject is everything, the content little or nothing. A severe study, such as classics or mathematics, is the thing wanted to train or brace the faculties. It does not matter whether it is in itself interesting or not. The student will find sufficient interest in the sense of power which he has to put forth in training for the great race with his competitors. "It is not knowledge," they say, " but the exercise you are forced to incur in acquiring knowledge, that we care about. Read and learn the classics simply for the discipline they afford to the understanding. You may, if it comes in your way, and does not interfere with your training, combine a literary pleasure with this mode of study; but that is no part of your education; as teachers we do not care to encourage it, we do not care to interpret for you the thought or feeling of your author; all such teaching is weak and rhetorical; we do not profess to examine into your capacity of receiving pleasure. Accurate and accomplished translation, effective composition in the style of the ancient authors, thorough grammatical and philological knowledge, these are our requirements. The training in exactness, in concentration, in logical habits, and in discernment of the niceties of expression, is the one thing with which we start you in life. Whether you have thought at all, or care to think about the questions which occupy and move the highest minds, is no affair of ours."

This theory, though I believe it to be one-sided and limited, has, from its very limitation and concentration of aim, been very effective in its practical application to education. It is, I think, a purely English theory of education; it has grown up within the last half century, and it is in the University of Cambridge that it has been and still is most fully realized. The rigor of intellectual training has probably never been carried to so high a pitch as in the preparation for the honors of the classical and mathematical triposes at Cambridge. The result of this education has told upon the world in those modes of intellectual and professional activity which require exactness of mind, concentration, justness of criticism, temperance of statement. Those who have been trained in such a system enjoy, in a high degree, immunity from intellectual weakness, vagueness, and extravagance. It might possibly be sufficient if the world were content to go on forever in its traditional modes of thinking and acting. Combined with

the pleasant social life of the University, it prepares
men to carry on the intellectual business of life in
accordance with established usage ; it trains to intellectual habits the politicians, lawyers, divines, and
critics of uneventful times. But our lot has been cast
in a more restless age, when the deepest questions
affecting our whole view of life are agitating all classes,
learned and unlearned alike, and are pressing for a
solution. We look for such solution partly to the
genius and patience of individual thinkers, partly to
the capacities of thinking and appreciating truth which
may be created and diffused by a larger and more philosophical education. In order to interpret the present
and to regulate the future progress of the world, the
speculative faculty must discern the full meaning of
the past; how, under previous conditions, man has
solved for himself, or failed to solve, his religious, philosophical, and political difficulties ; how he has built up
the fabric of his social life ; what charm he has realized
for himself in art and literature. To study the language of an ancient people, and yet to leave these questions unattempted, is surely to blind ourselves to the
highest interest and deepest meaning of our subject.
If it were not for a strong and ever-increasing sense of
this inexhaustible source of interest in the great writers
of antiquity, of the endless stimulus and food which
they afford to speculative energy, as well by the con-
trasts as by the analogies which they present to our
modern civilization, one could see, perhaps, without
much regret, classical studies altogether superseded by
studies of a more immediate utility.

23

This leads to a consideration of the opposite theory, at present indeed rather advocated than acted upon. " Can we not," it is said, " understand ' the ancient spirit' through the help of lectures, modern books on the subject, translations from the classics, without the unnecessary labor of acquiring an exact knowledge of two unfamiliar and difficult languages, essentially different in their structure from all the forms of speech now in use among men ? Nothing is gained by the mere difficulty of the process. Our object is to arrive at the result, the knowledge of the life and genius of antiquity, in the shortest, easiest, and pleasantest way." This is perhaps an extreme statement of the opposite theory of education, which makes nothing of discipline, everything of acquirement. Each of these theories appears to me to be true in what it affirms, false in what it denies. Each half-truth gains greatly, even in the position which it affirms, by admitting the counter half. The value of discipline is immensely enhanced when it is regarded as a process towards important results. A new and higher discipline is given to the mind by the active exercise of the faculties in thinking out the thoughts and reducing to order the impressions received in the sympathetic study and enjoyment of ancient literature. On the other hand, the easiest and shortest is not the surest way of realizing the results, perhaps is not compatible with permanently realizing them at all. There is all the difference in the world between imparting transient impressions and educating the steadfast sympathies of the mind. It is the same kind of difference that there is between passing rapidly in a railway carriage through a country rich in its natural beauty and historic associations, and exploring on foot all its heights and recesses, allowing its varied aspects to become part of our being, a lasting memory and source of joy,

" Felt in the blood and felt along the heart."

Is it unavoidable that we should carry this railway pace into our processes of education ? Are the requirements of our nineteenth century progress so peremptory ? After all, it is not universal information, whether pleasantly or painfully acquired, but more freedom and power, more insight and wisdom, that our intellectual being longs for. There is a danger for ordinary minds in trying to know too many things, and to know them too easily. Knowledge directly imparted may be a source both of usefulness and of immediate pleasure to an active mind ; but the toil and patience needed to bring a remote subject near, to make an unfamiliar subject familiar, may be the condition of more usefulness and more pleasure in the long run. I should fancy that both scholars and men of science would agree in this, that what they looked back upon with least dissatisfaction in their career, what they would now prize as the main source of their intellectual health and strength, was the strenuous toil which they underwent — ἱδρῶθ᾽ ὃν ἵδρωσα μόγῳ — in mastering for them-selves the essential difficulties of their subject ; what they looked upon with less satisfaction was the time spent on what was not essential, or in following wrong processes ; what they looked upon with least satisfaction of all was the easy methods they had adopted to gain some immediate result, to produce the show of acquirement, to impose for the moment on themselves and others.

I do not, however, for one moment wish to preach the doctrine of keeping up difficulties for the sake of the difficulty. In every important study or undertaking there is quite enough of absolutely essential difficulty to satisfy the requirements of the most rigorous advocate of discipline.

> " Pater ipse colendi,
>   Haud facilem esse viam voluit ; "

and mark the reason

> " Curis acuens mortalia corda."

The aim of the teacher should be to create in the mind of his pupil a real, independent, permanent insight into and sympathy with his subject, as distinct from a transient impression and vague enthusiasm about it. This aim will help him to distinguish between the kind of difficulty which it is good for the student to encounter, and that which it should be his teacher's part as far as possible, to spare him.

Intellectual difficulties must be distinguished from intellectual puzzles and intellectual burdens. The solution of the first braces the mind to meet the difficulties of thought and action which await the student in every serious pursuit of life. The solution of the second may be a pleasant amusement or a useless waste of time. The struggle with the last may be a source of permanent weariness and weakness to the mind.

It is quite right to train even a young boy to encounter difficulties suited to his age; but this discipline is adequately secured by the necessity of learning accurately the forms and inflections of the language he is studying, and of practically observing grammatical laws and distinctions in interpreting, with the help of a few simple rules, the sentences of an ancient author.

The conclusion to which we come on this point is, that there is no value whatever, but rather a great hinderance in the unmeaning and unnecessary difficulties with which classical studies have been too much encumbered; that it is the duty of every teacher to do his best to clear them away; that he should keep steadily before him the aim of awakening in every one of his pupils the power of independent insight into, and sympathy with, the various modes in which the spirit or genius of antiquity realized itself; and that he should strive to attain this result neither by the longest and most difficult, nor by the shortest and easiest, but by the surest and most intelligent, process. But after removing, to the best of our power, all unnecessary impediments to the independent mastery of the ancient languages and literatures, there still remains to be encountered a great deal of real difficulty, much more certainly than in the acquisition of a modern language or literature. In acquiring the mere vocabulary of two unfamiliar languages, such as ancient Greek and modern German, the mere strain on the memory may perhaps be nearly equal. But the intellectual difficulty of familiarizing ourselves with the structure of the ancient language is much greater, from the fact that

23 *

the logical and imaginative conditions under which the
ancient language was moulded were different from the
framework of our modern thinking. Consciously or
unconsciously, we must enter into these unfamiliar
modes of thought and imagination in interpreting the
meaning of an ancient writer; we must at every step
conform to intellectual laws and requirements different
from those to which we unconsciously conform in using
our own or any modern language. What we express
as an abstract relation of thought the ancients more
frequently express as concrete fact; what we express
as a number of independent statements, they express in
one complex, highly organized period; while the conditions of our language force us to a monotonous
observance of the order of construction, their richly
inflected languages enable them to vary, in many ways,
the structure of their sentences, in accordance with the
conditions of logical relation, rhetorical emphasis, and
rythmical cadence. The ideas which they realized out
of the relation of their circumstances to their inward
conditions of mind and feeling are different from those
which modern nations have realized from analogous
relations. Thus though we find that the words expressive of things discerned by the senses, and of the simpler states of feeling and simpler relations of life, may
often correspond completely with one another in the
ancient and modern languages, as, for instance, our
modern words *bread, wine, stone, dog, heart, liver, an-
ger, grief, father, king,* have their exact, or nearly their
exact, equivalents in Greek and Latin; yet in the great
number of words expressing complex modifications of

thought and sentiment there is no such exact equivalence. You cannot say, for instance, that there is any one English word which we can at all times use as equivalent with such words as *fides, religio, virtus, ingenium, humanitas, gravitas, pietas, officium*, and hundreds of other words expressive of the manifold diversities of idea that exist in the infinite world of consciousness. To find an English equivalent for such words in any particular passage, we must first realize to our minds all the shades of meaning which that word conveyed to a Roman, following in our minds the process by which each shade of meaning passed into the other; we must judge by the context which is the particular meaning there conveyed, and then we must find, out of several words, the exact English equivalent which may perhaps have no other point of coincidence with the Latin word. Though this may be a momentary process in the mind of an accomplished scholar, the facility and certainty with which he finds his equivalent English words are the results of a long-continued and severe training, not of his memory merely, but of his reflective power. Again, in translating from a modern into an ancient language, we become aware of another great difference between the two languages, consisting in the immense number of decayed metaphors which we vaguely employ in modern speech, and which very rarely correspond with the metaphorical uses of ancient speech. To realize and fully bring out all such differences between the ancient classical and the modern European languages is thus no mere exercise of verbal memory, but implies the constant use of highly-developed faculties, both of judgment and expression.

While, therefore, we rest the value of classical study not solely on its power as a discipline or exercise, but also on the variety of ways in which it animates and enriches the mind, we yet rank among the advantages of the study those essential difficulties which require the constant use of, and thereby afford a constant training to, the logical and rhetorical faculties. What mathematics are as a discipline in the sphere of scientific truth, that the study of language may be made in the sphere of ethical truth, — of that complex world of thought and feeling in which we truly live and have our being. In the words of the ancient languages are wrapped up a record of the past thought and experience of our race. Through the knowledge we acquire of these languages we cannot help familiarizing ourselves with some at least of the infinitely varied modes of intelligence and emotion through which the mind of man has passed. Thus, even if it were possible for a teacher to communicate, by means of lectures and translations from the classics, a true insight into the manifestations of the spirit of antiquity, the student would forfeit a large element of the educational value of classical study in foregoing the process of becoming familiar with the ancient languages. But to communicate this power of insight, independently of classical scholarship is, I believe, quite impossible. No doubt there have been men of genius — a Shakspeare or a Keats—who have got from a translation of a Latin or a Greek author, or even from the sight of some work of

art, a truer insight into antiquity than mere verbal
scholars will get in a lifetime. But it is not for men
of exceptional genius that our educational appliances
are wanted. They are independent of them ; they find
their mental food by processes unknown and unimag-
ined by common men.

The general conclusion, therefore, to which we come,
is that in classical study we are educated through the
active exertion of our understanding, combined with
our capacity of receiving impressions, and the spontaneous awakening of our ideas. Our aim must be to
unite these modes of intellectual progress, to make
the interpretation of the classical authors a process of
steady, continuous exertion, and at the same time to
find in them a source of literary impulse, and materials
for ethical and political reflection. The active exertion
of mastering the difficulties of the language ought
gradually to give place to another and higher kind of
active exertion — that of reducing into order and giving shape to the materials for thought which come to
us through the influence of ancient literature on our
imagination, and through the expansion of our ethical
and political sympathies. Thus the study of ancient
literature rises into the study of the philosophy of
history and of human life.

In regard to exercises, I attach importance to composition in Latin chiefly as an instrument of securing
accurate grammatical knowledge of the language. I
should expect all candidates for classical honors to translate from an English author into Latin prose, in such
a way as to show sound grammatical knowledge, and

a true perception of the essential differences between the ancient and modern idioms. Without practice in prose composition up to this extent at least, you can have no sure hold over the language. I am well aware that a very much higher standard than this is both aimed at and attained in English schools and universities; and I can, I hope, genuinely admire the finest results of modern scholarship in writing Latin prose and verse;

"Non equidem invideo, miror magis."

But I have long been convinced, and acted on the conviction, that this extreme refinement was not essential to the standard of scholarship attainable in the comparatively short time allowed for classical study in our Scottish universities, and that it could be attained by the majority even of our good scholars only by an expenditure of time and labor disproportioned to its value.

I should attach equal if not more importance to exercises in translation from Latin authors into English. This kind of exercise, if carefully performed in such a manner as to bring out in forcible idiomatic English the full truth, and nothing but the truth, of the author's meaning, is quite as efficient a discipline in scholarship, and is of more direct practical utility as a training of the rhetorical faculty, than composition in the ancient languages. But I attach the most importance of all to such exercises and essays as require thought and reasoning on the facts, feelings, and ideas presented to our contemplation in the ancient writers. Many persons, inadequately, I think, informed on the

subject, speak slightingly of such exercises, as capable
only of eliciting what is called crammed knowledge.
How far "cram" may tell in examinations or exercises
will absolutely depend on the competence or incompe-
tence of the examiner. If he can be imposed upon by
a mere superficial display of second-hand information,
got up for the occasion, or by the reproduction of
another man's views on a subject, and is altogether
incapable of appreciating originality of observation,
thought, and feeling on the part of the student, there
is a very great danger that such exercises as I am
speaking of may be unproductive of any good. But if
he sets before himself the object of attracting, suggest-
ing, and eliciting thought on the matters of most interest that meet the student in reading his author, he may
do more to awaken and educate his intelligence by the
questions which he thus proposes to him than by the
directer processes of teaching.

Before concluding this lecture there are one or two
other points which I must touch upon, though my
limits will not allow me to discuss them. The controversy as to the utility of classical studies, so long dormant, has again been revived. Scotland has been
made, in the first instance, the battle-field, but there
is little doubt that the war will soon be carried across
the Tweed. Three remarkable addresses, in which the
subject has been treated, have recently been delivered
to Scottish audiences by three men of great natural
gifts, great cultivation, and great eminence in public
life—Mr. Mill, Mr. Grant Duff, and Mr. Lowe. Though
in very different degrees, yet they all are opposed to

things as they now are. From the objections urged by Mr. Mill against the exclusive pretensions of classical study, and against the methods of study elsewhere in use, we in the Scottish universities need not withhold our absolute assent. We may also cordially offer to him the tribute of our gratitude for the noblest and justest vindication of the claims of ancient literature uttered in our time, or, I believe, in any time. And that these opinions of his are not of recent date, may be shown by a passage which I venture to extract from his earlier works, as sound and useful doctrine for this time :

" Not only do these literatures furnish examples of high finish and perfection in workmanship, to correct the slovenly habit of modern hasty writing, but they exhibit in the military and agricultural commonwealths of antiquity precisely that order of virtues in which a commercial society is apt to be deficient ; and they altogether show human nature on a grander scale, with less benevolence, but more patriotism ; less sentiment, but more self-control ; if a lower average of virtue, more striking individual examples of it ; fewer small goodnesses, but more greatness and appreciation of greatness ; more which tends to exalt the imagination and inspire high conceptions of the capabilities of human nature. If, as every one may see, the want of affinity of these studies to the modern mind is gradually lowering them in popular estimation, this is but a confirmation of the need of them, and renders it more incumbent upon those who have the power to do their utmost towards preventing their decline."

I will not venture at the end of this lecture to take up in detail the many points of difference suggested by the witty and pointed address delivered last Friday evening at the opening of the Philosophical Institution. The eminence of the speaker [1] will, I hope, call forth other champions, to whom the words "*impar congressus Achilli*" may not be so fatally applicable. With his opposition to the antiquated superstitions of classical teaching, the lessons on the loves of the gods and goddesses, the universal requirement of Latin verses, and the cram of commentators' theories about other commentators' theories on corrupt passages, of which he made so much, one may cordially agree. One may agree also with his protest against the preponderance enjoyed by classical and mathematical studies in determining the highest honors and emoluments of the English universities. But there one's agreement with his theory of a liberal education ends. Omitting many objections in detail, I may draw attention to the fact that the first principles he announced are not beyond question. It has already been pointed out that a fallacy is involved in one of his principles, namely, that we live in a world of things, not of words, and that it is more important to know the things. This account of the world is hardly exhaustive, unless "things" is made a very comprehensive term indeed. Besides outward objects and the words denoting them, there are ideas and sentiments and relations with which it is important for us to be familiar; and the ancient languages and literatures may be of use in imparting to us this form

---

[1] Right Honorable Robert Lowe. — [ED.

24

of knowledge. Another of his first principles seems to me not above question. Is it certain that university education should be practical rather than speculative? No one thinks of denying the use of practical aptitude in any calling; and though this cannot be imparted directly by university lectures or examinations, yet, in the higher kinds of calling, those which demand the application of general views to practice, the discipline of a university education is of inestimable service. But is it true that our speculative or critical faculties and our intellectual sympathies are of such little consequence — harmless contributions perhaps to the amusement of idle men — that their education may be left to the casual intercourse of society? Is it not the case that we cannot read an article in a newspaper or review, we cannot listen to a speech or a sermon, we cannot hold a serious conversation with any one on any subject worth talking about, without having to exercise whatever speculative capacity we may have, and to bring into use whatever speculative opinions and sympathies we have formed for ourselves, or have taken unquestioned from the current speech of society? We live in a world not of words and things only, but also of speculations; and if we have not educated our faculty of originating, or at least of judging of speculations, we are at the mercy of any sciolist, rhetorician, or fanatic who may be kind enough to take upon himself the office of forming our opinions and stimulating our feelings on the most important subjects of human thought. It is because I believe that liberal, as distinct from popular and professional, education, should be speculative rather than practical, should develop the

highest capacity of human thought and sympathy, that I
so strongly urge upon you the claims of classical study.

But while some of the objections to classical study
appear to me to be what the Greeks call βάναυσα, and
may best be answered by denying at the outset the
mechanical conception of the aims and objects of human
life which they presuppose, others, we must admit, are
forcible and formidable. In so far as these last are
directed against the exclusive pretensions of classical
teaching, they are reasonable, and deserve to prevail.
But such exclusive pretensions never have been put
forward in our Scottish universities. By far the most
formidable objection to my mind is, not that the classical languages and literatures are not in the highest
degree worth learning, but that we cannot teach them,
or do not in general succeed in teaching them. It may
be said — not, I acknowledge, without justice — that
a large number of boys who learn Latin and Greek
never acquire either language thoroughly ; that many
of the best verbal scholars remain ignorant of or un-
affected by the spirit and ideas of classical literature ;
that even those who have received the sound discipline
of scholarship and the rich culture of ancient literature
and philosophy, remain through life a great deal more
ignorant of other things than they need be or ought to
be. It is our duty and our interest to recognize the
truth of these reproaches, and to do our best to remove
them. I believe they can be removed by a liberal concession to the claims of other studies, and by modifying
the scope and improving the methods of classical teaching. For such modification and improvement we must
look to the good sense of our classical teachers in

schools and universities, to their living interest in their subject, and their power of making that interest live again in the minds of others. Their power and enthusiasm must spring from a large and genial appreciation of all the sources of interest, instruction, and pleasure which abound in ancient literature. This large and genial appreciation it should be the special office of the classical chairs in our universities to impart, in such a way that every classical school in the country should soon share in the impulse.

It is a question for those much interested in any one absorbing pursuit, how far they can combine their devotion to that pursuit or branch of knowledge with a many-sided interest in other branches of knowledge. It is a disputed question whether the true principle of education is that of opening the intelligence, in succession, to a variety of subjects of interest, or that of concentrating the faculties on a few great and important subjects. It seems to me that in what we may hope will soon assume the importance it deserves, namely the higher intellectual education of women, the first is the true principle; and also that the very highest order of minds among men is capable of uniting the variety of the first with the thoroughness of the second process; but that for the larger number of educated men, it is best to study thoroughly two or three great subjects mutually related, as, for instance, classical literature and modern philosophy, and in so far as they have energy and capacity, to combine this with enough general instruction to make them able to appreciate the pursuits of others. It is necessary to impose a limit on ourselves, but not too narrow a limit. Concentration, like every other great intellectual faculty, may be carried too far. Against the beneficial tendency of continuous devotion to any subject must be rated the depressing influence of monotony. A classical student may become a first-rate verbal scholar by devoting himself to classics alone ; but he never can realize the full worth of his subject without being also a student of mental and ethical philosophy, and of modern languages and literature. And every other real addition to our knowledge of man or nature will add to our interest in life, and will conduce to our moral growth by helping to free us from the dominion of our prejudices. There is, however, a danger of dissipating energy by attempting too much. Each man in settling this question for himself must take the measure of his own power and capacity.

It is not, however, without reason that the foremost place has in fact been assigned to this [classical] study. Grammar is the logic of common speech, and there are few educated men who are not sensible of the advantages they gained as boys from the steady practice of composition and translation, and from their introduction to etymology. The study of literature is the study, not indeed of the physcial, but of the intellectual and moral world we live in, and of the thoughts, lives, and characters of those men whose writings or whose memories succeeding generations have thought it worth while to preserve.

We are equally convinced that the best materials available to Englishmen for these studies are furnished by the languages and literature of Greece and Rome. From the regular structure of these languages, from

their logical accuracy of expression, from the comparative ease with which their etymology is traced and reduced to general laws, from their severe canons of taste
and style, from the very fact that they are " dead," and
have been handed down to us directly from the periods
of their highest perfection, comparatively untouched by
the inevitable process of degeneration and decay, they
are, beyond all doubt, the finest and most serviceable
models we have for the study of language./ As literature they supply the most graceful and some of the
noblest poetry, the finest eloquence, the deepest philosophy, the wisest historical writing ; and these excellences are such as to be appreciated keenly, though
inadequately, by young minds, and to leave, as in fact
they do, a lasting impression.   Besides this, it is at least
a reasonable opinion that this literature has a powerful
effect in moulding and animating the statesmanship
and political life of England.   Nor is it to be forgotten
that the whole civilization of modern Europe is really
built upon the foundations laid two thousand years ago
by two highly civilized nations on the shores of the
Mediterranean ; that their languages supply the key to
our modern tongues ; their poetry, history, philosophy,
and law, to the poetry and history, the philosophy and
jurisprudence, of modern times ; that this key can
seldom be acquired except in youth, and that the possession of it, as daily experience proves, and as those
who have it not will most readily acknowledge, is very
far from being merely a literary advantage.[1]

[1] This and the last part of page 281, is from the Report of the English
School Commissioners in favor of retaining the Study of the Classics.

XIV.

I AM prepared to vindicate the high place which has hitherto been allotted to languages in all the famous colleges of the Old World and the New, though I cannot defend the exclusive place which has been given them in some. Without entering upon the psychological question, whether the power of thinking by means of symbols be or be not an original faculty of the mind, or the physiological one, whether its seat, as M. Broca thinks he has proven, be in the left hemisphere of the brain, specially in the posterior part of the third frontal convolution of the left anterior lobe, I am prepared to maintain that it is a natural gift, early appearing and strong in youth. You see it in the young child acquiring its language so spontaneously, and delighting to ring its vocables the live-long day ; in the boy of nine or ten years of age, learning Latin — when he could not master a science — quite as quickly as the man of mature age. Now, in the systematic training of the mind, we should not set ourselves against, but rather fall in with, this natural tendency and facility. Boys can acquire a language when they are not able to wrestle with any other severe study ; and why should they

This Extract is from the Address delivered by James McCosh, D.D., LL.D., on " Academic Teaching in Europe," on the occasion of his Inauguration as President of the College of New Jersey, Princeton, October 27, 1868.

not be employed in what they are capable of doing?
There are persons forever telling us that children
should be taught to attend to " things " rather than
" words." But then words are " things," having an
important place in our bodily organization and mental
structure, in both of which the power of speech is one
of the things that raise us above the brutes. And then
it can be shown that it is mainly by language that we
come to get a knowledge of things. This arises not
merely from the circumstance that we get by far the
greater part of our knowledge from our fellow-men
through speech and writing, but because it is, in a
great measure, by words that we are induced, nay compelled, to observe, to compare, to abstract, to analyze,
to classify, to reason. How little can we know of things
without language? How little do deaf mutes know of
things till they are taught the use of signs? I have
known some of them considerably advanced in life
who not only did not know that the soul was immortal;
they did not know that the body was mortal. Children
obtain by far the larger part of their information from
parents, brothers, sisters, nurses, teachers, companions,
and fellow-men and women in general, and this comes
by language. But this is, after all, the least part; it
is in understanding and using intelligently words and
sentences that children are first taught to notice things
and their properties, to discern their differences and
perceive their resemblances. Nature presents us only
with particulars, which, as Plato remarked long ago,
are infinite, and therefore confusing, and the language
formed by our forefathers and inherited by us, puts

them into intelligible groups for us. Nature shows us only concretes, that is, objects with their varied qualities, that is, with complexities beyond the penetration of children, and language makes them intelligible by separating the parts and calling attention to common qualities. Nouns, verbs, adjectives, conjunctions, and other parts of speech in a cultivated tongue, introduce us to things, as men have thought about them in the use of their faculties, and combined them for general and for special purposes; primarily, no doubt, for their own use and advantage, but turning out to be a valuable inheritance to their children, who get access to things with the thought of ages superinduced upon them — as it were, set in a frame-work for us that we may study them more easily. In the phrases of a civilized tongue, we have a set of discriminations and comparisons spontaneously fashioned by our ancestors, often more fresh and subtile, always more immediately and practically useful, than those of the most advanced science. Then a new language introduces us to new generalizations and new abstractions, made, it may be, by a people of a different genius and differently situated, and thus widens and varies our view of things, and saves us from being the slaves of the words of our own tongue; saves us, in fact, from putting words for things, putting counters for money (as Hobbes says), which we should be apt to do if we knew only one word for the thing. Charles V. uttered a deep truth, whether he understood it or no, when he said that a man was as many times a man as he acquired a new tongue. Then, in learning a language grammatically,

whether our own or another, we have to learn or gather
rules and judiciously apply them, to see the rule in the
example and collect the rule out of the example ; and
in all this the more rudimentary intellectual powers,
not only the memory, but the apprehension and quickness of perception and discernment are as quite effectually called forth and ·disciplined as by any other study
in which the youthful mind is capacitated to engage.

I have been struggling to give expression in a few
sentences to thoughts which it would require a whole
lecture fully to unfold. Such considerations seem to
me to prove that we should continue to give to language an important — I have not said an exclusive —
place in the younger collegiate classes. Among languages a choice must be made, and there are three
which have such claims that every student should be
instructed in them ; and there are others which have
claims on those who have special aptitudes and desti-
nations in life. There is the Latin, important in itself,
and from the part which it has played. It has an educational value from the breadth, regularity, and logical
accuracy of its structure, giving us a fine specimen of
grammar, from its clear expression, and from its stately
methodical march, like that of a Roman army. It is
of inestimable value from its literature, second only to
that of Greece in the Old World, and to that of England and Germany in modern times, and a model
still to be looked to by English and by Germans, if
they would make progress as they have hitherto done.
Then, besides its intrinsic worth, it has historical value
as the mother of several other European languages, as

the Italian, the French, the Spanish, and Portuguese, to all of which it is the best introduction, and, as one of the venerated grandmothers of our own, ready to tell us of its descent, its lineage and its history; and, let us not forget, as the transmitter of ancient and eastern learning to modern times and western countries; and as the common language for ages in literature, philosophy, law, and theology, and thus containing treasures to which every educated man requires some time or other to have access. Then there is the Greek, the most subtile, delicate, and expressive of all old languages, embodying the fresh thoughts of the most intellectual people of the ancient world, and containing a literature which is unsurpassed, perhaps not equalled, for the loveliness, purity, and grace of its poetry, for the combined firmness and flexibility of its prose, as seen, for instance, in Plato, who can mount to the highest sublimities and go down to the lowest familiarities without falling—like the elephant's trunk, equally fitted to tear an oak or lift a straw. And it is never to be forgotten that it is the language of the New Testament; that it was the favorite language of the Reformers. Luther said: "If we do not keep up the tongues, we will not keep up the gospel"; and so the stream is still to be encouraged to flow on, if we would keep up the connection between Christianity and its fountain. A nation studiously giving up its attention to these tongues would be virtually cut off from the past, and would be apt to become stagnant, like a pool into which no streams flow, and from which none issue, instead of a lake receiving pure waters from above, and giving them out below. These languages differ widely from ours, but just because they so do, they serve a good purpose, letting us into a different order and style of thought, less analytic, more synthetic, as it is commonly said, more concrete, as I express it; that is, introducing us to things as they are, and in their natural connection. True, they are *dead* languages, but then, just because they are so, we can get a completed biography of them; and, as we dissect them, they lie passive, like bodies under the knife of the anatomist. As Hobbes expresses it, " they have put off flesh and blood to put on immortality "; they are dead, and yet they live; live in the works which have been written in them with their diversity of knowledge, living specially in their literature which is imperishable, which, for fitness of phraseology, brevity, clearness, directness, severity, are models for all ages, bringing us back to simplicity when we should err by extravagance; and to be specially studied by the rising generation in our time, when there is so much of looseness and inflation, stump oratory and sensationalism. It would be difficult to define it, but we all know what is meant by a *classical taste;* there are persons who seem to acquire its chaste color spontaneously, as the ancient Greeks and Romans must have done; but, in fact, it has been mainly fostered by living and breathing in the atmosphere of ancient Greece and Rome; and our youths may acquire it most readily by travelling to the same region where the air is ever pure and fresh. I believe that our language and literature will run a great risk of hopelessly degenerating, if we are not ever restrained and corrected, while we are enlivened and refreshed, by looking to these faultless models.

XV.

In the lore that has come down to us from other days, the student can still commune with the spirits of the illustrious dead. The philosophers, the orators, the historians, and poets of antiquity still speak to us in the very words which they chose for the dress of their undying thoughts. " Shining through the darkness of ages, they still remain stars of changeless and unequalled brilliancy." Their works have served to enrich and embellish the intellects of those who, in later times, have created the literature of their respective countries. All the civilized nations of the earth have drank from the same common fountain. Many of the most polished modern languages are but channels through which, from the same exhaustless reservoir, flow streams of knowledge, fertilizing and enriching the world of thought and feeling. The imagination of the poet, the eloquence of the orator, the understanding of the historian, and the critical acumen of the philosopher, have all been trained and matured by these same great teachers. The principles of their philosophy, poetry, and oratory, originated in the nature of man, and are as permanent and universal as the essential attributes of humanity. Hence they are adapted to

This Chapter is an Extract from an Article in the Biblical Repository for July, 1841, on " The Study of the Classics as an Intellectual Discipline," by Professor Edwin D. Sanborn, LL.D., of Dartmouth College.

all nations and all ages. They have been so freely adopted by subsequent writers, and so fully incorporated in their works, that their origin is almost forgotten, and they are regarded as the common property of the literati. The golden coin has been so often exchanged that its superscription is effaced, and the fortunate possessor now enjoys the reward of the original miner.

Thus the treasury of modern science and literature is replenished by the spoils of ages ; and our philosophers and poets are wearing laurels plucked from the brows of ancient sages and bards. Every generation adds something to the world's intellectual treasures. The literature of our own age, therefore, possesses elements as ancient as the origin of human civilization. There is not a civilized nation of past times to which our scholars are not indebted. They laid the foundations upon which we are building. They enriched the soil from which the human mind now derives its nutriment. They originated many of the arts and much of the literature which are reflecting honor upon our institutions.

The languages to which modern nations are most deeply indebted are thus beautifully characterized by H. N. Coleridge : " Greek — the shrine of the genius of the old world, as universal as our race ; as individual as ourselves ; of infinite flexibility ; of indefatigable strength ; with the complication and distinctness of nature herself ; with words like pictures ; with words like the gossamer film of summer, at once the variety and picturesqueness of Homer ; the gloom and intensity of Aeschylus ; not compressed to the closest by Thucydides, nor fathomed to the bottom by Plato; not sounding with all its thunders nor lit up with all its ardors under the Promethean torch of Demosthenes. And Latin — the voice of empire and of war, of law and of state; rigid in its construction, reluctantly yielding to the flowery yoke of Horace, although opening glimpses of Greek-like splendor in the occasional inspirations of Lucretius; proved to the utmost by Cicero, and by him found wanting, yet majestic in its barrenness, impressive in its conciseness; the true language of history; uniform in its air, whether touched by the stern and haughty Sallust, by the open and discursive Livy, or by the reserved and thoughtful Tacitus."

But it is not my object to eulogize the ancient languages. They have outlived the ravages of time and barbarism. Like the native diamond, they have acquired a higher polish by incessant use, and, in some instances, have received new lustre from the very blows that were dealt to mar their beauty. Omitting, therefore, the intrinsic excellence of these languages, as instruments of thought, and the rich materials of poetry, history, and philosophy, which they contain, let us contemplate the influence of a diligent and judicious study of them upon the development of the youthful mind.

The classics have probably been injured as much by indiscreet friends as by open enemies. When it is gravely announced that the classics are the storehouse of all knowledge, that every modern author only repeats, for the thousandth time, what was better said by the ancients, and that they are the only efficient helps

to a liberal education, the common sense of the intelligent reader revolts at such groundless assertions. We
do not affirm, therefore, that the ancients possessed all
wisdom — only that they were wise; nor that a knowledge of the classics is absolutely essential to a good
education — only that it is highly important; nor that
classical study should alone or chiefly occupy the student's attention — but that it ought to hold a prominent
place in every.system of education which claims to be
liberal. The design of all intellectual training is to
develop and strengthen the native faculties of the mind.
It does not aim at mere acquisition, but at origination.
Its design is, not so much to learn what others have
thought wisely, as to think wisely ourselves; not so
much to accumulate as to originate thoughts. It is
rather learning *how* to think than *what* to think; pro-
viding intellectual strength and skill rather than intellectual stores. The great object of the young student,
therefore, is to expand and invigorate the mind, to
promote an harmonious development of all its powers;
to improve the memory, control the attention, give
accuracy and discrimination to the judgment, refinement and elegance to the taste, and to impart to all
these faculties such a manly vigor and compactness as
will enable him to grapple successfully with the most
difficult and abstruse questions of philosophy, and, at
the same time, appreciate and enjoy the most splendid
creations of imagination. But some one may ask : Do
you pretend that the classics can accomplish this great
work alone ? Most certainly not. A mere classical
scholar is by no means a thoroughly educated man.

A complete education contemplates other objects besides intellectual culture. Man needs physical and
moral as well as mental training. He has a will to
be regulated, passions to be governed, appetites to be
checked, and affections to be cultivated. The influence
of classical study in these respects, it is not our object
now to discuss. We wish to show its utility as *an intellectual discipline;* and, be it remembered, while we
maintain the importance and excellence of such discipline, we do not exclude other sciences, or deny their
utility. We would not recommend the exclusive application of the mind to any department of knowledge.
It is only the combined influence of different studies
which can make the finished scholar, the able reasoner,
and deep thinker. While we make these concessions
in favor of other sciences, we may safely assert that
the study of the languages is the best discipline for the
tyro, and one of the most valuable helps to the mature
scholar. The mathematics and metaphysics are suited
to a more advanced stage of education, and are peculiarly adapted to develop the reasoning powers, though
less efficient in the cultivation of a correct taste, a
chastened imagination, and a tenacious memory.

A great part of the work of education is preparatory.
The foundation must be laid broad and deep before a
stable superstructure can be reared. How often have
we been told that the mind, like the body, requires exercise in order to its complete development? Who
does not know, that without that exercise, the mind
must forever remain infantile and weak? It should be
the first object of the teacher, therefore, to promote

25 *

intellectual activity. It is in vain to crowd the young mind with facts and theories; the understanding must be enlarged before it can contain; the judgment must be matured before it can decide; the memory must be strengthened before it can retain; the taste must be cultivated before it can distinguish. Knowledge cannot be poured into the mind like water into a cask — as the ancient sophists taught — without regard to capacity. As well might you teach the infant to walk, by presenting to his eye the process upon a canvass, as teach the young pupil to think by the bare presentation of facts. In both cases the child must exercise his own powers; and that he may properly exercise his mind, he must be furnished with appropriate subjects of contemplation. The proper stimulus must be applied, and a right direction given to his thoughts. If the material be such as to employ all the powers of the mind at once, time will be saved and great advantage secured. The mind is enlarged by expansion and not by accretion.

If the business of education has been properly stated, it follows that that course of study which most effectually secures the object of all mental training is the best. Let us now examine more particularly the claims of the classics to our attention. Let us notice their influence upon the individual faculties of the mind — the memory, the attention, judgment, imagination, taste, and reasoning powers.

1. In the acquisition of the words and grammatical forms of a new language, the memory is essentially improved. This is, perhaps, one of the least important results of this discipline. The memory is more easily

trained than any other faculty of the mind. Almost any exercise will be profitable to the memory of the child; still, in the process of a regular education, economy of time and mental advantage should determine our choice of means. If we take into view the collateral benefits which result from classical study as a discipline for the memory, its influence in creating mental capacity and stimulating to mental effort, by invigorating the mind, and, at the same time, furnishing the richest materials of thought, it may be questioned whether we can select a better exercise for the young student.

2. The study of the languages enables the student to command the attention at will, to fix it for any length of time upon a single point, and to form those habits of patient investigation and nice discrimination which are essential to intellectual eminence. This is the most difficult and painful part of the whole business of education. Indeed, it is difficult for the best trained minds to gain a perfect control of the attention so as to command it at will and concentrate it for a longer or a shorter period, upon a given subject. This habit is by no means the gift of nature. The mind naturally loves ease or amusement better than toil and solid improvement. It is disinclined to patient thought. It loves to indulge its own idle reveries, to sport with its own spontaneous musings, to brood over the creations of its own imagination, and to follow its own vagaries to the ends of the earth. " Every man who has instructed others," says Dr. Johnson, " can tell how much patience it requires to recall vagrant inattention, to stimulate

sluggish indifference, and to rectify absurd misapprehensions." "In order to grapple successfully with the difficulties of science, the mind should be brought to the task in a collected and unruffled state. No half-subdued gust of passion should start up ; no melancholy train of thought should pour in its muddy current ; no sudden start of skittish fancy or engrossing remembrance of darling diversion ; no dreams of romance should come in to ruffle the smooth surface. The whole soul should be only a mirror of thought, whose every image should be well defined and without distortion."

Such a perfect control of the emotions, passions, and thoughts can only be acquired by the truly philosophic mind, and that by intense application and rigid discipline. Still trial, effort, and practice may do much, even for the feeblest intellect. Confined attention is always irksome to the undisciplined mind, and it readily welcomes any amusing day-dream, which may help to expel unwelcome thoughts.

Now, it is found by long experience that the study of the languages is an excellent remedy for languid attention and intermittent application. It is impossible to advance a single step without careful attention. The interpretation of language requires thought, reflection, and reasoning. In the more difficult passages it requires undivided attention and intense application. The student must not only have a clear idea of the separate meaning of the words, but also of the thought presented to the reader by their combination. He must not only be familiar with the general meaning of each word, but he must know its particular meaning in the

passage he is examining. He must form a just conception of the import of each sentence, and of its relation
to the context. The precise thing indicated by every
word and every sentence must be presented to the
mental eye, and the exact shade of thought which lay
in the author's mind must be exhibited under new
forms and in new relations, so as not to lose one of its
original characteristics. This requires a careful attention to all the circumstances of the writer's situation,
the time, the place, and the cause of his writing. The
author's peculiar mental and physical constitution,
his mode of life, and habits of thinking should also be
investigated. Sometimes an author cannot be fully
understood and appreciated without an intimate knowledge of the geographical, commercial, and political condition, domestic manners, mental habits, private and
public life of the people to which he belonged. So that
frequently the whole field of ancient lore must be ex-
plored, and the whole world of antiquities be laid under
contribution to illustrate a single author.

The connection of each word, thought, and paragraph, with every other portion of the work, must be
carefully scrutinized, lest in translating we make the
writer contradict himself. The nature of the subject
discussed, and the logical sequence of the arguments
must also be noticed, so that our interpretation may not
be incongruous or irrelevant. This process requires a
vigorous exercise of the powers of invention and comprehension. Thus the mind is kept in a constant state
of healthy activity and pleasurable excitement. Its
natural appetency for new truths and new relations is

abundantly gratified. The pleasure of acquisition be-
guiles the tediousness of severe study, and the habit
of patient investigation and critical analysis is formed
without the consciousness of fatigue. " The power
of making nice distinctions and of separating things,
which, to the ignorant and inexperienced, appear alike,"
says Professor Stuart, "is one of the most important
powers ever acquired and exercised by the human
mind. I must believe that linguistic study, directed as
it ought to be, namely to acquire a knowledge of *things*
that are designated by the words of a foreign language,
is one of the most important means of improving and
strengthening the faculty of nice discernment that is
within the reach of a young man." The same author
acknowledges himself more indebted to this discipline
than to all his other studies. *The judgment* is also
called into active exercise during the whole process of
interpretation, in unravelling and recomposing every
sentence and paragraph, but more especially in analyzing an entire work. The same faculty may be
judiciously exercised in comparing synonymes, in determining their exact shades of difference, and in deciding
why a particular word is used in a given place instead
of another. In reading different authors their peculiarities may be noticed, their excellences or defects
compared, and their merits determined. In this way
even the young student may create for himself a standard of merit, and form some notion of a higher and
philosophical criticism. When he has once learned to
think with precision and to discriminate with accuracy,
he will easily command right words and forcible ex-

pression for the vehicle of his thoughts. The classical
student, if he have clear ideas and definite notions of
what he wishes to communicate, cannot want for words.
His familiarity with the best models will generally
secure him from inaccuracies in the use of language
and offences against taste.

3. The study of the classics tends to refine, chasten,
and exalt the imagination. Perhaps there is no one of
the native powers of the mind which usually exerts so
important an influence upon our happiness or misery
in this life as the imagination. If properly trained and
directed it may become the source of the most exquisite
pleasure ; if neglected and abused, of the most excru-
ciating torment. In those departments of literature
which are the peculiar province of the imagination, the
ancients stand unrivalled. In their poetry and oratory
the student is introduced to the most splendid creations
of genius. It is the prevailing opinion of some of our
best critics that the infancy of society is most favorable
to poetic excellence. Everything then is new. All
the impressions of the bard are fresh and vivid. The
current of his thoughts gushes out warm from nature's
living fount. As men advance in society they become
less susceptible to those lively emotions, excited by an
ardent imagination. They deal more in general ideas
and cold abstractions. The reasoning powers become
more acute, the imagination more tame. The experimental sciences, which require time for maturity, advance with the improvement of society, while poetry
remains stationary or retrogrades. " As civilization
advances," says Macaulay, " poetry almost necessarily

declines. In proportion as men know more and think more, they look less at individuals and more at classes. They therefore make better theories and worse poems."

If this theory be true the student can kindle the true poetic enthusiasm in his own bosom only by stealing a coal from the altar of the ancient muses. A thorough acquaintance with ancient poetry will undoubtedly give him a just notion of the office of the imagination in literature, and reveal to him the secret process by which this " shaping spirit " creates the magic wonders of its power. It is not enough that the scholar views and admires these unequalled productions of genius; he must become familiar with them and feel their influence. It is not sufficient to notice and treasure up the beautiful conceits and striking expressions of an author; but he must strive to reproduce in himself the inspiration of the bard and the enthusiasm of the orator. He must, for the time, forget self, and, in imagination at least, exchange places with the author, live in the very midst of the stirring scenes that called forth the orator's pathos or kindled the poet's fire, breathe in his spirit, be moved by the same impulses of feeling that actuated him, be touched by his sorrow, be melted by his tears, catch his fire, feel the same emotions of sublimity, and enjoy the same beauties that elevated or ravished his soul, soar with him in imagination, and train the whole intellectual being to like modes of thought. In this way he may acquire sufficient strength and nerve to wield the giant armor of men of other days.

By this process alone can the student become an

adept in classic lore. Some practical men may cry
out: "Enthusiasm! extravagance!" Admit that it is
enthusiasm. Great attainments were never made in
any branch of literature, science, or art, without some
degree of professional enthusiasm. This devotion of
eminent scholars and artists to their favorite pursuits
is the very secret of their success.

4. The taste is refined and matured by this same
discipline. By constant association with refined society
the individual is himself refined. The mind, in like
manner, is moulded by the objects it contemplates. By
long familiarity with these finished models of composition, the principles of philosophic criticism are gradually acquired, and a cultivated taste is unconsciously
formed, so that in writing the student instinctively
adopts what is beautiful in sentiment and faultless in
expression, and rejects what is vulgar and anomalous.
Though he may forget every word and every thought
he has ever learned from ancient authors, his time will
not have been lost. There still remains in the soul
"an intellectual residuum," a kind of mental precipi-
tate, which, though differing from all the elements that
were originally thrown into the intellectual crucible,
still contains their very essence and is superior to them
all. The student's taste is classical. And can we use
a more expressive epithet? Can there be higher praise?
After long acquaintance with classic excellences, he
has an intuitive perception of the beauties of a literary
production. He does not need to recur to the standard
he once used. He has risen from the condition of a
learner to that of judge, and his nice perception of the

26

beauties of a finished composition has become a part of his mental constitution. The man who has been thus educated, can scarcely become so degraded as to lose entirely his taste for the beautiful, the poetic, and the sublime in literature. Nor is this discipline, which thus forms the taste and polishes the mind, a mere unrequited toil, destitute of pleasure or profit. There is a pleasure in mere intellectual activity. We are so constituted that without exertion we cannot enjoy. Knowledge is the proper aliment of the soul, and the highest mental enjoyment results from the uninterrupted pursuit and the constant acquisition of new truths. A philosopher once said: " If the gods would grant me all knowledge I would not thank them for the boon ; but if they would grant me the everlasting pursuit of it I would render them everlasting thanks."

5. Classical study is eminently useful in strengthening the reasoning powers. The art of reasoning is one of the most complicated and difficult of all arts. It can be acquired only by long and laborious training. Perfection in this art would require all knowledge. The noblest productions of human reason have resulted from the combined influence of all liberal studies. The higher mathematics furnish an excellent discipline for minds that have already been partially matured by an appropriate early education. But as mathematical reasoning alone admits of absolute certainty, and all moral reasoning is based upon probabilities, classical study is found to be an excellent co-worker with the mathematics and metaphysics in preparing men for the diversified employments of life. In most of our daily avocations

we reason from probable evidence. The difficulty of
this process is increased by the ambiguity of human
language. In the business of translating from a foreign
tongue the mind is constantly employed in weighing
evidence and balancing probabilities. It is made familiar with the very process of reasoning which we need
to employ in the intercourse of life. " The mind,"
says Dugald Stewart, " in following any train of reasoning beyond the circle of the mathematical sciences,
must necessarily carry on, along with the logical deduction expressed in words, another logical process, of a
far nicer and more difficult nature, that of fixing, with
a rapidity which escapes our memory, the precise sense
of every word which is ambiguous, by the relation in
which it stands to the general scope of the argument."

Now this is precisely the student's occupation who is
translating a foreign language. He is incessantly employed in determining the meaning of words from the
connection in which they stand, constantly weighing
evidence and drawing conclusions, if he does not use a
translation ; for in that case he is only exercising his
memory. Each word has various significations. He
must carefully examine the sentence and then fix upon
the appropriate definition. In this way he is for years
training the mind to the most accurate discrimination
in comparing words and adjusting nice shades of meaning. Thus he learns to practise the most delicate and
difficult part of the art of reasoning. In what other
way could one become so intimately acquainted with
the right use of language which is the great instrument
of all ratiocination ? Without a minute knowledge of

definitions and of the nice shades of meaning which
result from the subject discussed and the connection
of the argument, no person can speak with precision,
or reason with force and perspicuity. Many eminent
teachers have been so fully convinced of the utility of
classical studies in invigorating and maturing the mental powers, that they give it as their opinion, that, if
two students of equal capacity be put upon a course of
study for six years — the one pursuing English studies
wholly, and the other devoting one third of the time to
the languages — at the end of the course the classical
student, by his superior discipline, will have acquired
a better English education aside from his knowledge of
the languages than the other. An eminent French
philosopher supposes if two boys were put to study —
the one upon the classics and the other upon the sciences — and, " on leaving the first class," the classical
scholar should, by some accident, lose every word he
had learned, but retain his intellectual powers in the
same state of maturity as before the loss, that this
scholar, beginning his acquisitions anew, would, at the
close of his course, be better educated and better prepared for the business of life than the other, who had
devoted the whole time to other pursuits. This may be
an extravagant opinion, yet by no means so extravagant
as many would suppose. It is undoubtedly true that
the time which many students think absolutely wasted
upon the classics, is the very seed-time of life. It is the
apprenticeship of mind; the time when they are acquiring strength and skill for greater effort; the time when
they are preparing their weapons for future warfare.

XVI.

AND now we come to the last tug of the war—Latin and Greek. Are they to go? Whoever says "Yes," I adhere to "No;" and if I could, I would say it in thunder. Here, too, however far I should go for pure addition, or however willing to allow a certain slight amount of option, I should be against any considerable subtraction. In the great English schools and universities they may wash away much, and welcome; but we in Scotland cannot spare any of our Greek and Latin. There are various grounds on which the continued study of Latin and Greek might be maintained. There is the well-known argument of the drill these languages give. The argument has been sneered at, but it is too stout to be overcome. There are few things of which I am more convinced. The first requisite in all education is training to accuracy; and it is my distinct experience, checked again and again by observation, that no ordinary agency has yet been invented comparable, for its stringency in clearing inaccuracy out of the mind of youth, to an exact school discipline in Latin. O yes! but we must have done with the mere study of words, you know; we must have a knowledge of things! This is the favorite form of expression

This Extract is from an Address delivered at the Ceremonial of Graduation at the University of Edinburgh, April 22, 1868, by Professor Masson.

with the anti-classicists — Things *versus* Words. I am
sorry to find Mr. Lowe, with his great strength and wit,
leading some of the worst forms of Philistinism, and
lending his authority to this particular clap-trap.
Things, indeed! Are things only pokers, shovels,
rocks, trees, fields, harbors at home, and townships in
Australia? Are not the thoughts of Plato things, and
Homer's heroes and battles, and the grand imaginations
and choral wails of Sophocles, and Demosthenes's bolts
of reasoning, and Livy's fine legends, and Horace's
consummate lyrics and maxims, and what Virgil musi-
cally chants, and the versatile speculations of Cicero,
or the more ferocious flamings of Lucretius? Is not
the whole life of the ancient world into which the
classics admit us also a world of things? May not
commerce with some of those things — let us say the
things in one of Sophocles's tragedies — be as edifying,
leave as many flakes and recollections of precious substance in the mind, as an hour among the pokers and
shovels and the commercial statistics of all our col-
onies? And if, as is argued, this commerce is best at
first hand; if there is an advantage in respect of matter
even, in that close and minute contact with the meaning of the classic authors which reading in the original
insures; and if, at the same time, one can drink in
only by that means the full beauty of the form, and
acquire a sense, even to fastidiousness, of what beauty
of form is for ever; if all this is true, and if (which
must always be remembered) the modern has still to
be added in full bulk, and all parts of it in their due
proportion, then I see not why classical studies, which

have certainly assisted in educating for us hitherto most of our ablest and best, need yet be abandoned. Have we advanced so far; are we so princely? But, again, about that statement that we must study things rather than words. What if there were a sense, not destitute of practical significance, in which things resolve themselves into words? This I will not argue, but I am entitled to assert, surely, that words are, at all events, one kind of things. Nay, more, not only are words things, but they are a most interesting and important class of things, and the study of them is about the most subtile and fruitful study on which man can engage. And here we are in sight of a final argument for classical learning, of a very special character, and not frequently referred to, but which ought to be of particular weight with the advocates of strict or positive science. Latin and Greek are not finished and stereotyped studies, any more than is logic, or chemistry, or political economy. They retain their names, but they sustain modifications from the course of general thought and knowledge. They imbibe what is around them, and grow, and change their color, by what they imbibe. The Latin and Greek training of the present century is different from that of the eighteenth, just as that was different from what had prevailed in the seventeenth, and the Latin and Greek, besides their other recommendations, have now a peculiar one. Being the two dead languages most minutely and grammatically taught in our schools and universities, and most worthy of being so taught, on account of the treasures to which they are the keys, they are

also, or they might be made also (along with our vernacular, and a mere hand-book of Indo-European or
other radicals), the most convenient illustrations and
furtherance of that new linguistic science, or general
Science of Language and Grammar, the prospects of
which are absolutely enormous. Philology, to use the
old name for it, promises to be a calculus of as great
potency for solving problems of the human past as
geology has been for solving problems of the pre-human
past, but of still greater exquisitness and complexity.
It is divisible into the allied sciences of glottology, or
the science of elementary vocalizations, their origin,
significance, and combinations historically into speech;
and mythology, or the science of the primitive, transmitted, and perhaps organic, imaginations and conceptions of the human race. Let any one look into even
such comparatively popular works as Professor Max
Müller's " Chips from a German Workshop ; " or the
American Professor Whitney's " Lectures on Language," and he will have an idea of what may come
out of the study of words. Why, you can see that,
through this study, scholars are already twining their
hands in the mane of back-rushing Time, and compell-
ing the monster to stand, and extracting from her some
of her obscurest secrets. Science against philology!
Why, philology is the latest of the sciences. The
physical sciences conspiring against linguistic studies !
Why, gentlemen, this is Joseph's half-brethren selling
him into Egypt, on account of his dreams of permanent
supremacy and his parti-colored coat.

XVII.

In the year 1778, in the midst of our revolutionary
conflict, when the resolution to maintain the Declaration
of Independence had become an unalterable purpose,
the brothers Samuel Phillips, of Andover, and John
Phillips, of Exeter — *par nobile fratrum* — under the
moving influence of the illustrious son of the former,
Samuel Phillips, Jr., of Andover, for " the safety and
happiness of the people," for " the good of mankind "
and the service of " our Heavenly Benefactor," founded
this Institution, the first incorporated Academy in New
England. They established it for a twofold purpose,
having for its secondary object the preparation of young
men for the business of teaching, and for those active
pursuits of life which require the practical application
of the mathematical and physical sciences, together with
a superior knowledge of the English tongue, but having
for its primary and great end the due preparation for a
university course, and the proper commencement and
foundation of that integral, symmetrical, and complete
culture, which involves the harmonious development
of all the higher faculties and capacities in their true
order and proportion, and which, in the words of Milton,

This Chapter is from an Address on " Classical Studies as a Part of Academic Education," delivered at the Dedication of the New Academic Hall
of Phillips Academy, Andover, Feb. 7, 1866, by Hon. Philip H. Sears, of
Boston.

" fits a man to perform justly, skilfully, and magnanimously all the offices, both private and public, of peace and war."

The importance and necessity of the secondary object and function of the institution they fully appreciated and insisted on, as their trustees have done ever since; but, in order that there might not be wanting to our rising nation those great supports and ornaments, the enlightened divine, jurist, statesman, scholar, and man of letters, and true scientific philosopher, they aimed principally to provide here the solid foundation for a truly liberal culture, planting the chief corner-stone thereof deep in the study of the classics. For the best discipline and cultivation of the highest powers of the human intellect, the reason, memory, imagination, and taste; for the best preparation for the learned professions, as well as for the duties of the republican citizen and patriot, and the Christian scholar; and, in the words of the founders, for furnishing the students " with such general maxims of conduct as may best enable them to pass through all the several connections and various scenes incident to human life, with ease, reputation, and comfort,"— they believed there was nothing so effective as thorough training in classical studies; and accordingly the successive trustees and instructors of this academy have faithfully carried into effect the original design and plan of education, devoting the first department to classical training, and the second department to the study of mathematical and physical science and the English language and literature.

The expediency and utility of such scientific and

English course as is here pursued, so extensive, complete, and efficient, and the importance of its influence in the community, have never been called in question ; on the contrary, the peculiar tendencies of our people and times secure to it from all, unqualified appreciation and commendation. But, from time to time, and especially in very recent times, under the influence of the answers made to the Parliamentary Commission upon the great schools of England by the scientific men of that country, the propriety of studying the classic languages, and particularly the Greek language, as part of an academic or collegiate education, has been made the subject of attacks the most elaborate and most widely spread abroad through popular channels, addressing the peculiar predispositions of our people, and calling perhaps for some defence of classical study on an occasion like this ; especially when, by the testimony of the same scientific men, by reasoning that never has been, nor can be, answered, and by the actual results of the career of this academy, the classical course here pursued may be not only perfectly vindicated, but commended to still higher and wider approval.

The favorite objections now so much in vogue against classical study as part of a liberal education, which most require our notice, may be stated in few words, and be answered, I believe, almost as briefly.

It is urged in these objections, First, that many desirous of obtaining superior education have no aptitude for classical studies, and therefore a different kind of study and discipline ought to be provided for them. Secondly, that the observing powers of the mind are

developed in the order of nature at an earlier age than
the powers of reflection and reasoning; that certain
branches of natural science are better fitted to train the
powers of observation than the study of the classics, and
therefore classical study ought to be removed from the
course of all early academic education. Thirdly, that
classical study is superfluous as a means of intellectual
discipline, being inferior for that purpose to the study
of the physical sciences and modern languages, which
alone are accounted of actual use in life, and therefore
these latter studies ought to supersede and replace the
classics; and, Fourthly, that the great progress of science
and increase of knowledge within the last half century,
together with the impatience felt in this country to
enter early into the active pursuits of life, make any
general scholarship, or general culture altogether impracticable, necessitate a minute subdivision of intellectual labor, and require that all preliminary general
education should be reduced to a minimum, and be
superseded in great measure by special professional
training.

These several objections, I need not say in this
presence, are founded mainly upon mistakes of fact,
or of reasoning, so evident to those familiar with the
subject, as to obviate the necessity of making any
elaborate reply.

That those who have no aptitude for classical study,
but have capacities alone adapted to the physical and
practical sciences, or modern utilitarian studies, should,
nevertheless, be obliged to pursue a classical course, no
advocate of classical studies in this country, and least

of all, any acting under the constitution of this academy, ever claims; the English department of this institution, the technological institutes, the scientific schools connected with our colleges, are peculiarly fitted for such. Let them enter there, and pursue the studies and adopt the vocations best suited to them.

Again, that the power of accurate external observation has commonly an earlier development than the powers of reflection, and that the early study of the elements of natural history will best train the mind in exact habits and methods of outward observation and classification, may be readily granted; but what the friends of classical study claim is, that the reflective and reasoning powers, when in the order of nature their active development does begin, equally require their proper nourishment, exercise, and discipline, and that thorough classical study is the proper and best nourishment and discipline.

According to the testimony given to the Parliamentary Commission by the scientific men, and especially by Sir Charles Lyell, Faraday, Owen, Carpenter, and Hooker, the development of the powers of accurate observation and classification, begins as early as the age of eight or nine years, and all the necessary gymnastic training of these powers may be completed by the age of twelve or fourteen years. According to the testimony of the same scientific men as well as upon common observation, the active, marked development of the reflective and reasoning powers begins ordinarily between the ages of thirteen and fifteen years, and their discipline ought then to commence, and to be continued through the course of academic and collegiate education. The statistics of this academy, on examination, show that the average age of entering the classical department through the whole period, from the first to the present time, does not differ much from fourteen years, the average age of entering during recent years being still greater, and only very few in recent years entering earlier than the age of thirteen; leaving ample time for the previous study of the common branches of English education, including elementary botany and zoölogy, at the public schools established under the laws of the commonwealth. The classical course of this academy begins, therefore, with the active normal development of the reflective and reasoning powers, and this classical course, with a suitable collateral course of mathematics to be duly continued in college, it is hardly too much to say, is the best conceivable discipline for the three years through which the course extends.

For the cultivation of the power and habit of internal, reflex observation of the mind's own processes of thought, feeling, and expression, — for the cultivation of the powers and habits of sustained, continuous attention, of persistent application, of nice discrimination, of searching and exact analysis, of moral or probable reasoning and consecutive reflection, of clear perception in attaining distinct ideas with the ability of precise expression, of well-trained judgment in weighing and comparing conflicting considerations, of abstraction, memory, shaping imagination, critical and refined taste; what discipline can be found or imagined, to be compared with thorough study of the classic languages and literature?

The study of language is at once an objective and a subjective study, and through its subjective part it is the best introduction of all to the genuine study of the philosophy of mind, the best introduction to that real knowledge of the mind and heart of man which is so essential in the professions of divinity and law, in the questions of history and of politics, in the arts of design, in all the active dealings of life, and is not less important as necessary preparation for the true philosophical study of nature. Call to mind for a moment in a summary and simple form the actual process of studying the languages. After learning the rules of grammar with appropriate illustrations, in attempting to render from the unknown tongue into the vernacular, the student has in the open volume before him simply a series of printed words, printed characters, that are in themselves mere arbitrary or phonetic signs; by means of the vocabulary and grammar he has suggested to him, in vernacular terms, the various possible ideas, relations, objects, or conceptions of objects which these words, phrases, and forms of construction may be used to represent; but before he can determine what particular thoughts or conceptions are actually intended to be there expressed, he is obliged to turn his attention inward upon his own consciousness, and call up there these various conceptions, and scan them carefully, and compare them exactly with the ascertained meanings in the sentence before him, if any there be, with the known values, to speak in mathematical phrase, or else with the several possible values within the determinate limits, until by much comparison and going backward and forward, to and fro, he is able at length to settle to his own satisfaction the true meaning of the whole sentence and of each of its parts. On the other hand, too, in undertaking to compose in the classic language or to translate into it, inasmuch as he cannot think in that language, and as scarcely any individual word of the vernacular tongue is precisely equivalent in meaning to any individual word of the classic tongue, he will be still more obliged to disrobe his thoughts of their vernacular garb, and look in upon them face to face, and ascertain definitely their real purport and extent, their quality and quantity, before he can express them precisely in classic phraseology. No one can reflect for a moment upon this simple, ordinary process of studying the languages without seeing at once how it contributes to the formation of some of the highest and most important intellectual habits. It takes the youth at an age when during his whole previous life his attention has been given to outward observation, and when the direct study of what Milton calls the "intellective abstractions of logic and metaphysics" would be altogether impossible, and turns the attention inward, and by an indirect method forms the habit of internal observation, and lays the foundation for the subsequent direct study of mental philosophy. And indeed, unless the power of internal observation be thus developed by the early study of languages, the study of mental philosophy itself at any period of life will too often become merely learning the speculations and conclusions of others, without any testing of them by direct inspection and study of actual consciousness.

The same process, it is equally evident, must produce by its direct effect, habitual clearness and precision, both of thought and expression, which Locke makes to be the most important work of education. It involves, too, necessarily close application and steady attention. It constantly exercises the understanding in analyzing, discriminating, comparing, in weighing and judging of probabilities of meaning, and thence forming conclusions: in short, in all the operations of practical logic; and when the student has to prepare himself also to answer the manifold questions that may be put to him in the manner illustrated so admirably in that invaluable work, "The Method of Classical Study," in respect to the composition, derivation, and affiliation of words, the peculiarities of idiom, the exact force of particles, phrases, and forms of construction, the arrangement and syntax of the whole, the comparison of the classic languages with each other, and with the English, as the basis for understanding universal grammar and the philosophy of language, together with all questions of ethnography, mythology, geography, history, biography, antiquities, and of the logic, the rhetoric, the style and art of composition of the author, what various resources, as well as powers, are not of necessity called into requisition ?

But how much all these various mental exercises and efforts are enlarged and intensified when the student in due course comes to the more difficult portions of classic study, to those condensed, elliptical speeches in Thucydides, or to those long, complicated passages of Livy, wherein the author, taking advantage of the pecu-

27 *

liar means for transposition in the arrangement and
collocation of words and clauses given to the classic
languages by their properties of inflection through de-
clension, conjugation, and comparison, thereby dispensing
so much with the use of prepositions, adverbs, auxiliaries,
and pronouns, for purposes of artistic effect, involves his
intricate sentences with clause enfolded within clause,
with qualification upon qualification, limitation after
limitation, governing words removed far from the words
governed, qualifying words far from those qualified,
but all the parts connected together by nicely adjusted
mechanism, and the whole almost as difficult of comprehension, and grasp, in one general view as the most
complicated pieces of modern machinery.   And yet the
work of comprehending and interpreting throughout is
to be accomplished by the student himself, through the
exertions of his own understanding, with such aid only,
often absolutely necessary, as the judicious teacher or
editor may think it wise to give.   For let it be remembered, that, by the methods of study here pursued, the
student of to-day, as truly as the student of three centuries ago, in endeavoring to make out the sense of
each successive passage or sentence of the classic author,
has to exercise his own faculties originally upon the
solution of the problem of its meaning.   With most
valuable aid upon the abstruse points, but without aid
in other parts, he has to work his way laboriously, per-
severingly through the difficulties of the question ; and
it is this patient, persistent, strenuous, intellectual
exertion, that most effectively develops into active energy
all the native powers of the understanding.

The physical sciences, evidently, cannot supply this place of classical studies as mental discipline. After the early study of botany and zoölogy for forming habits of observation and classification, the physical sciences for the most part are communicated to the student as general results already attained, illustrated by simple experiments, and requiring very little intellectual effort for their comprehension, or else they belong to a much later stage of education, after an advanced course of mathematics, like the mathematical parts of astronomy, optics, or electro-magnetism. They are not studied as original investigations of the student himself. In the language of Sir William Hamilton, " Merely to learn what has been already detected and detailed, calls out in the student the very feeblest effort of thought. Consequently, these [physical] studies tend the least to develop the understanding, and even leave it, for aught that they thus effect, in a state of comparative weakness and barbarism."[1] Not even the scientific men of England have ventured to claim for these studies any disciplinary influence to be compared with the classics. But yet that the physical sciences should be studied at some time before the close of the university course, for acquiring knowledge of their principles, and of the important truths embraced in their general results, the friends of classical study are ever among the foremost in maintaining. Nor need the great progress of science and increase of knowledge within the last half century deter any student from acquiring a mastery of the general principles and results of these sciences. Their

[1] Discussions, p. 705.

details belong only to the special cultivator of each science, and are of but little value to any one else. This very progress within the last half century has reduced these sciences to a more systematic form, and, instead of making the acquisition of their general principles and results more difficult, has rendered it far easier than ever before, as has been shown so clearly by Humboldt in his " Cosmos."

Neither, again, can the English, or any other modern language, take the place of the classic languages as the groundwork of intellectual training. Apart from manifold other defects, their relative lack of inflection and consequent use of particles, while denying to them the artistic capabilities of the ancient languages, at the same time impose upon them a comparatively fixed order in the collocation of words and clauses with little possibility of transposition or variation ; and this peculiarity alone would deprive them of a great part of the disciplinary power of the Greek and Latin tongues. In comparison with those tongues, the modern languages can hardly be said to have any grammar, except that inevitable grammar to which the logical laws of human thought subject them. Neither could any text-books be found, or prepared, to compare with the great classic text-books whose critical annotations are the work of ages. From the time that Plato and Aristotle discussed grammar as a part of logic,— from the time that Zenodotus developed its principles as an instrument for the criticism of the text of Homer, and Dionysius Thrax formulized them in Latin for the instruction of Roman youth, down to the latest grammatical or critical work of the German scholar of to-day, the classic languages and authors have been the perpetual subjects of critical study and commentary by the most acute and cultivated minds of twenty centuries. The classics are studied in an atmosphere of light. In comparison, no modern language or author can claim to have any critical exposition or commentary. These living languages rather are, and will be, studied chiefly for actual use in social and business intercourse, or in reading their literary and scientific works for the sake of the subject-matter, and these objects lead to entirely different methods of study, involving but little disciplinary influence.

But, what is far more important, the moulding taste, the ideals, the essential soul of modern literature, are vitally classic. The plastic spirit of Greece is the bond of affinity and sympathy running through all the works of modern genius, uniting them in a common republic of letters, and requiring for their appreciation a participation in the same spirit. In the words of Macaulay, from " that splendid literature of Greece have sprung all the strength, the wisdom, the freedom and the glory of the Western world. . . . . . What shall we say when we reflect that from hence have sprung, directly or indirectly, all the noblest creations of the human intellect ; that from hence were the vast accomplishments, and the brilliant fancy of Cicero, the withering fire of Juvenal, the plastic imagination of Dante, the humor of Cervantes, the comprehension of Bacon, the wit of Butler, the supreme and universal excellence of Shakspeare? All the triumphs of truth and genius over prejudice and power, in every country and in every age, have been the triumphs of Athens." Who, then, without imbibing the same spirit from the same original fountains, shall dream of entering into the inner genius of modern literature, of appreciating its highest artistic beauties, of enjoying its greatest charms, or of being able to make any genuine contributions to it? To cut off American mind from access to this primal source of inspiration, would be to insure a lapse into intellectual barbarism. To no literary man so much as to the American, is classical study essential. Well has it been said by De Tocqueville : " No literature places those fine qualities in which the writers of democracies are naturally deficient, in bolder relief than that of the ancients; no literature, therefore, ought to be more studied in democratic times."

Still more practically essential is classical study to the divine, the jurist, the scientific philosopher, and the. statesman. Protestant theology has been defined by Sir William Hamilton to be substantially " applied philology and criticism." Even though this be not the whole of Christian theology, certainly no man can be thought competent to instruct others in Christian truth who is himself unable to interpret the original writings in which alone the Christian oracles have been transmitted to us. The ordinary text-books, too, of the lawyer, are bristling over with Latin, and the earliest precedents of his profession are in the Latinized French of the Normans, neither of which can be understood without a familiar knowledge of the Latin language. Classical study is also the best, if not absolutely indispensable, preparation for that part of his professional duty which involves the interpretation of constitutions, statutes, ordinances, wills, contracts, and writings of every description. And if the lawyer aspire to that systematic knowledge of principles which constitutes the science of jurisprudence, he must of necessity resort constantly to those great works of the civil law, those peerless monuments of juridicial wisdom, which the Roman tongue contains.

For the right study and interpretation of nature, also, there is no better preparation than early classical training. The physical world, it must not be forgotten, is only a part, only one hemisphere, of the creation of God, and it cannot be understood or interpreted aright, without the light reflected upon it from the counterpart and correspondent hemisphere, which is the mind and soul of man. The physical inquirer, whose training has been wholly in physical pursuits, will find in nature nothing but the operation of mechanical and chemical forces; but the physical student, whose early attention through the study of the languages has been turned back upon the inner consciousness, and who has observed there the essential characteristics of free causality and rational design, will, like the great masters of antiquity, see nature everywhere pervaded and irradiated by the presence of upholding spiritual power, and will learn

"To look through nature up to nature's God."

For the republican statesman what school can be found like the history of the Grecian and Roman republics? What mistakes in that great contest which has just closed might not have been avoided through a more thoughtful study of classic history? With the facts of that history vividly or clearly in mind, who could disbelieve the possibility or the likelihood of civil conflicts in a federate or a consolidated republic? Who delay to gird up all the strength of the nation in the outset for a contest of " Greek meeting Greek " ? Our most distinguished Massachusetts statesmen of classical scholarship, Everett, Quincy, Webster, Choate, foresaw the approaching conflict, and had they all survived in their vigor, they would all undoubtedly in 1861 as in 1831 have brought to the support of the government and flag of their country the united resources of their great statesmanship and eloquence. The same classic history equally supplies an inexhaustible storehouse of political instruction for the future emergencies of the nation and the State.

XVIII.

It might well be matter of surprise that the great masters of antiquity, whose works have stood the test of two thousand years, should at this late day be summoned before the tribunal of public opinion, their merits closely scrutinized, questioned, doubted, and in some cases passionately disputed. It might, I say, be matter of surprise, had we not all observed and felt the revolutionary character of the present age. There has been for years past a strong tendency to overturn old systems, however hallowed; to dispute old opinions, however established by the lapse of ages; and to carry the work of revolution and reform from the halls of legislation to the halls of learning. These stirring movements of the awakened and excited mind, have doubtless swept away many systems and theories that had their origin in an age of darkness, and were unfit for an age of light. They have taught men to examine, compare, think, decide, and act for themselves. But it becomes a momentous inquiry for us who are in the very vortex of the troubled waters, whether there is not great danger, as well as advantage, in our present situation; whether we may not, in the giddy whirl, neglect too much the old landmarks, and make shipwreck on the ocean of change.

This Chapter is from a Lecture "On Classical Learning," delivered at Boston, before the American Institute of Instruction, by Cornelius C. Felton, Tutor in Greek (afterwards Professor and President), in Harvard University, August, 1830.

The adversaries of classical learning assert that 'the main reason for giving such importance to the ancient masters in a course of liberal education was, in former times, the fact that they were the only teachers. The moderns had not yet begun that series of researches and discoveries which have been so splendidly exhibited in these latter days. The physical, moral, intellectual sciences were unknown, save as the sages of the Academy and the Porch had taught them. The genius of modern poetry was voiceless, or breathed only harsh strains in the barbarous Latinity of the Monks. It was, therefore, correct and proper that recourse should be had to their instructions, for want of better. But now the case is widely different; the tables are turned. The ancients were not wiser than we are, but we are wiser than they. We have carried on and perfected what they only began. They might have been giants, we grant, and we may be pigmies; but then we have the advantage of being upon their shoulders, and of course see farther. Shall we then continue to look with their eyes?' Such is the reasoning of the more moderate and rational among the opposers of classical learning.

Others have entered into the controversy with a spirit of violence and denunciation, altogether unbecoming gentlemen and scholars. The advocates of classical learning have been held up to the ridicule of the public as the bigoted adherents to a useless and cumbrous system, because they are too idle and selfish to admit the lights of modern improvement. They have been charged with palming off upon the world a cheap and trifling stock of words, a parade of verbal niceties, for the genuine learning which is to prepare young men to act their parts well in the great drama of life. A tone of bitterness, a rancor like that of personal hostility and family quarrels, has assailed them, and the whole armory of sarcasm has been exhausted. But denunciation and anathema are not to be reasoned with, — " and who can refute a sneer ? " It often happens, we well know, that the most violent are the most ignorant. Men have derided the wit and wisdom of antiquity, who are unable to explain a classical allusion, or interpret a Latin sentence. Smatterers have assailed the reputation and denounced the writings of the mightiest of Grecian philosophers, to whom the curious inquirers into the mysteries of the Greek alphabet, would turn in vain for light. And yet the opinions of such men, unworthy as they are of confidence, derive from their impudent assurance an authority against which reason and good sense and sound learning are for a time of little avail. But the calm and rational sceptics have stated their questions and deserve a reply. An exposition of the claims that classical learning still maintains upon our attention and respect, will contain that reply.

Much wit has been expended in ridiculing the pursuits of the philologist. But true philosophy regards every manifestation of mind, whether in the forms of language, the creations of poetry, the abstractions of science, or the godlike gift of oratory, as worthy of its study. The mind, the essential and immortal part of man, is not to be contemned in any one of its thousandfold aspects and operations. Among the most curious

and subtile of these operations, the process unfolded by
the development of speech may fairly be classed. This
gift, so universal, so indispensable, like the air we breathe,
is scarcely valued because its loss is rarely felt. ' But
let us reflect a moment upon its infinite importance,
and we cannot, with anything like the spirit of true
philosophy, scorn its study as a puerile and trifling
object. That power by which all other powers are
guided and fashioned, by which all emotions are described, by which all the playful efforts of fancy are
made distinct to the perceptions of others, by which,
more than by all our powers besides, the creations of
genius are illustrated — and language the instrument
of that power, the most ingenious and finished of all
instruments — can it indeed be so small, so contemptible,
as to fix justly upon those engaged in its study the
scornful epithets of " word-weighers," and " gerund-
grinders" ? Language opens a wide and curious field
to the observation of those whose pursuits lead them to
trace the intricate phenomena of intellect. The great
difficulty in studying the philosophy of mind, arises
from the impalpable nature of the objects to be scanned
in that study. Language is one of the modes, and a
most essential one, by which the operations of intellect
are distinctly made visible. In studying language,
therefore, we are in fact studying mind, through the
agency of its most purely intellectual instrument. In
mastering language, we not only attain the power of
wielding this most efficient instrument, but we make
ourselves familiar with the results, and we comprehend
the compass of those gifts which make us feel that we

are " fearfully and wonderfully made." Such pursuits can have no other tendency than to strengthen and elevate the mind, and prepare it, consequently, to act with energy, dignity, and success, upon the various objects presented to it in life. But it is said, the student of language is employed about words to the neglect of things. I cannot help calling such reasoning, or rather such assertions, for it is not reasoning, poor, unmeaning cant. Wasting time upon words to the neglect of things! Are not words realities? Have they not a separate, an independent existence? Nay, more; have they not a power to stir up the soul, to sway nations even, such as no other things ever possessed or ever can possess? Did not the words of Demosthenes carry more dread to the heart of Philip than the arms of Athens and the fortresses of her tributary cities? Have not the words of Homer touched the hearts and roused the imaginations of myriads, many centuries since the walls of Troy and the armaments of Greece perished from the face of the earth, and the site of Priam's capital was lost from the memories of men? It is true that the trifling and quibbling of some philologists give a plausible air to the objections raised against these studies. But would you condemn the mathematics, because one votary of the science declared his contempt for Paradise Lost — a work which proved no truth by a chain of geometrical or algebraic reasoning? Would you reject geology because an enthusiast values a stone, apparently worthless, more than a splendid product of imagination? Would you shut your mind against the beautiful science of botany because you

28*

have seen one so absorbed in its study that he would expend more anxious care in rearing a puny hot-house plant, than in alleviating sorrow or saving life? Are you prepared to throw away the hopes of religion, because a few bigots, attaching an over-strained importance to trifles, make it appear absurd, and strip it of almost every attribute that can command your respect? Analogy, I am aware, is not argument; but the same kind of reasoning, which is aimed at philological studies, might be aimed with equal success against every science we value, every truth we hold sacred.

Such are some of the general considerations that recommend the study of language. But the classical languages, besides these, have other and peculiar claims upon our attention. No one will for a moment dispute the importance of understanding the full power of our vernacular tongue. I assume this as a fact beyond discussion and argument. I assert, moreover, the impossibility of doing this without the aid of Greek and Latin.

The Latin was formed chiefly from a modification of Greek. The Romans drew largely from Grecian fountains, both in language and literature; and vain would be his labors, who should essay to comprehend the efforts of Roman genius, without first listening to the instructions of Rome's literary masters.

In the division of the Roman empire and the formation of modern states, other languages arose from the ruins of the Latin. Four of the principal dialects of modern Europe bear so strong a resemblance to the parent tongue, that a knowledge of the latter makes the attainment of the former an affair of trifling labor. Other languages of Europe, and our own among the rest, are derived but in part from the Latin; and I assert that so far as that part goes, a knowledge of Latin is essential to one who would understand it fully, and wield it with certainty and effect. Nearly all our words of Roman origin retain the radical meaning of their primitives. Their general import may, it is true, be gathered from English usage; but the peculiar, the nicely critical propriety of their application, is unknown save to the classical scholar; and all others, who attempt to write their own mother tongue, especially in the discussion of literary subjects, are liable to mar their pages by slight inaccuracies of style, and inaccuracies in the use of single words, which destroy their claim to the honor of being classical models of composition. Such is the inevitable result of the natural progress of the human mind. Had we lived in the time of the ancients, and they in ours, the case would have been reversed. They would have drawn instruction from our writings; their languages would have received an infusion from ours; and to learn the exact quality of that infusion, they must have traced it to its fountain head with us. We do not compromise one particle of our claim to originality, by admitting the necessity of resorting to ancient tongues, in order to learn our own. It is only admitting, in the spirit of philosophy, what the natural course of human thought, and our relative position to the great civilized nations who have gone before us, make it incumbent on us, as reasoning men to admit. Perhaps the exceptions may be urged of such men as Franklin, who have written our language in great purity and elegance, without having been trained in the discipline of classical schools. If I grant that these apparent exceptions are exceptions in fact, I might defend my position by the plea that a few exceptions never invalidate a general rule; and I might array in reply to every single exception five hundred examples in which the rule holds good. But there is little argument to be drawn from the literary powers of Dr. Franklin against the utility of classical learning. According to his own statements, his style was formed by closely imitating the best models of English composition — the papers of the Spectator — which, we all know, are from the pens of the most accomplished classical scholars England has ever produced. The purity, simplicity, and beauty of Dr. Franklin's style, therefore, is, after all, the consequence of an exquisite taste in ancient literature ; although with him it comes at second hand. Is any one prepared to say that the language of Franklin would not have been more bold, more stirring, more eloquent, had his mind, after having been cultivated and refined in the study of antiquity, given free scope to its acknowledged powers, and acted by its own resistless impulses, untrammelled by the fetters of imitation.

Not only our language, but our literature, is closely dependent on the classical. The fine conceptions, the productions of the beautiful fancy of the ancients, have exerted so strong an influence upon the tone and genius of the elder English literature, that one half of the beauties of the latter are-lost sight of without a knowledge of the former. The great writers of England have been filled to overflowing with classic lore. The history and poetry and oratory of Greece and Rome, have lent them their tributary aids; the sages of antiquity have poured out their richest treasures to illustrate, adorn, and enforce the glorious conceptions of English intellect. Classical allusions and illustrations tastefully employed, are enchanting to a cultivated mind. In English literature they are used with a skill and beauty that form one of its most delightful traits. This does not arise from, nor does it argue, a want of originality. It would be impossible to prevent such influences of the literature of one age upon that of another, except by entire ignorance of everything that does not come within our own experience. We may complain of it, if we please, but we cannot change the order of time, and place ourselves at the beginning of the history of our race. The ancients were before us, and we have studied them, and cannot help it. We cannot read our own writers without being constantly reminded of those great men. The law of progress requires that it should be so.

Fortunate, indeed, is it for us, that the creations of Grecian genius were guided by such unerring taste. The intellectual character of that gifted nation was formed under the happiest auspices. Nature was lavish of her beauties upon her favored land ; but she did not convert it into a region of oriental softness. Every influence that tended to give refinement and elegance to the mind was there felt ; but refinement and elegance were made to stop at the proper limits, and never allowed to

become degenerate and effeminate. **Her** free and oft-
times tumultuous politics gave energy, her matchless
climate infused vivacity and cheerfulness, her scenery
inspired a pure taste and an exquisite perception of
beauty. The human form was developed in its fairest
proportions. The majestic and intellectual head, the
finely expanded frame, the active and airy and graceful
motion, gave to artists the prototypes of their chiselled
gods. Add to this their beautiful modes of instruction:
music and science uniting to give at once a humanized
and manly tone to the character, in the groves of the
Academy, on the places of public resort, by the wisest,
best, and most eloquent from among them, with the
noblest specimens of art all around them, the marble
almost waking into life, the canvass glowing with the
hues of heaven — and we cannot wonder at the perfection of Grecian taste ; we cannot but congratulate ourselves, that a race so favored, so gifted, were called to
preside over the beginnings and direct the destinies of
intellectual Europe ; that the Genius of Greece yet lives,
as fresh, as bright, as beautiful as her own blue hills,
sunny skies, and green isles.

Another additional consideration in favor of the study
of ancient languages, is the fact that they are more finished than any others. The perfection of the Greek
tongue has always been the admiration of scholars. Its
flexibility, its exhaustless vocabulary, its power of increasing that vocabulary at will by the use of compounds,
make it an admirable vehicle for the communication of
thought, even to the nicest shades ; while its unrivalled
harmony imparts to poetry a richness and beauty beyond

the capacity of any modern tongue. The principles and power of language are here more fully unfolded ; the philosophy of rhetoric is more thoroughly displayed. Add to this, the Greek grammar is now fixed and settled. There it is, beyond the reach of change, an object of study, to be resorted to at any time, ever perfect, ever beautiful. But beyond and above the study of mere language, I know of no better intellectual discipline than to determine the meaning of an ancient author. The principles of grammar are to be applied by the reason and the judgment ; the situation of the author must be vividly presented to the mind by the memory and the imagination ; the connection of the passage in question with the context, is to be closely scrutanized ; the style of ancient thought to be taken into consideration, and, after thus exercising the most important of our powers, the purport of a difficult passage may be settled. This is precisely the course of reflection and reasoning which men must follow, in determining the proper conduct for many difficult conjunctures in life ; it is acting upon probabilities.

Such is the process, and such the discipline, of determining single passages. Of a similar and more elevated kind, is the intellectual effort of comprehending the entire worth of an author. It is not enough barely to give his works a hasty perusal, or even a careful perusal, with a knowledge of the language simply. The student who would enter fully into the merits of a classical author, must take himself out of the influences immediately around him ; must transport himself back to a remote age : must lay aside the associations most familiar to him; must forget his country, his prejudices, his superior light, and place himself upon a level with the intellect whose labors he essays to comprehend. Few are the minds that would not be benefited by such a process. We are disposed to permit our thoughts and feelings to repose too much upon the objects nearest us ; and thus a constant reference to self becomes the habitual direction of our thoughts. What was the character of the age in which he lived ? what was the religion ? how far did it gain a hold upon the minds of cultivated men ? to what extent did it influence the tone of poetry ? what were the philosophical theories, and how far were they true, and how extensively were they believed ? what was the character of the nation, and what had been its historical career ? what was the state of political parties and what was the government ? what were the doctrines held by each, and wherein did they differ, and how far was the individual mind of the author in question wrought upon by all these influences — are questions which should be asked, and, as far as possible, answered, by the scholar who would do himself and literature full justice, by the mode in which he pursues his classical studies. I am aware that such is not often the path followed by the scholars of our country ; but I do sincerely believe that the worth of classical learning will never be realized until some such method is adopted. I know, too, it involves a depth of thought and a wide range of studies, from which we are apt to shrink in alarm, and ask ourselves if there is not some shorter way to attain the object; but reason, as I think, decides without appeal, that such is the price of genuine classical erudition.

Knowledge of the sort I have described, may not lead to the invention of a single new mechanical agent; it may not be the direct means of increasing our fortunes a single dollar. But it will give us an enlarged view of our nature; it will disclose the workings of our common powers under influences widely differing from any that have acted upon ourselves; it will teach us to judge charitably of others' minds and hearts; it will teach us that intellect and sensibility and genius have existed beyond the narrow circle in which we have moved — beyond the limits of our country—centuries before our age. Such lessons are needed in the every-day concerns of life. Those who say that the classics are of no practical use—those even who say that they are merely ornamental in a liberal education, show an entire forgetfulness of their most striking and obvious effects. They are eminently practical. They require the most practical modes of reasoning to comprehend them; they give the most practical views of our nature; they prepare the professional man for his labors, by presenting a field of practically similar labor, before he enters upon its special duties. I have no hesitation in asserting, that a mind long trained in unfolding the meaning and worth of classical authors, by the course of inquiries I have described, will be eminently prepared for the intricate investigations of the profession of law.

If, then, it be desirable that our young scholars should be trained up in classical pursuits, and in such a manner as best to fit them for the duties of life, it is

29

evident a general change must be made. Those who
are devoted to the business of instruction must enter
more deeply, more philosophically, into the spirit of the
classics than has been common among us in these latter
times. We must put forth our best energies to master
the treasures of learning, and awaken in our pupils an
enthusiasm for similar pursuits. In the whole circle
of the learned professions, I know of none which presents nobler topics of eloquence, more exciting and
elevating subjects of reflection, and, I may add, more
useful fields of labor, than that of a man of letters.
Indolence and stupidity have no part nor lot here;
every power is called upon; every moral feeling is
confirmed, and every honorable aspiration may be
gratified. It is not my purpose to eulogize the profession of a teacher; but when I see many engaging in
it with dread, and leaving it with pleasure; when I
hear it spoken of as a fit resort for the drudge and the
blockhead; I cannot but ask, if the explanation of the
authors of the ancient world — embracing, as it does,
such a depth and variety of learning; admitting, as it
does, the highest flights of imagination and eloquence;
employing, as it does, thousands of the first intellects
of the first intellectual country on earth, — I cannot
but ask, if it *is* a fit resort for a drudge or a blockhead;
if it *is* a pursuit to be adopted with dread, and relin-
quished with pleasure. My answer to these questions
would be one and decided.

XIX.

I HAVE spoken of two classes of study, the mathematics and ancient languages, as complementary and supplemental. This may be made evident by a few general considerations. The demonstrations of pure mathematics, and of the physical sciences which depend on the mathematics for their most subtile and irrefragable proofs, start from axioms which are universally and necessarily true. No multiplication of examples can make them appear more true, nor can any lapse of time or change of circumstances diminish their validity. Their conclusion, then, must be equally certain ; and the student, in advancing from step to step, feels always the delightful assurance that he is standing upon solid ground, and that no power can change his convictions. It may not be a great conclusion that he has reached, but it is a sure one. But in order to this certainty, he must exercise the most careful discrimination respecting his premises and every individual process in the reasoning. Now, this habit of judging from indisputable facts and not from feeling or prejudice or bare authority, this habit of exactness and discrimination, of eliminating every possible source of error, of including everything

This Extract is from the Address delivered by Rev. Samuel Gilman Brown, D.D., on the occasion of his Inauguration as President of Hamilton College, Clinton, New York, July 17, 1867.

essential to the process before you, and of excluding everything indifferent or accidental, and therefore only disturbing or confusing, is one of the most valuable in life. "There are more false facts in the world," as Sir William Hamilton quotes from that eminent medical philosopher, Dr. William Cullen, " than false theories." It seems sometimes as if one could hardly overestimate the importance of exactness and precision as mental habits.

But then a large part, far the largest part, of our reasoning processes in actual life are not demonstrative, but what are called moral or probable ; where sound arguments exist on both sides, and we are obliged to form our conclusions according to the preponderance of testimony ; where we are to weigh, and not merely to number ; where there are conflicting judgments and contrary statements ; where facts are not all within our reach, or are presented with distortion, and colored to suit the occasion ; where we deal not with nature alone, with her fixed facts and immutable laws, but with men, *varios et mutabiles semper.* And here will he who has been disciplined to form his judgments from premises somewhat intangible and indefinable ; to determine the consequents from antecedents a little variable and uncertain ; to discriminate between the nicest shades of thought, and see which will best fit all the demands of a severe intellect and a pure taste ; who has become familiar with the infinite, evanescent, indescribable forms of thought, sentiment, passion, conviction, habit, which languages and letters have revealed to him in the great domain of imagination and history, and ethics and polity,— have an insight, a soundness of judgment, a discriminating sense, which pure science or the study of nature with her fixed certainties cannot give. The analysis and translation of languages has given him precisely the discipline which he needs. What an endless amount of comparison and reasoning, of balancing of probabilities, and forming of independent judgments and expressing them in the best forms, the student has gone through with in the careful reading of a single classical author. Hence every student of the higher professions, especially of law and theology, feels the special advantage which he derives from this kind of training.

Let me suggest a little more particularly, that there is no study which calls into play at the same moment so many of the mental faculties, and those of quite diverse character, as the languages; not only do we exercise the powers of judgment, discrimination, and reasoning, but our sympathies, our taste, our sense of the fitting and the beautiful. What logic so subtile as the logic of grammar? What pleasure more pure and inspiring than that which we get in mastering the thought, and rising to the comprehension of the poetic beauties of some of the master minds of the world? To these studies, too, the majority of young students, with fair opportunities, apply themselves with a natural aptitude. During all our younger years we are perforce learning language, in one aspect undoubtedly a difficult task, where absolute perfection is unattainable, for who ever yet mastered his own tongue? but in another aspect, an easy and delicious exercise of the faculties, for we are constantly making positive progress, and a child, if he has fitting opportunities, seems to learn two

or three languages at once with the same ease as one.
Nor can we easily overestimate the value of translation,
so that it be at once accurate and elegant, the transfer-
rence of the full power, precision, and beauty of thought
from one tongue to another, as an aid to our own
powers. What comprehensive attention, what concentration of mind, what intuitive perceptions of mental
peculiarities, tastes, and habits, what knowledge of subtile allusions, what feeling, what plasticity of mind,
adapting itself instinctively to every varying emotion,
before we begin to satisfy ourselves in the effort; so that
to excel in this really fine art is proof itself of a mind
of the most admirable structure.

But the study of languages, say some, helps only to
expression, not to the thought expressed ; to the form,
not to the substance. Taking this for the moment as
something like an adequate statement, that it only helps
us to represent that which we acquire with other aid,
do we fully understand what great praise this is ? Do
we remember that a word fitly spoken is like apples of
gold in pictures of silver ? that as social beings, a great
part of our duty in life lies in the power of expression ? in bringing truths, from whatever source acquired,
to bear upon our fellows for their advantage ? Do we
remember as we should, that the necessity of advocating the cause of righteousness, and resisting the
machinations of dishonesty and craft, is as ancient as
justice and as permanent as religion ? So that if the
value of the study of language were confined to the
giving us a good vocabulary, and enabling us to express
our thoughts and emotions in a manner the most vigor-

ous or persuasive, it would help us to a function of
almost universal necessity, and which we cannot afford
to neglect or slight.

But we may look much further than this : at the
general enlargement of mind produced by the study of
the language of a great and powerful people. " So often
as I learn a language, so often do I become a man," is
not an epigrammatic expression without meaning. How,
indeed, can you enter into the inner life of a people so
well as by reading their thought in their own idiomatic
tongue ? We gain our impression, not at second-hand,
but from our own observation. Can any description
give us an idea of the eager, passionate, versatile, philosophic, art-loving Greek, equal to that which we gain
from Homer and Thucydides, from Plato and Sophocles ? or of the proud, imperious, conquering Roman,
like that which Sallust and Virgil and Cicero unconsciously reveal ? A nation's thought, its aspirations,
its ambition, its faith shines through its literature.
Every page is illumined or darkened by the spirit that
pervades it. The great difference between ancient and
modern intellectual and moral life ; between classic art
and romantic ; between Sophocles and Shakspeare ; between Phidias and Michael Angelo ; the history of ideas ;
the great march of civilization ; can be realized fully
only as we become permeated with the spirit of the
times and the nations ; and this it is almost impossible
to do without some acquaintance with that most won
derful of products and of agencies, a nation's language.

Nor is the actual knowledge which is directly or incidentally imparted to the student of a language by any

means small in amount or trivial in value. He is introduced of necessity to the history of new nations; to
a knowledge of their science and art, their civil polity
and their domestic customs, their military conquests
and the tranquil pursuits of peace. His thoughts are
carried beyond the sphere in which he of necessity is
constantly busy; beyond the petty annoyances of daily
life. He becomes insensibly emancipated from the
tyranny of narrow tastes and provincial habits. You
could less easily make of him a man of one idea, of
sectional ambitions, of impoverished sympathies. It
surely should be one purpose, also, of a liberal education
to give the student some taste of the most thoughtful
and influencing literatures of the world. And how can
this be done with any fairness and completeness, if you
omit those writers who fairly governed the philosophic
thought of the world for sixteen centuries, and who,
after all our culture, remain still models of style, illustrious examples of the most refined and perfect literary
composition that the world has ever seen? Why it was,
and how, that they acquired such marvellous skill, it is
not worth the while for us to stop to inquire. Whether
the cause lay in their artistic culture, in their greater
deliberateness of work (no steam-driven press or impor-
tunate public urging them for copy), in their obedience
to the Horatian principle, *nonum prematur in annum*,
and of course in repeated criticism and eliminations
and emendations, in their stern fidelity to the demands
of a pure taste, their resolute purpose of perfection, so
far as unflinching labor could secure it, or in their finer
mould, the rare texture of mental material, the exquisite
symmetry of development, and the indescribable com-

pleteness and harmony of discipline and attainment, or all these causes combined, the fact remains confirmed by the judgment of all generations. But what stimulant is there for a generous, enthusiastic, and resolute mind, at once so pure and so strong, as the contemplation of excellence? Was there not a world of truth in the saying of the ardent young Greek, that "the victory of Miltiades would not suffer him to sleep"? Place ever before the eager mind of the learner models of attainment and excellence, point out wherein their virtues consist and how they were gained, by what self-denial and resolute endeavor they must have been won, if you would teach him to be both modest and aspiring, to be ambitious of true excellence rather than of temporary popularity.

There is yet another point of considerable consequence not very often alluded to. Have you considered what a marvellous product is any language, even the most meagre? How in its very vocabulary, its forms and euphonic changes, it embodies the mental growth and modifications of thousands of minds? How much more wonderful it is than the works of any one who uses it? that no one can be said to be absolute master of any tongue? that the most discursive or profound thinkers carry on their grand processes of reasoning and imagination far within the limits of the unbounded domain of a nation's speech?

Language is the ever-living, self-evolving product of the most vital powers, no more to be absolutely fixed than the action of the mind itself. It is Coleridge, I think, who somewhere says, that the history of a word may be more important than that of a campaign. And if the naturalist finds a pure and intense pleasure in observing the habits of reptiles and fishes, if he thinks the toil of years well repaid when he absolutely determines the shape and hue of the wild bird's wing, or the the processes of the coral insect, should not the student of a nation's philosophy and poetry, within a domain whose boundaries ever recede as he approaches them, feel his mind expand with a new delight, and be conscious of the growth of new power?

Nor is the study of the ancients without a certain moral discipline, which is not of small account. In the midst of our intense life, of our indomitable self-assurance, legitimately born of our marvellous national progress, of our almost unchecked prosperity, it will do us no harm to feel, as we only can feel through familiarity with their works, that "great heroes lived before Agamemnon," and that to no age and no nation has been committed the supremacy of the earth. We are in no danger of failing through excess of diffidence. If modesty be not our national virtue, it is still a beautiful one; a necessary result too, or should be, of the best education. The finest, purest, most attractive, most sacred minds, are those which to masterly attainment and delicate culture, add the winning grace which beautifies and charms. And I know not by what means open to our public education we can so well imbue the student with the proper feeling as to all high literary attainment, as by bringing him into close and daily contact with those whom he may imitate but cannot excel; who have worn their crowns so long, and whom he honors not alone, but in company with the noblest and best-taught of modern minds.

XX.

A DEAD language: what a sad and solemn expression! Trite enough, I own; but to a reflective mind, none the less sad and solemn; for in the death of which it speaks are involved deaths untold, innumerable.

I can understand what is meant by " a Dead Sea"; and should suppose it to be a sheet of water cut off from all intercourse with the main ocean; never rising with its flow; never sinking with its ebb; never skimmed by the sail of commerce; never flapped by wing of wandering bird; undisturberd by the bustle of the restless world; but slumbering in a desolate wilderness, far from the track of caravan or railway or steamship, in a stagnant and tide-forgotten and unheeded repose.

The chance-directed efforts of an enterprising traveller exhumed, but recently, the sculptured monuments of a dead civilization. We then learned that Nineveh and Babylon were not only the homes of conquering kings, but the seats of tranquil learning and treasured science, before ever a fleet had sailed from Aulis, or the eagles had promised empire to the watcher on the green Palatine.

This Extract is from Day Dreams of a Schoolmaster — the Chapter entitled " Dead Languages " — by Professor D'Arcy W. Thompson, of Queens College, Galway, Ireland.

The language of priestly and kingly Etruria is revealed to us only by dim marks upon vase or tablet, or
by melancholy inscriptions on sepulchral stones. That
is, indeed, a language unquestionably dead.

But can such a term be applied to that Hellenic
speech that in the Iliad has rolled, like the great Father
of Waters, its course unhindered down three thousand
years; that in Pindar still soars heavenwards, staring
at the sun ; that rises and falls in Plato with the long,
sequacious music of an Aeolian lute ; that moves stately
and black-stoled in Aeschylus ; that reverberates with
laughter half-Olympian in Aristophanes ; that pierces
with a trumpet-sound in Demosthenes ; that smells of
crocuses in Theocritus ; that chirrups like a balm-
cricket in Anacreon ? If it be dead, then what language
is alive ?

Or again, is that old Italian speech dead and gone,
that murmurs in Lucretius a ceaseless, solemn monotone
of sea-shell sound ; that in Virgil flows, like the Eri-
danus, calmly but majestically through rich lowlands,
fringed with tall poplars and rimmed with grassy banks ;
that quivers to wild strings of passion in Catullus ; that
wimples like a beck in Ovid ; that coos in Tibullus like
the turtle; that sparkles in Horace like a well-cut
diamond ?

No: Heaven forbid it! No! Pile upon these twin
daughters of Omphacan Zeus mountains of Grammars
and Grammatical Exercises and Latin Readers and
Greek Delectuses and Graduses and Dictionaries and
Lexicons, until Ossa is dwarfed and Pelion is a wart.
Let dull, colossal Pedantry — unconscious handmaid of

the Abstract Bagman—with her tons of lumbal lead press heavily on the prostrate forms. For a while they may lie, breathless and exhausted; but when that is grown again wherein their great strength lay, then will they make a mighty effort, and fling high in air the accumulated scoria of ages: like a hailstorm in the surrounding sea will fall the fragments of a million gerund-stones; and the divine Twain will clothe themselves anew in their old strength and beauty, and sit down by the side of Zeus Omphaeus, exulting in glory.

No, no! The music of Homer will die with the choral chants of the Messiah, and the strains of Pindar with the symphonies of Beethoven: *una dies dabit exitio* Aristophanes and Cervantes and Molière; the Mantuan will go hand in hand to oblivion with the Florentine, *divinus Magister cum Discipulo diviniore;* the Metamorphoses of Ovid will decay with the fantastic tale of Ariosto and the music of Don Giovanni; Horace will fade out of ken, linked arm in arm with that sweet fellow epicure, Montaigne; Antigone will be forgotten maybe a short century before Cordelia; and Plato and Aristotle will be entombed beneath the Mausoleum that covers for ever the thoughts of Bacon, Kepler, Newton, and Laplace.

Moreover, before the last echoes of Greece and Rome shall have died away, a Slavonian horde will throng the Morea and the Cyclades; and in some crumbling cathedral, Catholicism will have chanted, for the last time, its own *Nunc dimittis* in the grand imperial language of the City of the Seven Hills.

When all this shall have come about, then may it be said with truth: "Rome is dead; and Athens is no more! the words of whose wise ones. went out into all lands, and the songs of whose singing-men to the ends of the world: their pomp and their glory have gone down with them into the pit."

But, gentle reader, long, long before this desolation shall have come about, you and I will be lying in a very sorry plight, with a strange and not beautiful expression on our human countenances; our quips, our cranks, our oddities all gone: quite chapfallen. Yes, friend, a very long while indeed, before all this shall have come about.

XXI.

WHAT position is to be held henceforth by the Classics? That is the main question now for directors of liberal education. Let us approach it in a rational spirit, neither defending the Classics with fanatical devotion, nor assailing them as though they were criminal usurpers; but placing ourselves, if we can, at the true point of view, and considering what measure of change is really required. Nobody concurred more cordially, or took part more actively, than I did in breaking down the monopoly of the Classics and welcoming the new studies in my own University; but I wish to avoid alike the bigotry of conservatism and the bigotry of innovation.

Undoubtedly the intrinsic value of the Classics has been greatly diminished since the period of the Revival of Learning, when they were first adopted as the staple of high education. There was, at that time, no other literature worthy of the name; no philosophy but the arid speculations of the schoolmen; no history but the monkish chronicle; no oratory but the monkish homily; no poetry but the monkish hymn. The Greek and Latin languages were then the caskets in which all the treasures of intellect were enclosed: and it was as the key to

This Extract is from a Paper on "University Education," read before the American Social Science Association, at Albany, February 17, 1869, by Professor Goldwin Smith.

that casket, not as a mental gymnasium, that Grammar
was established as the prime instrument of education
for both sexes alike.   In fact, it was expected that
Greek and Latin, as alone containing any writings
worth a cultivated man's notice, would be the languages, we may almost say the vernacular languages,
of the cultivated world ; and the universal practice of
Latin composition in prose and verse, no doubt, had
reference to this expectation: Erasmus and Politian did
not suppose themselves to be writing in a dead language : they supposed themselves to be writing in one
of the only two languages in which writings would live.
But we have now not only a modern literature, but
three or four modern literatures, each of them equal
to the ancient in intellectual power, and of course far
superior to it in depth and range both of thought and
sentiment, and in nearness to our personal interests
and feelings.

Nor is this all; the claim of literature and philosophy
altogether to monopolize the higher education, or even
to be its principal elements, is challenged by Physical Science, which in the sixteenth century had not
advanced beyond the Physical Works of Aristotle.

These are evidently strong grounds for a revision
of the system.   On the other hand, the superiority of
Greek and Latin as languages, and as instruments of
linguistic training, to the modern languages, appears to
me to be undiminished.   In fact, it is constantly increasing, since a flood of extraneous and heterogeneous
elements, themselves to a great extent classical, though
often hideously barbarized, is constantly flowing into

the modern languages, principally through the vocabulary of Physical Science. Greek, especially, if you compare it with any modern tongue, seems from its symmetry, its richness of inflection, its unlimited power of forming compounds, its liberty of arranging the words of a sentence in the order of thought, alone worthy to be the organ of the human mind. So marked is this superiority, indeed, that I can hardly believe that the destinies of the two ancient languages are yet accomplished, or feel sure that Latin will not some day be again the language of Law, and Greek the language of Philosophy and Science. So far, therefore, as linguistic studies are an essential part of education — so far as the habit of analyzing language is necessary or conducive to the perfection of the powers of thought, Greek and Latin seem to me still to hold their ground. The only linguistic study which can compete with them, as it appears to me, is that of our own language, which, though eminently wanting in the peculiar qualities which I have noted in the Greek, makes up for that want by some peculiar qualities of its own, but above all, by its vast practical importance as the organ of our daily thoughts, constantly reacting on the thoughts which it expresses. At all events, the culture of the English tongue is a duty to which the attention of all educators ought to be turned. Cultivate your language and it is one of the highest instruments of civilization: neglect it and it becomes a vehicle of barbarism.

The usefulness of a knowledge of modern languages is beyond question. But we now suppose ourselves to

30*

be laying out a course of general culture, and we must consider what is conducive to culture, not merely what is useful. The power of reading the modern languages is acquired with great facility by any one who has undergone the linguistic training of Classical education, especially in the use of French, Italian, and Spanish, to which Latin is the master-key. The power of speaking a language can be acquired to perfection only in the country in which it is spoken; and it is there acquired with such ease that to go to a university for it would seem a waste of time. At Oxford we have declined, hitherto, to admit the modern languages into the University course, except so far as a knowledge of them may be useful to candidates for honors in the School of Modern History: but we have an institution for teaching them called the Taylor Institution, with four teachers, German, French, Italian, and Spanish, a Professor of Modern Literature and a library of foreign books and periodicals. Two scholarships are given annually, by examination, to the most proficient among the students, and the examination is conducted in such a manner as to test, as far as possible, not merely a conversational knowledge of the languages, but the critical and literary acquaintance with them which could alone be thought an equivalent for classical scholarship and a worthy product of high culture. But the winners are so often students of foreign parentage, or who have lived abroad, as to suggest a strong mistrust of the value of proficiency in these studies as a criterion of the proper work of a university; and when I was last at Oxford there were thoughts of abolishing the scholarships altogether, as being useless for Academical purposes, and of applying the fund to the other objects of the Institution.

A Classical education ought to include, and that which a candidate for honors received at Oxford did include, besides a philological knowledge of the Greek and Latin languages, a thorough acquaintance with the works of the best Classical authors, philosophers, and historians, as well as orators and poets. As I have already said, the ancients, in every department of literature, are surpassed by the moderns in present interest. But taken as a whole they still seem to me to constitute the best manual of humanity. For this purpose they have even an advantage in being remote from the questions and the emotions of the present time. We have been asked whether a knowledge of Goethe, for instance, is not as valuable as a knowledge of any author of antiquity. One answer to that question is, that to study Goethe with profit, the mind of the student must be tolerably mature, able in some measure to appreciate the influences, religious, philosophical, political, and personal, under which Goethe wrote, to take a stand above those influences, and calmly to discriminate, in their complex result, truth from falsehood, good from evil. But this is too much to expect from a youth under education brought into contact with such a writer as Goethe. The Classics present humanity entire, but with transparent simplicity, with statuesque calmness, free from modern bias or influence, near to our sympathies (for Homer's nature is ours), but far from our controversies and

passions. It would be difficult to suggest any course
of modern philosophy, history, oratory, and poetry of
which the same could be said.

There are more ways than one of teaching the Classics. They may be taught dryly and pedantically; or
they may be taught as a man of cultivated and comprehensive mind would teach them, enlarging their scope
and increasing their interest by commentary and modern illustration. Supposing the style of teaching to be
the highest, are there any better text-books of history
even now than Thucydides and Tacitus, — is there
any better text-book of politics than the treatise of
Aristotle ?

In point of form, at all events, and as models and
schools of pure taste, the classical writers are still peerless. Our use of the term "classical" to denote faultless
beauty of form is a popular testimony to the fact. On
different races nature bestows different gifts. The
Greek she endowed above all races with the sense of
beauty. I saw the other day, in the house of a friend,
an excellent judge of art, two casts, one of a great
work of Michael Angelo, the other of a great work of
Phidias, hanging side by side : and my friend pointed
out how superior, not of course in poetry or depth
of sentiment, but in artistic beauty, was the master-
piece of the Greek. There is no part of our old classical
system which is more decisively condemned than the
general practice of Greek and Latin versification. But
even this practice exacted, in the first place, a very intimate acquaintance with the Greek and Latin poets,
and, in the second place, cultivated the taste for form.

I have heard one of the most experienced chiefs of the English press remark that his best writers had generally been men who had excelled at school and college in verse composition. It is not in a new country, where the historical monuments and works of art which in old countries cultivate the sense of beauty are for the present necessarily wanting, that we can afford to expel the beauties of the Classics from our course of education without finding something to supply their place.

Of course we may have translations; and it is time that some really good English translations should be made. But great poets cannot be translated at all; great orators cannot be adequately translated: no works can be adequately translated of which, as of the works of Plato and Tacitus, a principal excellence is the style.

The fatal objection to classical education, as it has fallen under my experience in my own country, is, that it fails with the great mass of the students. The great mass of the students — though so many years of their life are mainly occupied in the study — at the end of their course have not acquired a sufficient knowledge of Latin and Greek to read the ancient authors with facility, to appreciate their beauties, or to receive from them any mental culture beyond the mere exercise of the faculties involved in getting up any subject for an examination. They have read only a few authors, translate them with difficulty, and on leaving the University lay them and all classical studies aside forever. Whether these same men could be brought to study with success any other subject requiring as much mental effort as the Classics, or to undergo high training of any kind, may be doutful. The increase of industry at Oxford which I mentioned as having followed the adoption of the elective system of studies is found mainly in the school of which modern history is the staple: and, with all due loyalty to the subject of which I am Professor, I must say that the intellectual effort undergone in getting up a certain amount of modern history for examination, does not seem to me to be of the severest kind. As a mental discipline, and a mode of acquiring mental power, I could never place it on a par with the classical school.

XXII.

THE most commonly understood result of University studies is the acquisition of knowledge. It is the business of the teacher in each department to know what is known of his subject, if possible, to add to what is known, and to impart freely what he has discovered or acquired. It is the business of the learner to avail himself, as far as he is able, of the stores of knowledge which are placed within his reach in books and in oral instruction. To raise the fabric of scientific attainment, tier after tier, adding fact to fact, law to law, theory to theory, that is one view of the work that we are taking in hand.

And, certainly, if the word "knowledge" is taken in the widest sense, and if the knowledge so conceived is pursued with the entire heart, without disturbance from any narrower motive, there can hardly be a nobler aim. In this highest aspect, there is much truth in the Socratic paradox, that knowledge is identical with virtue. But no single term can actually express "the chief end of man," and even the great name of knowledge, when used alone, is apt to become limited in meaning. The mere accumulation and arrangement

This Chapter is from an Address on "The End of Liberal Education," delivered at the opening of the United College in the University of St. Andrews, Nov. 8, 1868, by Rev. L. Campbell, Professor of Greek.

of facts and theories may be an endless labor, but it
may also be barren of result. Great stores of learning
may be unfruitful, where there is no living energy;
and, as the theologian speculates on the possibility of
having all faith without the gift of charity, so it may
be said to be equally conceivable that a man may have
" all knowledge," and yet have no mind.

And the idea of knowledge becomes still further
lowered, and the desire of knowledge, which exists
naturally in all men, is still more enfeebled, when the
pursuit of knowledge is recommended for the mere sake
of power. " How did Such-an-one lay the foundation
of his princely fortune ? " " He got schooling enough
to make him an exciseman; that was the first step."
This answer exemplifies, certainly in a rudimentary
form, one way of looking at the usefulness of knowledge;
and it is, perhaps, better that education should be
valued on such grounds as these, than if it were not
valued at all; but such a conception of the advantages
of learning is hardly adequate as an ideal, although it
has sometimes been appealed to as a fundamental principle, or so-called canon of ponderation. The great
author of the saying, " Knowledge is power," has himself taught us ever to look beyond immediate results.
We are not, he says, like Atalanta, to stop to pick up
an apple while we are running in the race.

Knowledge, then, is not by itself a sufficient expression of our object; first, because the word is apt to
suggest a mere abstract notion; and, secondly, because
when thus narrowed it is liable to be tacitly regarded
as a means rather than as an end.

Another definition of the aim of study, perhaps more suited to the subjective spirit of this age, is intellectual culture. This notion may help to supplement the too abstract or objective conception of knowledge. It may be said the test of a real education is not what a man knows, nor even what he can do, but what is the condition of his mental powers. The true process of teaching is not like that of filling a vessel from without, or impressing a mould on some yielding and merely passive substance, but consists rather in developing conscious activities from within ; and the consummation of the process is not an aggregation of knowledges, or a bundle of accomplishments, but the harmonious development of mind, the cultivation of an intelligent and thoughtful spirit. I might enlarge on this aspect of our common purpose, which may suggest many practical inferences to those who will consider it deeply ; but I will only observe, before passing on, that intellectual excellence or beauty, like knowledge, may, or may not, be an adequate expression of our ideal, according to the extent of signification which we attach to the term. We cannot aim higher than perfection — all depends on our notion of what is included in perfection. And here that secret egotism, which is the source of so many weaknesses, creeps in and tempts men to rest short of what is really highest, by thinking of self-culture apart from the love of truth and the practical good of men. The subjective form of expression is thus liable to misconception, as well as the more objective form. So difficult is it to keep a firm grasp of the whole of anything, especially of a thing so

complex as a human life. For education can only be
truly estimated in relation to life as a whole; and
hence the design of education is something more than
the amassing of information; more, even, than the
cultivation of mental faculties. It is the enlargement
and elevation of the whole nature — the growth of
individuals and communities towards the measure of
the perfect man.

The analytical spirit of modern times, may I add,
the logical tendency of our own nation, leads us to
think of human life and character in a fragmentary
and disjointed way. Not contented with ideal distinctions between things which can have no life when put
asunder, we are prone to separate and oppose them.
We set the heart against the intellect, feeling against
reason, formal against real truth, forgetting that no
true life is possible in which both sides of each antithe-
sis are not combined. There can be no sound theory
of education in which any element of humanity is lost
sight of. And university education is only a stage in
that larger scheme of progress which for the individual
extends over the whole of life, and for the community,
embraces the welfare of every class. In that scheme,
it has an appropriate place and work, but this separate
function is vitally related to the whole, from which no
part can be isolated without losing use and meaning;
and therefore, although the object of our meeting here
is chiefly and directly an intellectual one, whether this
be regarded as the acquisition and diffusion of knowledge, or the promotion of mental culture, yet this
purely intellectual aim, noble in itself, cannot have

free course unless it is animated by a still greater purpose — the formation and growth of character, the knowledge of self, the diffusion of right principles of action in private and public.

I now turn to the consideration of a department in which I am more at home.[1]

The periodical reaction against classical studies seems to have again set in. Their partial or entire abolition was advocated about a twelvemonth since, in a well-known speech, on grounds which tell almost equally against every form of liberal education. If by " things *versus* words " is meant familiarity with material objects, as distinguished from the products of the mind; if " truth, not falsehood " means the mere inculcation of traditional beliefs, without the deeper study of the history of opinion; above all, if the highest training is to be in things that are nearest and most immediately useful, I do not see why the Faculty of Arts in our universities should exist another day. The advanced teaching of the physical sciences must be proscribed equally with that of classics. The pulpit and the industrial school, with some machinery in the shape of seminaries for keeping up the traditions of the several professions or crafts, would supply all the educational wants of the age. On the other hand, the defenders of these studies appear to me to omit some reasons which might be urged in their support. To revert once more to the premises laid down at first, the study of the classics

---

[1] He had been speaking of mental and moral Philosophy and Mathematics.

is to be maintained as a branch of science, as a means of culture, and as an engine of progress.

1. The study of Greek and Roman antiquity is, for western nations, the first and most important chapter in the science of man, in the several departments of language, poetry, religion, politics, and speculative philosophy. Thanks to the wonderful labors of earlier and later scholars, this lesson is more intelligible than formerly. The materials of the science are ready to our hand, and are in that state of preparation in which scientific inquiry becomes most fruitful in results. If the grammar of the ancient languages, and the mere verbal study of their literature, was a sufficient education for great men a few generations since, will not the more philosophical analysis of their language, as compared with others, the more critical and comprehensive interpretation of their great writers, still form a valuable preparation for the science which begins to absorb all sciences — the history of thought? Shall we withdraw this study from education just when it is becoming clearer and more universally interesting, and, if that is to be a reason, when European antiquity is coming nearer to us than ever before? Are we to cease educating men in critical and historical inquiry, and that, in the name of freedom of thought, when questions of sacred criticism are among the burning questions of the day? Are we to throw away the best means of creating the power of realizing modes of thinking remote from our own, just when that power is becoming of the highest practical value?

2. This leads to the second consideration; for is not

this very power the highest evidence of culture, the essence of an enlarged and liberal spirit? The value of classical studies in this respect has been so often stated, and has so recently found a worthy exponent in our Lord Rector, that I need only remark that the exercise of composition in the ancient languages has other uses besides that of familiarizing us with their idioms and vocabularies. It is one means among several of enabling the student to live in the ancient world, and to realize something of the subtile beauties of classical thought and speech; for scholarship is not a crude mass of information, but a habit of mind, a mould not impressed from without, but fashioned from within, through intercourse with the great of old, with the " select men," who were the leading spirits of great nations when the world was young.

3. And the result of such a habit ought to be something more than is usually expressed in the term " culture." The earliest name of the study is the most suggestive: Rerum humaniorum scientia — the study of what is more essentially human. The outcome of such a study should be an enlarged humanity, a growing consciousness of the higher things in man, an increased perception of the inward power and freedom of the human spirit. It is well that this should be combined with those other perceptions of order and uniformity and law which are so much strengthened by the sciences of nature. It is well that both should be carried up by reflection into the still higher region of philosophical inquiry. But it is a matter of common experience that the mind that has not been thus brought

31*

into contact with the past, and trained to follow the various movements of early thought, sees less of what is deepest in the life of man, and is ever liable to be enslaved by the newest physical hypothesis, or, what is sometimes the same thing, the newest metaphysical generalization.

While thus urging the claims of philology to continued recognition, I am quite ready to concede that we shall lose nothing by judiciously making room for other subjects, and that the most hopeful thing that can be said of our methods of teaching is that they have begun to change.

The consideration of student-life is not completed with a survey of the curriculum of study. In remarking more generally on some of the principles which should guide us in our work here, I wish still to keep in view what I said at first, that our object is something more than knowledge or mental culture — something which may be better described as personal progress. Human nature is complex, and, if we are chiefly engaged with a part only, we must not forget that that part is tended by us for the sake of the whole. Fine character alone ennobles intellect, and that intellectual training is not worth much which has no effect in elevating character.

It is a phenomenon not less sad than frequent to see the defects of the school-boy perpetuated in later life. There are characters whose growth seems to be arrested at a certain point, like a leaf that has been nipped, or a a tree stunted by some prevailing wind. There are latent excellences and possibilities of greatness, which remain undeveloped, until, like green corn in November, they have no more chance of ripening in this world. In observing such things in ourselves and others, the reflection naturally arises: Could not education do more for us than it does? If the habit of self-criticism and of correcting faults were once begun, could it so entirely cease? Could men be so indifferent to the decision of important questions, if the love of truth were more inculcated in youth? Could that sacred ardor be then extinguished "more utterly," as Plato says, "than Heraclitus's sun, in that it is never re-illumed"? If consciousness were once fully alive, would not the result be more perceptible in the upward growth of character?

For what is the root of self-improvement? Why is the work of individual progress begun earlier and continued longer by some than others? We are apt to attribute this to an instinctive prescience, which out-runs experience, and much is no doubt due to an original gift; but this gift shows itself in the quickness and firmness with which the intimations of experience are seized. The first warning that some course of action, or the overgrowth of some quality in us, is likely to be hurtful to ourselves or others, may be accepted with manly faith, or may be childishly rejected. The worth and nobleness of some act which is not required by common opinion may be apprehended, or may pass by us unperceived. In such perceptions as these lies the secret of true originality. And their development depends greatly on the early cultivation of a habit of reflection, which to some men seems to come naturally, but can surely in some degree be formed in most men by education.

The most ordinary lesson contains the type of all true human growth, in the consciousness of new powers alternating with the consciousness of deficiency. And these two are most thoroughly combined in the most perfect method, which consists, not merely in reading and hearing and reproducing what is heard and read, or even in original efforts generally approved or condemned. That mind is sure to run to waste which is not frequently subjected to friendly but unsparing criticism. To invite such criticism, and to lay it well to heart, is the wisdom of every learner. To know how to bestow it, not discouragingly, but convincingly, and with stimulative effect, is one of the highest gifts of the teacher. It is by this means, more than by any other, that the mind is trained to set the love of truth before the love of display. " I am one of those," says Socrates, " who would gladly be refuted if I say anything that is not true, and gladly would refute another who was in error ; but, of the two, would rather be refuted, inasmuch as it is a greater gain to be one's self delivered from the greatest of all evils, than to be the means of deliverance to another."

The simple love of truth is a greater thing than intellectual power. Without this, all other gifts and acquirements are so many means of going further astray. Reason is made the minister of prejudice. Opinions which happen to suit the temper are hastily caught up, and all the resources of ingenuity and learning are spent in defending them. The love of truth is the meeting-point of intellect and character, improving both the heart and head. When this eye of the soul is dimmed, the greatest mind has but a discolored and shadowy prospect of men and things.

This helps us to distinguish between verbal and real discussion, and shows the one to be as worthless as the other is valuable. This teaches that intellectual moderation and repose, which is the best safeguard against rhetorical extravagances and perverse reasoning. This raises us above the pettiness of viewing knowledge as a mere means of gain. I would not speak slightingly of any motive which is deeply infixed in human nature, and has the power of inspiring great and continued effort; and the desire of rising in the world and establishing a position for one's self undoubtedly has a certain use. But as the ruling motive of a life, as an ideal of practice, as the mainspring of character, the determination to get up in life is simply vulgarizing. That is, indeed, a low and poor ambition into which there does not enter some dream of truth and good, of unending progress in knowledge and in virtue, of real and lasting service to mankind,

INDEX.

A.

Accuracy of thought and expressions promoted by the study of the Classics, 305.

Age at which the study of the Classics should be commenced, 61, 63, 70.

Analytical faculty; strengthened by the study of the Classics, 17.

Antiquity, Classical, the whole subject inexhaustible, 259.

Arago's opinion as to the value of classical studies, 111.

Attention, influence of classical studies on the powers of, 294, 295.

B.

Brown, Pres. Samuel G., extract from his Inaugural Address 339–346.

C.

Choate's, Rufus, fondness for classical studies, 256.

Classics and Classical Studies, the question of their proper position in a system of education, one of great interest, 1; causes of the high position occupied by them for so long a time, 2–5; that at the revival of learning there was no literature worthy of the name in existence except the Classics, 3; that Latin was then the language of the church and the vernacular language of learned men, 3; that classical subjects then furnished the chief materials for thought, 4; that the foundation of seminaries of learning was contemporaneous with the revival of learning, 4; that the educational field was then occupied exclusively by the Classics, 4; question of the tenableness of the position occupied hitherto by the Classics, 5; they are not entitled to an exclusive position among studies, 13; are entitled to a central position, 15, 281, 282, 286; they cannot effect the whole of our mental culture, 19; effect of classical studies on the memory, 19; on

J.

K.

L.